Cinema and the Indian
National Emergency

WORLD CINEMA SERIES

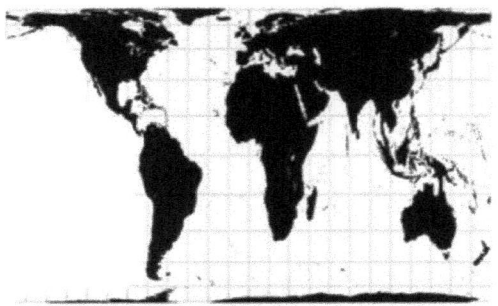

Series Editors:

Lúcia Nagib, Professor of Film at the University of Reading
Julian Ross, Research Fellow at the Leiden University
Advisory Board: Laura Mulvey (UK), Robert Stam (USA), Ismail Xavier
(Brazil), Dudley Andrew (USA)

The *World Cinema series* aims to reveal and celebrate the richness and complexity of film art across the globe, exploring a wide variety of cinemas set within their own cultures and as they interconnect in a global context. The books in the series will represent innovative scholarship, in tune with the multicultural character of contemporary audiences. Drawing upon an international authorship, they will challenge outdated conceptions of world cinema and provide new ways of understanding a field at the centre of film studies in an era of transnational networks.

Published and forthcoming in the World Cinema series:

Allegory in Iranian Cinema: The Aesthetics of Poetry and Resistance, Michelle Langford

Animation in the Middle East: Practice and Aesthetics from Baghdad to Casablanca, Stefanie Van de Peer

Basque Cinema: A Cultural and Political History, Rob Stone and Maria Pilar Rodriguez

Brazil on Screen: Cinema Novo, New Cinema, Utopia,

Lúcia Nagib
Brazilian Cinema and the Aesthetic of Ruins, Guilherme Carréra

Cinema in the Arab World: New Histories, New Approaches, Edited by Philippe Meers, Daniel Biltereyst and Ifdal Elsaket

Contemporary New Zealand Cinema, Edited by Ian Conrich and Stuart Murray

The Cinema of Sri Lanka: South Asian Film in Texts and Contexts,
Ian Conrich

The New Generation in Chinese Animation,
Shaopeng Chen

The Spanish Fantastic: Contemporary Filmmaking in Horror, Fantasy and Sci-fi,
Shelagh-Rowan Legg

Theorizing World Cinema,
Edited by Lúcia Nagib, Chris Perriam and Rajinder Dudrah

Women and Global Documentary: Practices and Perspectives in the 21st Century
Edited by Najmeh Moradiyan-Rizi and Shilyh Warren

Queries, ideas and submissions to
Series Editor: Professor Lúcia Nagib
l.nagib@reading.ac.uk
Series Editor: Dr. Julian Ross
j.a.ross@hum.leidenuniv.nl
Commissioning Editor at Bloomsbury: Veidehi Hans
Veidehi.Hans@bloomsbury.com

Cinema and the Indian National Emergency

Histories and Afterlives

Edited by

Parichay Patra

Dibyakusum Ray

BLOOMSBURY ACADEMIC

LONDON • NEW YORK • OXFORD • NEW DELHI • SYDNEY

BLOOMSBURY ACADEMIC
Bloomsbury Publishing Plc, 50 Bedford Square, London, WC1B 3DP, UK
Bloomsbury Publishing Inc, 1385 Broadway, New York, NY 10018, USA
Bloomsbury Publishing Ireland, 29 Earlsfort Terrace, Dublin 2, D02 AY28, Ireland

BLOOMSBURY, BLOOMSBURY ACADEMIC and the Diana logo are trademarks of
Bloomsbury Publishing Plc

First published in Great Britain 2025

Cover design: Ben Anslow

Cover image: Strict checking was enforced of the visitors to the Supreme Courts
by policemen in view of the hearing of ''Kissa Kursi Ka'' case in New Delhi on
Monday-November 26, 1979.

Contributor: Keystone Press / Alamy Stock Photo

A catalogue record for this book is available from the British Library.

ISBN: HB: 978-1-3503-7113-2
PB: 978-1-3503-7117-0
ePDF: 978-1-3503-7115-6
eBook: 978-1-3503-7114-9

Series: World Cinema

Typeset by Deanta Global Publishing Services, Chennai, India
Printed and bound in Great Britain

For product safety related questions contact productsafety@bloomsbury.com.

To find out more about our authors and books visit www.bloomsbury.com and
sign up for our newsletters.

Contents

Editors and contributors

Editors

Parichay Patra is Assistant Professor at the School of Liberal Arts, Indian Institute of Technology Jodhpur, India.

Dibyakusum Ray is Assistant Professor at the Department of Humanities and Social Sciences, Indian Institute of Technology Ropar, India.

Contributors

Vinzenz Hediger is Professor of Cinema Studies at Goethe University Frankfurt am Main, Germany. He is a co-founder of the European Network for Cinema and Media Studies, NECS (www.necs.org), and the founding editor of Zeitschrift für Medienwissenschaft (www.zfmedienwissenschaft.de).

Ashish Rajadhyaksha is an independent film researcher based in Bengaluru, India.

Someswar Bhowmik is the retired director of the Educational Multimedia Research Centre (EMRC), St. Xavier's College, Kolkata, India.

Amrit Gangar is an independent film curator-programmer, film society activist and film historian based in Mumbai, India.

Sudha Tiwari is Assistant Professor of History, School of Liberal Studies and Media, UPES, Dehradun, India.

Ritika Kaushik is Assistant Professor in Film and Television Studies, University of Warwick, UK.

Vinayak Das Gupta is Associate Professor in the School of Humanities and Social Sciences, Shiv Nadar Institute of Eminence, India.

Ananya Juneja is a teaching and research assistant at the School of Humanities and Social Sciences, Shiv Nadar Institute of Eminence, India.

Vikrant Dadawala is Assistant Professor of English at York University, Toronto, Canada.

Ranjani Mazumdar is Professor of Cinema Studies at the School of Arts and Aesthetics, Jawaharlal Nehru University, India.

Kaushik Bhaumik is Associate Professor of Cinema Studies, School of Arts and Aesthetics, Jawaharlal Nehru University, India.

Figures

Acknowledgements

The editors would like to thank the Scheme for Promotion of Academic and Research Collaboration (SPARC) of the Ministry of Education, Government of India, for its financial support for the project that resulted in this volume. Lúcia Nagib and Julian Ross, the two editors of the Bloomsbury World Cinema Series, provided the much-needed encouragement for this volume as it gradually evolved over time. The anonymous reviewers provided significant suggestions that must be acknowledged. The editors also like to thank Tulika Books and Ashish Rajadhyaksha for allowing the reprint of excerpts from his *John-Ghatak-Tarkovsky: Citizens, Filmmakers, Hackers* (2023). The editors thank their respective students for their immense help, the list includes Satvik Gupta, Sagar Das, Pooja Radhakrishnan, Bhairab Barman, Parnika Agarwal, Samya Brata Roy and Swarnima Banerjee.

Foreword

India, a global laboratory of democracy in and through film

Vinzenz Hediger

India is the largest democracy in the world: close to one billion voters were called to the polls in the 2024 election, more than the population of any other country save for China. India is also the most important film-producing country in the world: more than 1,800 feature films are made by the different regional language industries each year, roughly three times the output of the Hollywood film industry. These are impressive statistics. But correlation is not causation, and on the face of it, there is little reason to assume that these two sets of facts are connected.

And yet.

Much like the other large-scale multi-ethnic democracy, the United States, Indian democracy has significant flaws (which is not to say that ethnically more homogeneous democracies are without problems). In the United States, gerrymandering and the electoral college prevent all votes from being counted equally, leading to a system in which a rural white minority rules over a more diverse urban majority, with the urban majority paying most of the bills. India, a country which can lay claim to centuries of tradition in public deliberation (Sen 2012, 3–33), has been described by Partha Chatterjee, among others (2021), as an empire rather than a nation state, and one that has been ruled since independence by political and economic elites who had not always entirely emancipated themselves from the mind frame of feudalist landownership.

And for all their democratic spirit and traditions, the United States and India similarly face enduring authoritarian threats from within. The ghost of the imperial presidency with limitless powers and negligible accountability has haunted the United States at least since Nixon, and the Supreme Court's recent ruling granting virtual immunity to presidents for all official acts during their time in office has further ensconced authoritarianism in the heart of American democracy. Furthermore, democracy, as per Adam Przeworski, is a system in which parties lose elections and accept defeat (2019), and we have now reached a point in US history where one party no longer accepts defeat, as shown by the violent insurrection led by the outgoing president on 6 January 2021. In India, the authoritarian threat today comes in the form of a political ideology that has its origins in the colonial era but is now ascendant and aims to exclude from the polity a significant share of the population based on religion. But there is a secular threat as well. For most of its post-independence history, India was ruled by a secular family dynasty legitimized by elections, which is now into its fourth generation, and in the second generation, this dynastic rule culminated in the Emergency, the temporary suspension of a bundle of core civil rights under the de facto dictatorship of Prime Minister Indira Gandhi from 1975 to 1977.

Cinema, the paradigmatic mass art, which emerges at just around the same time as sociology and the epistemic figure of the mass itself, has often been deemed an enemy of democracy. The reigning consensus in post-war Europe was that cinema was complicit in the rise of fascism in Europe in the 1920s and 1930s. Siegfried Kracauer read the entirety of Weimar cinema as a prefiguration of Hitler and Nazism (1947). Similarly, in today's online video culture, we can find the story of Trump's rise to power told in the popular form of American action movie trailers, and some proponents of the Weimar analogy read Trump campaign videos as the second coming of Leni Riefenstahl.[1]

However, even in flawed democracies, cinema can also be read, as Alain Badiou puts it, as a 'democratic emblem' (2005). Cinema, as both an onscreen space and a social site, is a space of imaginary equality and democratic possibility. In the United States, most of the wealth is inherited, leading to what Michelle Obama has recently described as 'the affirmative action of generational wealth'. One of the few areas where people can hope to achieve success irrespective of their origin, education, or parents' wealth is the entertainment industry, particularly the film industry. Talent and star power, those elusive qualities which the camera alone captures, are sufficient. The United States has also elected a former actor and a reality TV star to the highest office in the land. What is more, film has projected American ideas of democracy and prosperity around the world. Facilitating the export of Hollywood films has been a core element of US trade policy since the 1920s, and the structures of feeling of what William Appleman Williams has described as the American 'empire as a way of life' have been built up and cultivated, to a large extent, through film (1982). As for India – for all of Gandhi's 'cinephobia', as Ravi Vasudevan calls it – Indian politicians after independence have always sought the proximity of film stars, hoping to tap into fandom as a vicarious source of democratic legitimacy. The current dispensation is no exception. Sometimes film stars have themselves entered politics, most notably the star duo of M. G. Ramachandran and Jayalalithaa, who turned their fan clubs into parties and became successive first ministers of the state of Tamil Nadu (Srinivas 2006). But Ashish Rajadhyaksha goes one step further and argues that the only place where the idea of equality enshrined in the Indian Constitution – a legal document for which its main author B. R. Ambedkar used the 'Jim Crow' race laws of the US post-reconstruction era as a negative blueprint (Mukherjee 2009) – has ever become a reality, however fleetingly, is the cinema hall, with its egalitarian audience (Rajadhyaksha 1998).

The correlation between India as the biggest democracy and the biggest film-producing country does matter, then. The question is how to understand its dynamics. Another seemingly unrelated question is why someone not from India, or not working on India, should care.

This book emerged from a research project which focused on film in the lead-up to, during, and in the wake of the Emergency. As the editors have explained in the introduction, the book is funded by the currently dominant political regime, possibly with the intention of highlighting the authoritarian tendencies of the dynastic rule of the opposition. Presumably, then, this book is informed by politics, and it has to be informed about politics. Underlying the book is what may be called as a reverse-Schmittianism. If Carl Schmitt, the crown jurist of the Nazis, argued that the sovereign is not the people but she who decides over the state of exception – which also means, from a philosophical point of view, that the state of exception nullifies not just the practice but the principle of democratic rule. Then the contributions to this book are bracketed together by the assumption that there is something important to be learnt about democratic rule precisely in the moment of its suspension, and in this case specifically by studying the configuration of the demos in and through the cinema.

The approach chosen by the editors and their authors is not that of lofty theoretical speculation. Rather, they study the moving image with a view to the legal and institutional frameworks and bureaucratic practices which regulate and enable its production and circulation. What the book offers is a series of snapshots including Amrit Gangar's discussion of cineclubs during the Emergency, Sudha Tiwari's analysis of the transformation of the public film funding system, Ritika Kaushik's study of the bureaucratic logics of state documentary film, Parichay Patra's reflection on how the Emergency rendered seemingly apolitical films political, Dibyakusum Ray's examination of popular cinema's retroactive conferral of legitimacy on the Emergency, and Kaushik Baumik's exploration of its long-term effects on independent filmmaking in Bengal. Taken together, these snap shots coalesce into a comprehensive view of the micromechanics of governance in and through film in mid-1970s India and beyond.

Three insights emerging from the ensemble are particularly striking. First, the extent to which the policies of the Emergency were driven by economic motives rather than by a desire to clamp down on political discourse. Ashok Mody has recently argued that India's post-independence economic and industrial policy suffered from a focus on large-scale industrial plant projects and elite education exemplified by the IITs at the expense of investments in primary and secondary education and manufacturing by small and mid-size companies (Mody 2023). For Mody, this misguided focus, inspired in roughly equal parts by the model of Britain and that of the Soviet Union, helps explain why South Korea, which did focus on education and manufacturing after 1945, is now one of the most prosperous countries in the world while growth in India continues to remain relatively flat, to the point where Bangladesh has recently overtaken India in GDP. As Mody himself points out and as the authors of this volume powerfully demonstrate, cinema was an important indicator of this stagnation in the lead-up to the Emergency, whether in the form of the Javed-Salim's angry young man films or Satyajit Ray's city trilogy. The extent to which the government shifts the focus from a quest for cultural diversity and educational value to a search for commercial success in its film-related policies during the Emergency offers a textbook case of a blindly comprehensive, panicky top-down attempt to spur economic growth as the cure for political problems and a source of legitimacy. Second, the film-related policies and particularly the handling of censorship can be read as an indicator of the extent to which the Emergency revealed the imperial core of the federal republic that India nominally is. As a matter of course, censorship is handled by the central government, which becomes particularly active and interventionist during the Emergency. And third, the contributions taken together recall the adage that nobody emerges from life under a dictatorship unscathed. In the synoptic view of the Emergency that the contributions offer, they demonstrate that even a short period of authoritarian rule leaves scars that can take a long time to heal and that continue to shape life decades after the event. In that sense, this book is also a cautionary tale with a view to the future of not just India but other democracies currently under pressure and threat around the world.

This alone should answer the question of why someone not from India or working on India should read this book. But there is another reason.

In political science and political theory, democracy continues to be discussed with a focus on the relatively closed system of the nation state. In the wake of the end of the Cold War and the collapse of the Soviet empire, most of its former subjects have chosen the path of liberal democracy and integration into the Western European political and economic system. But efforts to export liberal democracy to the Middle East by military force led the United States over the last three decades have failed, at a high price to those whose lives these efforts were supposed to improve.[2] The Western utopian vision of a globalized system of free trade and free and fair elections for all now seems elusive and has been scaled down to a focus on global trade alone.

However, cinema, the emblem of democracy, has always transcended national boundaries, and because of that any national film industry – including Hollywood and Bombay cinema – requires international markets to sustain itself in the long run. As early as the 1930s, almost half of Hollywood's revenue came from abroad; now it is more than 50 per cent. And Hindi cinema has long since been – and perhaps somewhat paradoxically, considering that it comes from a Hindu majority country – the Muslim world art, at least judging by the map of countries and regions where these films find their largest audiences outside of India. One effect of cinema's global circulation is that it creates heterotopic spaces not bound by national boundaries.

One such space could recently be experienced in Switzerland.

On 10 August 2024, Shah Rukh Khan received a lifetime achievement award at the Locarno Film Festival, one of the oldest and most prestigious film festivals in the world. On that Saturday night, the Locarno piazza became one of cinema's paradigmatic heterotopic spaces.

Appearing on the stage of the festival's signature open-air cinema in the central piazza of this small town in the Italian-speaking part of Switzerland in front of close to 10,000 people, Shah Rukh Khan spoke about his career, his philosophy of acting, and he tipped his hat to his host country, in which he had been shooting films for more than three decades, including such perennial favourites as *Dilwale Dulhania Le Jayenge* (*DDLJ*, 1995). The award ceremony elicited comprehensive press coverage in the Swiss, German and Austrian press. To their readers, these publications consistently introduced SRK as the 'world's biggest film star nobody knows', in which 'nobody' could be said to refer to the entire world except for the audience of European legacy media and European film festivals. However, the Locarno award for SRK was not so much geared towards the local or regional moviegoing crowd as it was to a broader, even global audience not yet present in Locarno. Had the Locarno audience been the main target, the festival could have screened one of SRK's films for the piazza audience to introduce them to his work. *Dil Se* (1998) would have been a great fit for a screening on the first Saturday of the festival, when traditionally a good part of the political elite of Switzerland is in attendance, or *DDLJ*, of course, because of all the scenic views shot in Switzerland's Bernese Oberland. Instead, on 10 August 2024, Locarno screened a recent Swiss film, which the audience politely endured. And so, to this day, *Lagaan*, which won the audience award in 2001, remains the only commercial Hindi film ever to have been screened in Europe's greatest open-air cinema. The real audience of the lifetime achievement award were SRK fans elsewhere, not just in India but across the Middle East and in countries like Malaysia and Indonesia: the new global middle classes who are increasingly patronizing European tourist destinations. SRK's Locarno lifetime achievement award was sponsored by the Ascona-Locarno tourism association. Ascona is a picturesque fishing village near Locarno and one of Switzerland's most visited tourist destinations. When Indian film crews started shooting films in volume in Switzerland in the 1980s, they focused on Gstaad and its surroundings, a north-of-the-alps hill station surrounded by lush green pastures and snow-capped mountains in the distance, a perfect substitute for the then-increasingly unsafe shooting location of Kashmir. At first, nobody in Switzerland paid much attention to the visitors except for a few tour operators who made Indian film crew logistics their speciality, at a premium to their customers. The Swiss only started paying attention when they registered a significant uptick in Indian tourists in the 1990s. Initially, the New Indian Cinema tourists were travelling in groups and confined to specific hotels, often somewhat run down, as their food tastes and general behaviour were deemed incompatible with the standards expected of patrons in high-end Swiss hotels (incidentally, these standards were established by English upper-class travellers who discovered Switzerland as a tourist destination in the nineteenth century, just as Britain was tightening its hold over India during the Raj). Today, however, Indian film tourism has become an integral part of the Swiss tourism industry, a change perhaps best illustrated by the fact that the Victoria-Jungfrau Hotel in Interlaken, a five-star palace on par with the Taj and Oberoi hotels, now has a luxury suite named after Yash Chopra, the pioneer of Indian film shoots in Switzerland.[3] Back in Locarno, the town's storied Grand Hotel, the original site of the festival screenings, is currently under renovation and will reopen, together with another luxury hotel further downtown, in 2026. These new luxury hotels will need Asian patrons to thrive. Clearly, the Locarno award for SRK was designed to put the southern parts of Switzerland on the map of Indian and Asian film tourism.

What this anecdote can help to illustrate is an ongoing shift towards what Pakistani writer Fatima Bhutto, in a paean to SRK and other new global players in the culture industries, has described as the emergence of a 'new world order of cultural production' (Bhutto 2019). Yet for the 10,000 Eurocentric cinephiles on the Locarno piazza that August night, the few 'somebodies' as opposed to the 'nobodies' who know SRK, that is, most of the rest of the world, it was entirely possible to remain largely unaware of the fact that the terrain has been shifting from under their feet for some time now.

For the time being.

Because the heterotopic space of the Locarno piazza is about to turn into the melodramatic space of global democracy, in which some people realize that they are late to the action and might be in danger of missing it.

One of the formative films of my childhood was *Der Erfinder* (*The Inventor*, 1981), a Swiss film directed by Kurt Gloor. Bruno Ganz stars as a farmer who invents a caterpillar vehicle to facilitate the cultivation of steep slopes. He sacrifices his health and fortune to this invention, but finally, he obtains a patent writ for it. On the way home from the lawyer's office, he catches a movie show. The First World War is drawing to a close, and the programme includes a newsreel showing tanks in action. The farmer realizes that someone else got there first and loses his mind.

The lesson I took away from this film is that it is important to go to the cinema before it is too late. Today, that lesson would be that it is important to study Indian cinema, and particularly its relationship to democracy, before it is too late.

Introduction

Dibyakusum Ray and Parichay Patra

The idea of this edited collection germinated a few years ago when our team received a grant from the Ministry of Human Resource Development (now rechristened as the Ministry of Education), Govt. of India, to work on the Indian Emergency of 1975–7 and its many implications for film and media. The project included designing specialized courses for students, organizing workshops and seminars, and the plan for a book. Two workshops and one seminar were organized, the first of them at the Indian Institute of Technology Ropar in chilly Punjab in December 2019. Then a global emergency set in with the onslaught of an invisible enemy, and we went virtual for the rest of the events. The workshops and seminars were astonishingly vibrant, with their throbbing, pulsating atmosphere built up with the active participation of scholars of many generations, those who stood witness to the Indian Emergency and those who read/heard/wrote/webbed about/on it. An eclectic choice of speakers added to the heterogeneity of the event, as senior cinema studies scholars, young historians and digital humanities experts, ace archivists and hardened activists joined us in the discussion. This book intends to document such debates, discussions and dissensions.

The Indian Emergency of 1975–7 is considered a cataclysmic event in a modernizing, postcolonial India. The so-called 'world's largest democracy', for the first (and arguably only) time in its history, suspended the democratic rights of its citizens for nearly two years. Indira Gandhi, the charismatic prime minister who was at the helm during 'Hindu' India's decisive victory over its Islamic neighbouring state Pakistan in the 1971 War, was hailed as the unquestionable leader of the nation, a demi-goddess, as her party received an unprecedented electoral mandate in the 1971 general elections by unleashing 'a huge wave of patriotic sentiment' (Guha 2008: 461). For social scientists, Gandhi presented 'ruthless real politik' (Nandy 1980) and collapsed the party organization into the government (Hewitt 2008: 93). Sudipta Kaviraj has critically explored how her reign can be segmented into specific periods, each of which has been marked by historic events (Kaviraj 1986).

However, the popular faith placed on Gandhi's government started to fade with severe food shortages, economic crises, widespread student unrest and the rise of Maoist insurgency in several states. The opposition parties formed a strong but unusual alliance against her with the pro-Soviet leftists and Hindu Right groups coming together. Her electoral victory in a parliamentary seat in the Indian state of Uttar Pradesh was invalidated by an Indian court for the allegations of electoral malpractice. Gandhi was running her government under the garb of a populist socialism for long. Now, with the state's 'capacity of democratic governance' challenged by the sudden upsurge of democratic mobilization (Hewitt 2008: 1), Gandhi responded to the time by declaring a state of National Emergency at the midnight of 25 June 1975, with the suspension of fundamental constitutional rights, imposition of fundamental duties on the citizens, and a ruthless suppression of democratic and insurgent oppositional forces. Problematic amendments to the constitution, the declaration of an infamous 20-point programme, the incarceration of opposition leaders, custodial torture, police atrocities, extrajudicial killings of radical activists and insurgents, eviction and forced sterilization of the urban poor in the name of urban beautification, and several other manifestations of dictatorial rule followed. In 1977, with the restoration of democratic processes, Gandhi's party lost the general elections decisively.

The Emergency generated many forms of responses, immediate and otherwise. Immediate responses included a number of prison writings and memoirs (Banerjee 1980; Tyler 1977; Kapoor 2016). Journalistic accounts of the events abounded (Nayar 2013), bureaucrats associated with the Indira Gandhi regime recounted their experiences in the power corridors of the Emergency (Dhar 2000). Maoist insurgency and state repression gave birth to a radical reimagination of the social science archive in India/South Asia, with the emergence of a now-renowned historiographic school called the 'Subaltern Studies'. The indebtedness of this new school to the insurgency, its radical politicality and rereading of Indian modernity was explicitly acknowledged in the works of historians associated with the school (Chakrabarty 2002). South Asian historians or South Asianists of other geopolitical locations explored many nuances of the event and political responses to it (Hewitt 2008; Guha

2017; Prakash 2019; Lockwood 2020; Jaffrelot and Anil 2020), sometimes producing significant documentation of its specific aspects (see Srirupa Roy's archive on the Long Emergency). Social anthropologists offered ethnographic investigations into the neighbourhoods in the underbelly of Delhi that were victimized during the Emergency (Tarlo 2003).

Despite the growing social science corpus on the Emergency (the French South Asianist Jaffrelot's work appeared as recently as 2021 and addresses the Emergency as India's first dictatorship in unequivocal terms), its profound implications for Indian cinemas remain mostly unaddressed. A wider and all-encompassing volume on the 1970s and its legacies in India's cinemas (Joshi and Dudrah 2014) engages with a broader scenario and its contemporary remnants, while M. Madhava Prasad's Marxist-ideological history of Bombay cinema deals specifically with the 1970s Amitabh Bachchan-starrer 'angry young man' films (1998). Ashish Rajadhyaksha's reverse historiography of Indian cinema in the time of celluloid, public experience, and statist use is one of the rare instances where the Emergency has been considered one of the major moments of crisis for Indian cinema, and the state-control on cinema's many lives, along with the emergent aesthetic practices, was addressed (2009). Rajadhyaksha has long been working on the largest database on Indian cinema, known as Indiancine.ma, and the database includes specific sections on the 1970s, even if they are yet to be fully developed (and perhaps not meant to be so as an ever-developing open archive).

When we started working on the project, this visible dearth in Indian cinema studies troubled us. The incumbent government decided to fund our project for reasons that are obvious; it is spearheaded by the Hindu Right group that formed the alliance against Indira Gandhi during the Emergency and contributed to her downfall in the aftermath. An Emergency project seems like a safer, even desired option, as work on the past Emergency may lead to amnesia in the present. However, cinema can and does subvert what the state desires it to be, as evidenced by the cine-politics during the Emergency. This book situates itself within this cinematic trajectory of the Emergency, tracing its many lives across the cinemas of India and beyond.

The Indian state that brought in the Emergency tried to exert its influence over the domain of cinema through a careful development of a double-edged controlling mechanism. In Althusserian terms, the state truly created a repressive censorship apparatus with strong colonial residues, something which has received scholarly attention in recent times (Mazzarella 2013; Bhowmik 2009). Several censorship debates during the Emergency might be located in the film chamber of commerce magazines and film society publications in the 1970s, where the Information and Broadcasting Minister's heated arguments with the film industry people featured strongly. More atrocious instances of film bans and the confiscation of available 35 mm prints can also be found. The censorship issue was gradually extended into the ethical and moral domains of what films should or should not depict, as the state carefully crafted a developmentalist plan for cinematic showcasing beyond mere propaganda.

The ideological apparatus, unarguably more complex than the former, included the state's investment in the making of a 'national' art-house cinema for India, something which resulted in an Indian New Wave of the 1970s. But this New Cinema was essentially heterogeneous, spread across many production centres and cinematic cultures and often foiled the state's strategies for a sponsored cinema. Some filmmakers formed collectives and resorted to crowdfunding instead of relying on the subvention of the Indian state. Moreover, a fierce public debate was initiated on the fundamental aspects of the art-house economy, on whether state subsidy/loan is necessary for the realization of a cinema that cannot guarantee profits.

This collection of essays critically considers the many modes of state control over cinema and the latter's politicality during dictatorial rule. It begins with the many histories of Indian cinematic institutions and their politics, specifically during the Emergency. Its accounts include the institutional histories of state agencies as well as those of non-state actors (such as film societies) that continued to live double lives under an oppressive state. It does not leave out the curious politics of film curation during the Emergency, something which may have strongly determined filmgoing activities and film society publics in urban centres such as Bombay, a city that was (and still is) the space that housed the 'national popular' cinema. From such histories, it proceeds to the mediatized representations of the Emergency and the many legal and extra-legal nuances of the censoring mechanism. Then, in the contemporary, it concerns itself with two aspects of the past, the possibilities of archiving/remembering and its probable afterlives in cinemas and elsewhere.

Cinematic discussions and associations in other Asian locations in the long 1970s never escape the inevitability of the 'state of exception' of various forms and its implications for cinema in the Global South. The Martial Law periods in Southeast and East Asian nations find their place in the discussions of Taiwanese and Filipino New Waves (Reynaud 2019; Patra and Lim 2021). Indian cinema studies, as the rationale for this book argues, engaged inadequately with its own moment of crisis and state of exception. This provocative absence/inadequacy has helped this book in raising many questions that exist at the intersectional areas between cinema studies, South Asian studies and contemporary history.

In addition to that, it places Indian cinema history within the wider network of Global South cinemas through the prism of the global dictatorial of the 1970s. The exceptional status that Indian cinema has always claimed for itself, along with many other reasons, has thwarted any movement beyond the purview of the national cinema. At present, the advent of transnational cinema as a research method has offered a counterpoint to this overt emphasis on national cinema studies. This book attempts to initiate a much-needed dialogue in this domain, hoping to move beyond the insularity that has often characterized Indian cinema studies.

The book, hence, is divided into two broadly thematic parts: historical and filmic, with the former developing a significant part of the volume. At the same time, such thematic bifurcation is inefficacious here, as the chapters dealing with the documentary history of Emergency and beyond often veer into filmic examples and cinematic analysis. The obverse is equally true.

Ashish Rajadhyaksha's chapter opens the volume and is a reprint of excerpts from his most recent work, *John-Ghatak-Tarkovsky: Citizens, Filmmakers, Hackers* (2023). The book was necessitated by the Film and Television Institute of India (FTII) student protests, but its implications go far beyond its immediate context. With his exploration of the Indian state's 'cinephobia' across ages and especially during the Emergency, Rajadhyaksha delves deep into the state's fear of and mode of disciplining the medium of cinema, its process of producing an ideal citizen-subject as spectator, the judiciary's mode of becoming the 'interpretative authority' in the legal processes involving cinema and other issues. With an increasing, overwhelming shadow of censorship, threat of policing, Film Finance Corporation's (FFC) changing policies towards filmmakers in the 1970s, Rajadhyaksha underlines the challenges posed by cinema to the state and sets the tone for the present volume.

Much in the vein of Rajadhyaksha's chapter, Someswar Bhowmik's 'Not by Emergency Alone: An Unending Saga of Political Repression and Content Control' continues its sweeping historical summary of the Emergency and one of its many crimes – censorship – with frequent forays into specific films as case studies. Starting from the Central Board of Film Certification (CBFC) era of film censorship in the early 1950s, Bhowmik recounts the tradition of silencing cinematic voice(s), visible in its ugliest form during the 1970s. In the book, he is also the first author to cite the 'White Paper on Misuse of Mass Media' – a declaration by the government of India published in 1977 that elaborated the 'rationale' behind mass censorship of popular media at that time. In this connection, Bhowmik cites the fates of films like *Aandhi* (1975), *Aandolan* (1995), *Kissa Kursi Ka* (1978), as well as the documentary films by S. Sukhdev, elaborating the double standards and creative interference of the state into the domains of artistic expression. The censorship and dominance, however, were not unresisted.

Amrit Gangar, in the following chapter 'State: A Patron and a Tyrant: Indian Film Society Movement in "Emergency" Times', narrates a history of cinematic belligerence that ran parallel to the account of media censorship. Gangar's essay talks about the majorly combative relationship between the 1970s Indira Gandhi regime and the Film Society Movement – a parallel cinema endeavour in India which attempted to combine vision, passion, social justice and a decidedly non-bureaucratic approach to filmmaking (Majumdar 2006). Referring to not only films but also to posters, photographs and palimpsests that depict the micro-history of counter-narratives of the dictatorship (especially through film society-backed art-house productions like *Kabani Nadi Chuvannappol* and *Kranti Ki Tarang* etc.), Gangar traverses the narrative of resistance up until Ashish Avikuntak's *Aapothkalin Trikalika: The Kali of Emergency* (2016).

While this sweeping yet cogent historiography continues in Sudha Tiwari's 'The Emergency, FFC/NFDC and New Cinema in India (1970s)', her essay is also the first of the three 'archival historiography' papers (followed by Ritika Kaushik and Vinayak Das Gupta-Ananya Juneja). Like Gangar and Bhowmik, Tiwari's chapter has a broad temporal spectrum at its core – she tracks the history of state-sponsored film production systems, from FFC to National Film Development Corporation (NFDC). She also focuses on the seemingly paradoxical enthusiasm of Indira Gandhi in state-sponsored parallel films during the initial years of her governance, since Gandhi herself facilitated these organizations' demise during the Emergency and after. Analyzing interviews, anecdotes and film-texts in equal measure, Tiwari's chapter is a suitable opening to the intensively archival methodology of Ritika Kaushik.

Ritika Kaushik's contribution critically reconsiders the 'Film 20' programme and other Emergency efforts made by the Films Division, focusing mostly on S. Sukhdev and Goutam Ghoshe, with significant archival unearthing, looking at the internal production files and memos of the state-owned mass media. However, it does not construct the history of the institution and its filmmaking efforts through the conventional binary of control and agency. Instead, it problematizes existing narratives and offers an exciting micro-history through its nuanced reading of power relations, of the complex negotiations between the state and such non-state actors as independent filmmakers, of conflicting responses to cinema, and of multimodal debates around questions of autonomy, choice-making and so on. Kaushik's explorations of complexities and idiosyncrasies disallow us to read the state-filmmaker relation through a conventional lens and resist reducing even state-sponsored documentaries to the reductive category of propaganda cinema. Her narrative aligns well with the work of the Emergency-anthropologist Emma Tarlo, who regarded the socio-administrative relations produced by the Emergency as far more ambiguous than they appear.

Vinayak Das Gupta and Ananya Juneja's chapter has several sections focusing on different aspects of the idea of archiving the Emergency. While one fragment of the chapter seeks to engage with select Bombay cinemas (or, in its own terms, with a limited dataset) during the Emergency and the extremities of the latter, it concentrates more on the theories of/on the concept of the archive, its colonial origin, the authorial control over it, the creation of silence, and the archive's association with public memory and public history of traumatic events of the past. Using such conceptual apparatuses as testimony, anecdote, and an Agambenian idea of witness, it shows how the traditional archive fails to accommodate oral testimonies of trauma while the new, digital archival projects devoted to the Partition, the Emergency, and other cataclysmic events succeed despite their ephemerality.

Vikrant Dadawala approaches the Film Division and the curious career of S. Sukhdev with a considerably different approach. Despite having his archival evidence, Dadawala relies more on the visual archives, the images and the process of image-making that may raise significant questions on the cinematic lineage of the Emergency. He draws our attention to the myriad possibilities of cinema contributing to the political and historical archive of the postcolonial Indian state before and during the National Emergency, while engaging with filmmakers from opposite ends of the political spectrum, such as Sukhdev and Anand Patwardhan. The aesthetic choices of the filmmakers and the materiality of the film form inform his essay significantly. In his ingenious method, the 'tragedy' of the developmental state becomes associated with the literary connotations and consequences associated with tragedy itself, with the disillusioned 'anagnorisis' and 'hubris' of Indian democracy opening the chapter up towards a consideration of relevant literature in Hindi and Bengali.

Ranjani Mazumdar brings in new media research in this context as her chapter traces the circulation of documentaries on the Emergency through and as video fragments, print materials, YouTube images and other free-flowing, flickering audiovisual stuff that she addresses as 'atmospheric media' à la Mark B. Hansen. Through these dispersed and chaotic forms, she focuses on the experiential dimension of this media as an environment. Situating political memory of the Emergency in the contemporary context of authoritarian politics, she emphasizes on the archive effect and its significance for the historian/filmmaker.

For the remaining part, the book shifts from the archival-historical to a filmic-textual mode. Parichay Patra's chapter, 'In Defence of a Not-So-Political Cinema', diligently keeps its focus on the elusive definition of 'Political Cinema', attempting to trace the films contemporaneous to the Emergency, which, in Patra's own words, 'became' political due to the sociopolitical convergence that formed their background. Drawing frequently from the 'non-filmic' theoretical canon, Patra talks about the avant-garde films of Mani Kaul and Kumar Shahani and their formalistic experimentation that defeats any apparent political reading of them. And yet, Patra asserts, films like *Ashad Ka Ek Din* (1971) did put forward a surreptitious rejection of creative sterility, dictatorship and autocracy through a dense maze of theatrical and literary tropes.

Dibyakusum Ray's 'From "Dictatorship" to Dictatorship: The Dynamics of Alien and "Legitimized" Authoritarianism in 1980s Popular Hindi Films' is the only chapter dedicated to popular films. The chapter is also notable for its temporal departure from Emergency as it presents a detailed analysis of dictatorship as a self-repeating trope. How is the 1970s 'dictatorship' viewed by the action-adventure genre of the 1980s? And, more troublingly, how (and why) does cinematic autocrats gain narrative approval in a country plagued by post-authoritarian trauma?

Ray's methodology of temporally reconfiguring the 1970s authoritarianism finds a suitable echo in Kaushik Bhaumik's 'The Long 1970s: Anjan Dutt as Archive, Some Interfaces' – the concluding chapter of this book due to its sweeping scope, axial to the cinematic figurations of Bengali actor-director Anjan Dutt. Unique in its methodology, Bhaumik's essay talks about Dutt's four-decade-long career as an unconventional leading man, musician and director, embodying the crisis of ideology and moral vacillation following the Emergency. Post-Gandhi political turmoils, the rise of neoliberalism, the emergence of right-wing politics – Bhaumik tracks these watershed moments through Dutt's career, depicting him as an ideological flaneur representing the quintessential, rootless creative thinker of India.

While the afterlife of the National Emergency is covered mostly by Bhaumik's chapter on a contemporary filmmaker who often engages with the long 1970s, it might also be noted how many other chapters in the present volume offer references, albeit opaquely, to the many emergencies that plagued Indian democracy, including the draconian regime of Narendra Modi that has sparked raw debates on the nature of a possibly undeclared Emergency and India's possible decline into an electoral autocracy. The Emergency of 1975 is being remembered in the Indian Parliament amidst heated arguments as we are on the threshold of fifty years of it, and the ruling coalition is interested in raising the issue at the discomfort of the Indian National Congress-led opposition. On the other hand, after the historic Indian General Election outcomes of 2024 where the present regime has suffered a considerable setback, the election is being compared to that of 1977, which saw the downfall of Indira Gandhi. So the Emergency has regained relevance on the streets, in political discussions and dissensus that is extended beyond the purview of the state.

In this context, the publication of the present volume seems apt and timely, with its scope getting much wider than what we could initially assume. However, we need to accept a major limitation of this volume. None of the chapters engage with the Emergency's consequences for cinemas of South India, even though Snehalata Reddy's incarceration during the Emergency and subsequent demise after release[1] makes her one of the most significant instances of what Ashish Rajadhyaksha once addressed as 'dying in the cause of cinema', albeit in a different context.[2]

The editors thank the Scheme for Promotion of Academic and Research Collaboration (SPARC) of the Ministry of Education, Government of India, for its generous financial support that made this book (and the research that went before it) possible. Topics that this volume has not addressed will surely be considered by future researchers, with the present one serving as a vantage point for taking off.

1

The fear of cinema

Ashish Rajadhyaksha

Cinephobia. The term was first introduced into Indian film studies by Ravi Vasudevan to mean both a fear and hatred of the cinema, the opposite of cine*philia* or love for not just the films one may like, but the cinema itself. M. S. S. Pandian later usefully transformed it into something more specific. According to him, the elite, modernist, upper-caste fear of 'low' popular culture would further translate into an ideology of the state – an essential fear of something it could not control. His major example of state cinephobia was the Tamil Congress leader C. Rajagopalachari, who made multiple pronouncements about cinema, expressing the view (for instance) in 1939 that there is 'so much objectionable matter in the films prepared in India' that the objection that they are 'anti-Indian' 'pales into insignificance' (Pandian 2014, 952).

A rather deeper cinephobia is evidenced in Mahatma Gandhi's occasional and under-discussed pronouncements about film. In 1929, he considered the cinema to be central to a 'satanic' modernity into which everybody had sunk. We are, Gandhi warned, 'in the midst of a raging fire' of the 'cinema, the stage, the race course, the drinking booth and the opium den' (1929, 216–17). In 1936, when Gandhi made the tactical argument that despite his avowed 'disapproval of cinemas, races, share market, gambling and the like', perhaps the time to confront the cinema was not now – since as a 'practical reformer' he needed to take into consideration 'what vices are ripe for being publicly dealt with' (1939, 378) – his views drew a protest. K. A. Abbas, in a famous rejoinder addressed directly to Gandhi, wondered how he could possibly have such opinions when, by his own admission, he had never seen a film. While some films did, Abbas admitted, 'exploit the baser passions of man to make money', they are also capable of bringing in a 'socially useful and morally uplifting element'. You could, for example, make documentaries, work with education, provide news. He listed a few Indian films that offered such content, typically saint films like *Sant Tukaram*, *Sant Tulsidas*, *Seeta* and *Vidyapati*, and reform socials like *Janmabhoomi*, *Dharti Mata* and *Aadmi*.[1]

Abbas believed, sincerely it seems, that the usual moralist 'good cinema' argument would work, but he clearly hadn't understood Gandhi. The cinephobic was not only against bad films but against the *cinema itself*. 'Sitting in a closed theatre', Gandhi wrote in May 1947, 'one feels suffocated'. If he had his way, he would 'see to it that all the cinemas and theatres in India were converted into spinning halls and factories for handicrafts of all kinds' (1947b, 150). In December 1947, he went further and described the cinema as unsanitary, against which one needed to purify oneself.

> You should follow the rules of sanitation. Why do you need a cinema here? Instead of this, you can perform the various plays and stage dramas known to us. The cinema will only make you spend money. Then you will also learn to gamble and fall into other evil habits. (Gandhi 1947a, 121)

The problem was certainly far more basic than anything that could be solved merely by making better films. The filmmaker-weaver's job was to sanitize film, atone for its apparatus and cleanse the movie theatre.

—

Cinephobia entered into a new era of dangerous politics in 1969–70, when India transitioned into a popular democracy. An increasingly heterogeneous opposition, drawn for the first time since Independence from the peasantry, the lower castes and tribes, and other oppressed minorities, challenged (in Rajni Kothari's words) a 'small but powerful, educated, urban middle class controlling major, technological and financial institutions and in full command over the policy process and the decision-making framework' (Kothari 1988b, 273–74). The cinema, an extreme form of unregulated and lumpenized popular culture capable of arousing the masses and throwing up a rabid leadership in who knew what uncontrollable form, had become an instrument of this opposition – unless, that is, it were somehow contained.

The Khosla Committee charged its *régisseur* with several new responsibilities. These included sanitizing the system with a fervour that at times recalled Gandhi. As an exemplary citizen, and human incarnate of the law of Article

19, the director's liberal freedoms would be zealously protected by the courts *on the condition* that the director also publicly demonstrated his use of such freedoms in a responsible way – as Govind Nihalani was commended for doing by Justice Sabyasachi Mukharji when making *Tamas*, in which he successfully drew 'a lesson from our country's past history to . . . rise above religious barriers and treat one another with kindness, sympathy and affection'. It is, says Mukharji, only possible 'for a motion picture to convey such a message . . . [this is a filmmaking] achievement of great social value'.[2] This can only happen if the director literally leads by example: demonstrates how the 'reasonable restrictions' on free speech actually work, and how they can be translated into the aesthetic-technical practices of scriptwriting, shooting, editing and sound-mixing. Khosla outlines how this can be done through a comparison of two Hindi films, *Farz* and *Man Ka Meet*, with Ingmar Bergman's *Wedding Swedish Style* and Michelangelo Antonioni's *Blow Up*. The Hindi films had strange and incomprehensible sequences in which

> the heroine . . . shakes her hips backwards and forwards and sideways . . . no school or college girl would dance in this manner in front of a stranger, nor is such dancing at all resorted to by any of our young people . . . [it] may almost be called the performance of a unilateral act of coitus.[3]

On the other hand, while Bergman and Antonioni also deal with sexual content, they do so in a sensitive way without any attempt to deprave and, on the way, even produce 'a slice of life'.

In 1970, this law of the cinema was made explicit in a major Supreme Court judgement, which defined a concept that Madhava Prasad has christened 'cinepolitics' (Prasad 2014). At its most basic, it is a cinematic enactment of several conventions of popular democracy, played out as a narrative-spectatorial pact both inside a movie theatre – in the way films are made, in the multiple conventions of shooting, editing and sound used – and outside it, in the way stardom, or fan behaviour, expands into social and political realms.

A state-appointed *regisseur* – a *sarkari* Bergman, if you like – practising a state-endorsed cinematic realism now came to embody 'a secularized, contractual aspect' of film direction, says Prasad (1998, 20–21). The director would work on behalf of a new kind of 'citizen-spectator' whose stern, interpretative authority would 'brook no challenge from the frame of representation'. The cinematic apparatus would also become the censor's apparatus. Censorship posed specific challenges to Realism, including how to confront it, how to skirt around it with multiple conventions, like cutaways and wink-and-nudge interpretations of seemingly legitimate content. Since the early 1980s (more precisely, following the amendment to the Certification Rules in 1983) these challenges came to define the filmmaker's skill. They also repurposed the censor into a film appreciation instructor, as the CBFC began giving extensive advice in its certification process on how filmmakers needed to remake their films, what bits of dialogue needed cutting, what acceptable substitutes to use, how sequences might be re-shot or re-edited.

Cinema and the Abbas judgement

Thirty years after his open letter to Gandhi, K. A. Abbas re-entered the picture with another intervention. He was a member of the Khosla Committee and, dissatisfied with its debates, he made a short film, *A Tale of Four Cities*, with the explicit purpose of challenging first the Committee and then the Censor Board itself. In a meeting of the Khosla Committee, the chairman of the Censor Board had denied that there was any political censorship in a way that provoked Abbas deeply. 'They never had any social or political themes to which anyone might object. They only knew dancing, singing and hip-swinging. That provoked me to challenge the statement' (Abbas 1977, 477). And so he made this short film, screened it, and when, as expected, his brothel scene was objected to, he filed a petition with the Supreme Court. In an extraordinary 'screenplay' about the events leading up to the trial – a story about a 'film sixteen minutes long' that was 'produced in the interests of Truth and Justice', but which became an 'eleven month-long feature' that could now be titled 'A Tale of Censorship' – Abbas recounts the campaign: from the time he first applied for a censor certificate for the film on 23 December 1968 to when he wrote a letter on 20 July 1969 refusing to carry out cuts, stating to the court that

> I think, once for all, the Supreme Court will have to decide the issue of whether a documentary of social protest can be banned or distorted under the cover of clauses which were originally intended to eliminate obscenity and pornography. That is where I propose to take the issue, besides the court

of informed public opinion. This is not a threat. It is a promise. (Abbas 1970, 110–11)

When the government relented and offered an unchanged version of the Universal certificate, Abbas further amended his petition to either be 'able to challenge pre-censorship itself as offensive to freedom of speech and expression, [or alternatively] . . . to challenge the provisions of the [Indian Cinematography] Act and the rules, orders and directions under this Act, as vague and arbitrary'.[4] He did this, he said, because he 'wanted to put the censorship machinery in the docks'.

The judgement interpreted Abbas's petition with some gratitude as a filmmaker's noble effort to clear up once and for all the 'void for vagueness' doctrine that had beset the law and taken it 'to the verge of extinction' in all areas 'except in the ever-shrinking area of obscenity'. Justice Hidayatullah then followed up with an extended textual summary of what he thought *A Tale of Four Cities* was actually about. It was a graphic judicial embodiment of the legal gaze and (what Prasad calls) its 'interpretative authority'.

[*A Tale of Four Cities*] is in black and white and is silent except for a song which the labourers sing while doing work and some background music and sounds for stage effect. The film, in motion sequences or still shots, shows contrasting scenes of palatial buildings, hotels and factories, evidence of the prosperity of a few, and shanties, huts and slums, evidence of poverty of the masses. These scenes alternate and in between are other scenes showing sweating labourers working to build the former and those showing the squalid private life of these labourers. . . . Sometimes the inmates, becoming aware of the photographer, quickly withdraw themselves. Then we see one of the inmates shutting a window and afterwards we see the hands of a woman holding some currency notes and a male hand plucking away most of them leaving only a very few in the hands of the female. The suggestion in the first scene is that a customer is being entertained behind closed shutters and in the next sequence that the amount received is shared between the pimp and the prostitute, the former taking almost the whole of the money. The sequence continues and for the first time the woman who shut the window is again seen. She sits at the dressing table, combs her hair, glances at the two love-birds in a cage and looks around the room as if it were a cage. Then she goes behind a screen and emerges in other clothes and prepares for bed. She sleeps and dreams of her life before she took the present path.

There is nothing else in the film to be noticed either by us or by the public for which it is intended.[5]

There is no doubting to be permitted here, no ambiguity, no apophenic overinterpretation, no covert, wink-and-nudge, subversive content. While the legally enfranchised gaze of the citizen–spectator can admit to a diversity of reality, it cannot – when it becomes an act of citizenship – permit a diversification of perception, says Madhava Prasad. 'To admit that the eye's choice of objects from a field of perception could be arbitrary and unpredictable would be to jeopardize reality itself and would lead to anarchy' (Prasad 1998, 22–3). What you see is what you (should be able to) get.

What did Abbas get? Seen in one way, a lot. A Film Censorship Appellate Tribunal (or FCAT) was instituted of 'eminent persons' to exist independent of the government, a landmark in the history of film censorship in India, which was disbanded in April 2021 by the Modi-II regime. On the other hand, Chief Justice Hidayatullah reinstated both state cinephobia and the cleansing *regisseur*, and effectively claimed Abbas's support in his endeavour to do so. The judge thanked Abbas, reiterated his discomfort with censorship, but also parallelly the need for some kind of mechanism given the cinema's alarming ability to produce images 'more true to life than . . . any other form of representative art'. What was required, Hidayatullah concluded, was that film be isolated for special treatment different from 'that of other forms of art and expression'. The problem of the cinema continued to lie in its unregulated excesses.

Who is a filmmaker?-1: *Circa* 1975

In 1974, Anant Namjoshi, Minister of Education in Vasantdada Patil's Congress government in Maharashtra, wrote a curious short story in *The Illustrated Weekly of India*. Titled 'Should Students Run Universities?' (Namjoshi 1974), it was written in theatrical style as a fictional conversation between the author and an anonymous young student. The student complains that they are 'nobodies' in an institution that, the author says, is 'run for you and for you alone, my young friends'. The student is not impressed: 'our syllabi are outdated and outmoded'. Namjoshi is building up to his big point: his proposed Maharashtra Universities Act, in which an elected Students Council would be formally recognized and given representation on every university's Senate.

A year later almost to the day, Namjoshi's party did the very opposite of that promise. It declared the Emergency. This is, of course, a controversial moment in Indian political history. The Emergency has been framed, for example by Rajni Kothari, as a combination of paramilitary forces and 'techno-managers' cracking down on the very people that Indira Gandhi had mobilized in a new era of mass politics (Kothari 1988a, 2227). The 1970s saw a 'steady and systematic destruction of institutions' as charismatic individuals taking on 'mythical qualities' found themselves 'bolstered . . . by a powerful imagery of threats and dangers, of enemies that must be dealt with . . . as anti-national and against national interest'. A central aspect of the uprisings that presaged the Emergency had been student militancy on and off the campus, the very students now widely characterized under the crackdown as 'lumpens' – hedonist males with no interest in education, art or anything that made for the good life.

The Navnirman movement in Gujarat in 1973–4, followed by the Bihar agitation led by the Chhatra Yuva Sangharsh Vahini in 1974, were the immediate political triggers for the declaration of the Emergency in 1975. During the Emergency, student action was quelled by a repressive state apparatus as students were forced underground, arrested, imprisoned, killed and abducted. Its repeal in 1977 saw the full-scale return of militancy. In 1978 the Students Anti Fee-Rise Action Committee (SAFAC), a Bombay-based coalition of the Vidhyarti Pradharthi Sanghathna (VPS), PROYOM and the All India Students Federation (AISF) led a stunningly successful operation in which they physically took over the Fort offices of Bombay University for a day, declared among themselves a Vice Chancellor and other office bearers, passed several executive orders, and then one by one melted into the crowd gathered outside, even as the military was summoned to surround the campus ('Bombay University Occupied!, Story of a Student' 2015). Between 1979 and 1990, multiple issues – primarily around caste-based reservations and fee rises – saw students take over the frontline of political action, making for a long-term ancestor to the agitations in Delhi, Kolkata and Hyderabad over 2016–19.[6]

The late 1970s' student ferment across the nation was presumably unaware of – and even had they known, would have been largely unimpressed by – the small bit of action at the Film and Television Institute of India (FTII) in January 1975, when twenty-two acting course students complained that they weren't getting good roles in diploma films. A later FTII strike in 1977 attracted marginally more interest, in part because of its connection with Information and Broadcasting Minister Vidyacharan Shukla's complicated investments in the film industry that sought to, as reported in *Screen*, 'misuse . . . censorship, the raw stock supply scheme and the machinery of film exports to bully and blackmail the industry into lending film . . . as a medium of political propaganda' ('Shukla's Twenty Month Reign of Terror: Industry Speaks Out At Last' 1977). Mostly, however, FTII did not exist within the university imagination, and its internal grievances remained closed to the world, despite the occasional attention gathered by, for example, September 1984, when the entire student body *gheraoed* the Governing Council over a dispute around the right to change course electives and were hauled off *en masse* by the police.

To the acting students, the problem was straightforward. As Naseeruddin Shah recounts it, young student directors would 'cast anyone they liked, acting student or not', while several students of acting 'went through their two years without once facing a camera'. Meanwhile directors were making films 'with titles like (and I exaggerate a bit but only a bit) *Apocalypsis-cum-Genesis, And unto the Cosmic Void, Madhyasuryaya Mrigtrishna, Tribheeshan ka Teevra Maadhyam*'.[7] When Hrishikesh Mukherjee tried explaining 'in words of two syllables why in movies the director is so much more important than the actor', he was asked by students 'to cut the baby talk'.

> Without mincing words, but deleting the expletives that rise like bile every time I recall all this, we student actors thought there was something mighty rotten with this situation. It stank. Apart from the fact of student actors missing out on what should have been an assured part of their training not being perceived as an injustice, it just didn't seem to sit well with anyone that we actors were asking to be considered as essential participants in the making of the films, on par with the technicians.

Challenges to the 'director system'

How do we look back, as we develop our project of reading the nation into the campus, on a weird strike like this one? There is, for one, graphic evidence of the *regisseur*-in-formation. The 'director system' of filmmaking was a European import borrowed from the theatre to replace an earlier 'cameraman system'. It survived in Hollywood only for a short period before it was itself jettisoned by the industrial production line. In India after the War, and following the decline of the studio era, the director was more often the star-impresario, a Raj Kapoor or a V. Shantaram, fronting several murky financial systems that lay beneath. When the *regisseur* was adopted by the Indian state in the 1970s, it turned controversial. There was a tacit hierarchy at work, with the film director at the top of an 'above-the-line' list and acting, minus the star, somewhere at the bottom. Although actors led the way for recognition, they were followed by cinematographers who fought for the right to be upgraded to Directors of Photography and receive 'co-authorship' status,[8] scenarists who demanded copyright contracts and royalty for usage, and lyrics-writers and singers who too asserted intellectual property rights over their different contributions.[9] Actors received no such rights. By August 1975, a new two-year integrated course did away with the acting course entirely. It was effectively outsourced to the National School of Drama, with the FTII only offering six-month advanced courses for its final year students, which too were then done away with.

Many of the student films Naseeruddin Shah mocks reveal precisely this tension. One that is clearly referenced in his sarcastic list is Arun Khopkar's 1974 short fiction film, *Teevra Madhyam*, an exploration of the political role of art through the moral centre of a young classical singer (Smita Patil's first screen role) surrounded by student activists. Quotations include Caudwell on how 'Bernard Shaw became a mere entertainer for the bourgeoisie', and 'a revolutionary laughs only once, when he hears the last laugh'. In one scene, male student activists are preparing for an anti-fee-rise *morcha*.

One of them, played by Saeed Mirza, prints leaflets on a cyclostyling machine. Another, played by Ketan Mehta, describes a scene he considers funny, in which a rich student willing to pay higher fees sees this problem as someone else's. Returning even to a film like this, we get to unearth a rather more complicated convergence: between politics playing out in the filmmakers' work and in the actions occurring on the campus – not least, we shall soon see, those of Saeed Mirza and Ketan Mehta.

We shall see this convergence manifested on campus (in Mehta's *Holi* and the 1977 strike) and off it, especially in the birth of film co-operatives (Yukt, later Odessa) that spilled over beyond the frame and thus also beyond orthodox institutional limitations. As politics converged with cinema, it split the *regisseur* apart. The conflict between the director's creative rights as against the cinema's capacity to accommodate the 'hordes' – the multitude walking in *morchas* against the fee-rise now turned into normative film spectators – would enter a wider public domain. The multiple FTII strikes would become interesting punctuations in that astonishing, under-discussed convergence.

The fear of noise

In 1971, Satyajit Ray waded in with his own idea of what the refurbished Indian *regisseur* needed to bear in mind. Such a filmmaker had of course to be the bearer of free speech, and thus needed to keep alive his 'urge for self-expression, common to all artists'. However, this urge had to be tempered by the equally pressing need to 'establish rapport with an audience'. For all the success of the film society movement, of which he was himself a founder and a key representative, Ray was sceptical of the governmental project to convert a 'perceptive minority' of the public into 'patrons of . . . art theatres', or for the cinema to truly claim for itself the *niche* safe spaces that the other arts possessed. Even if such a possibility exists, Ray asserted, it still needed filmmakers to have a plan that would make their productions accountable, financially and otherwise, to the state.[10]

Ray was speaking at a time of serious crisis for independent filmmakers. Specifically, the crisis was to do with the fact that many films made with government loans – including critically acclaimed ones – were getting no release to reach their audiences, were being frozen out of the distribution system, and had begun defaulting on their debt. The Film Finance Corporation (FFC) was implementing draconian measures to recover its money. An FFC representative was quoted as saying that they would go after filmmakers in every way possible. 'We will not relent, we will follow. But if (the filmmaker) goes completely out of business and he has no assets to declare and there is nothing to his credit . . . naturally, the amount has to be written off' ('Committee on Public Undertakings (1975–76): 79th Report: Film Finance Corporation').

—

Of course, it was more complicated. The arrival of lightweight Arriflex cameras meant that, for the first time, filmmakers were freed up to displace script- and location-bound cinema with the introduction of *verité* noise: to bring into the frame what new media theorist Hito Steyerl would decades later call 'dirty data'.[11] An early example of such data came about in the late 1960s when Mrinal Sen, one of the pioneers of the New Cinema movement that the FFC was then supporting, began shooting political processions in Calcutta with, as he said, little clarity on how, if at all, he would use the footage. In the event, Sen used this footage across his Calcutta trilogy and in his *Bhuvan Shome*. By 1971 the numerous rallies that he had filmed had coalesced into a specific direction as they directly took on the Congress government of Chief Minister Siddhartha Shankar Ray, gradually turning violent with attacks on statues of nationalist leaders and clashing directly with the police. In 1971 itself, the year that Sen references in his film, the colonial Bengal Suppression of Terrorist Outrages Act of 1936 was replaced by the Prevention of Violent Activities Bill, even as the violence turned systemic with retaliatory police crackdowns killing over 4,000 young supporters of the Communist Party of India (Marxist-Leninist) (the official figure was 1,783).

In 1972, *Calcutta 71* received a limited commercial release at Chowringhee's Metro Cinema. Several of the documentary shots inserted into the film's finale suddenly found a whole new meaning as students came to screenings to spot their friends among the pictured crowds. 'Young boys . . . would keep coming back', Sen said later. 'People with their family and their friends. They would watch [the film] over and over again, just for another glimpse of their friend' (Sen 2003, 67). The scenes began providing unexpected evidence of people in the crowd who had later disappeared or been killed in police encounters. As the screenings became something of a regular political event for activists to meet nightly, police began mounting surveillance every time and everywhere that *Calcutta 71* was shown. New controversy followed as the footage pot converted into diverse forms of textual 'noise' and spilled over into debates that may have had nothing to do with the film Sen believed he had made. Arguments took place: Sen first told students he had begun shooting *Calcutta 71* only in September 1971, but then admitted, as activists confronted him with faces on the screen whom they knew had disappeared well before then, that he may have also used street footage from as far back as 1969.

By 1971, cinephobia had taken on a yet further dimension, closer to what Steyerl has called 'apophenia', or the fear of 'perception of patterns within random data'. 'Pattern recognition resonates with the wider question of political recognition', she writes, for 'who is recognized on a political level and as what? As a subject? A person? A legitimate category of the population? (Steyerl 2016)'

Ray's view on the filmmaker's responsibility – a responsibility that he was effectively accusing Sen of having abdicated – was driven by a clearly apophenic fear of rampant misinterpretation, precisely such as what the students were indulging in at the Metro screenings. This directorial abdication is to him evidenced in Sen's self-indulgent, 'modish narrative devices' in *Akash Kusum* and *Bhuvan Shome* (Basu and Dasgupta 1992, 38). Ray spoke of *Bhuvan Shome* as something that 'looks a bit like its French counterpart, but is essentially old-fashioned and Indian beneath its trendy habit'. If *Bhuvan Shome* was, at base, no more than a story of 'Big Bad Bureaucrat reformed by Rustic Belle', such a story could well be equally plausibly told in 'a simple but forceful language' shorn of unnecessary excess.

—

Earlier, in 1968, the FFC had expanded its operations to include distribution and export; by 1973 it was channelling all imported celluloid raw stock; and by 1974 (after the withdrawal of the MPEAA from the Indian market) it was importing foreign films for local distribution. At this time it began dangling a carrot of loans to 'modest but off-beat films of talented and promising people in the field', with the stick that these filmmakers use this chance to create 'an effective instrument for the promotion of national culture, education and healthy entertainment'.[12] In 1976, at the height of the Emergency, a year after the strike of the acting students and Ghatak's sage advice on how to have a name befitting a filmmaker, carrot-and-stick was further sharpened into a financial-cum-aesthetic strategy: where you could at once be an independent filmmaker *and* support a state project, make your own 'artistic' film *and* have a 'reasonable prospect of being commercially successful'. It would be a 'balanced view', and it would follow an art-house 'check list' including the 'following criteria . . . for granting loans: (1) *Human interest* in the story; (2) *Indianness* in theme and approach; (3) *Characters* with whom the audience can identify; (4)

Dramatic content.[13] Much of this was extrapolated from the advice Ray gave to young filmmakers in 1971, including that they should always make films with a 'well worked out scenario' revealing 'a modicum of craftsmanship' (Ray [1976] 1994, 98–9), not only aesthetic necessities but economically vital.

Being *regisseurs* and thus defenders of free speech, India's independent filmmakers were by default on the same side of the political fence. Opposing Emergency censorship was the easy part. The problem deepened and then led to, as one critic called it, 'schismatic warfare' between the independent filmmakers themselves, when it began implicating a larger, more elusive and infinitely more problematic state project around cinematic realism (Masud 1980, 83–8). Iqbal Masud saw it as a divide between the cinema's 'radicals and its gradualists', 'root and branch' filmmakers conflicting with 'gradual change' filmmakers. For many, there was nothing reformist about 'gradual change'.

For all their avowed opposition to the Emergency, in freezing a film's overt content – in reproducing the chilling Hidayatullah diktat that the film means only *this* and *nothing else* – filmmakers found themselves effectively reproducing the functions of the censor. Justice Mukharji, speaking on *Tamas*, warned filmmakers that they needed to rise to the challenge of 'meeting the explosively expanding cinema menace'.[14] The menace had, he said, to be 'strictly policed': and you can read the dark hint that if the textuality police (a.k.a. film directors) didn't supervise the narrative adequately, the actual police would step in.

(excerpts from 'Reinventing the Regisseur', in *John-Ghatak-Tarkovsky: Citizens, Filmmakers, Hackers*, 45–59, New Delhi: Tulika, 2023).

Not by Emergency alone

An unending saga of political repression and content control

Someswar Bhowmik

The phenomenon

Post-independence, India has witnessed (political) Emergency being declared thrice. However, the term 'Emergency' invariably evokes memories of the third and most controversial of these three instances so far – between 25 June 1975 and 21 March 1977. It was imposed during the reign of Mrs Indira Gandhi as the Prime Minister and was based on perceived imminent threats (both internal and external) to the Indian state and polity. To ward off those threats, the regime promptly suspended citizens' rights under Articles 14 (Equality before the law), 21 (Right to life and personal liberty) and 22 (Rights of persons arrested or detained) of the Constitution. This was followed by the suspension of Article 19. While it guarantees fundamental rights of free speech and expression, peaceful assembly, associations and unions, freedom of movement, freedom to hold and dispose of property in any part of the country and freedom to practice any profession, occupation or trade, it also enumerates limitations on these freedoms, terming these as 'reasonable restrictions'.

However, the Emergency witnessed complete cessation of the fundamental rights on the pretext of three major considerations: (1) economic productivity and social justice were more important than civil liberties and freedom of expression; (2) the media and sections of people in India were seriously hindering the State's efforts to promote economic productivity and social justice; and (3) a drastic contraction of civil liberties and press rights would advance the State's ability to promote those causes.

The worst sufferer among the media during the Emergency was the print medium, which was practically free from any measure of content control by the government after independence. The State promptly imposed stringent pre-censorship under the Defence and Internal Security of India Rules (DISIR) on 26 June 1975, a day after the proclamation of the Emergency. It also scaled up the indirect methods of manipulation by: (1) denying allocation of government advertising and newsprint; (2) forcibly merging news agencies; (3) threatening newspaper publishers, journalists and individual shareholders, both directly and indirectly; (4) detaining and arresting Indian journalists and deporting foreign ones; (5) seizing presses; and (6) cancelling Certificate of Registration of newspapers and periodicals and forfeiting their security deposits.

Fortunately, the phase of pre-censorship of the press was short-lived. It was lifted after the surprise declaration of snap parliamentary elections, which Mrs Gandhi lost resoundingly. A new coalition government restored, with immediate effect, the fundamental rights and civil liberties that were curtailed during the Emergency. Within six months of coming to power at the centre, it also published a 'White Paper on the Misuse of Media during the Emergency'.[1] True to its name, it focused only on some *temporary* aberrations perpetrated by a *short-lived* dispensation. This may be true of the press, but it is a false narrative as far as the film medium is concerned.

Generally, any cultural dissemination is a direct transaction involving the messenger (author/creator) and receiver (reader/audience/connoisseur). However, in the realm of film culture in India, the State foils this direct transaction by filtering and often sanitizing the message before allowing it to be placed in the public domain. This is pre-censorship of film.

Cinema in India has suffered more than a century of pre-censorship, out of which close to eight decades have elapsed in the post-independence era. This era has unfolded a complex saga of the Indian State keeping the cinematic medium in chains despite granting its citizens a constitutionally protected right to free speech and expression. And its application so far has generated a long list of serious abuses – of bureaucratic prerogative, of official position, of constitutional leverage – for political purpose.

One has therefore to contextualize the Emergency of 1975–7 vis-à-vis the film censorship machinery in India. Unlike in the press, neither pre-censorship of films nor political control of cinema was an Emergency-specific phenomenon. Truth be told, political narratives have unfolded in myriad and diverse forms on either side of the Emergency. The Emergency was just a microcosm of the State's political machinations with cinema.

State surveillance of films before Emergency

The most intriguing feature of film censorship in India is that it has straddled both the colonial era and the postcolonial one without a break.

Film censorship was introduced in 1920 under the aegis of the Indian Cinematograph Act 1918. The then British rulers were determined that cinema should serve, unflinchingly, their colonial interests.

The philosophy of film censorship in pre-independence India evinced three basic parameters:

1. to deny the Indian audience any access to communist or socialist ideals reflected in the Soviet cinema;
2. to ensure that the spirit of freedom and independence did not reach the audience of a colonized country regularly through the American films; and
3. to prevent the crystallization of the nationalist paradigm in Indian cinema.

It is, however, significant that the British rulers chose to foreground 'the safety of the audience and the prevention of degrading or moral performances' to camouflage their real, that is political, intentions. The Regional Censor Boards that were set up were largely autonomous.

Rulers of independent India surprised everybody by choosing to carry forward the system of film censorship in the postcolonial era, but in a different guise. There was no reversal in the official negative perception about the film medium, on moral and ethical grounds. It was rather reinforced by the enunciation of a postcolonial 'political' perception, different from the one that emerged in the colonial era. Rhetoric about scientific temperament, rationality, freedom, justice, rights, modernism, progress and development flaunted by the national(ist) leaders did not affect the film censorship machinery. Cinema remained equally vulnerable to administrative pressures and susceptible to the politicians' malice in the new era. By 1952, this postcolonial infrastructure for film censorship was firmly in place.

In 1951, film censorship was brought under the unified command of a Central Board of Film Censors (henceforth CBFC). Such centralization was a direct affront to the spirit of federalism enshrined in the Indian Constitution of 1950. But this was an indication that the leaders of independent India were more committed to building a unitary State structure than creating a genuinely federal system. It was, moreover, a fulfilment of their political agenda regarding cinema. Like their colonialist predecessors, they were also keen that cinema should serve their broad political objectives, which involved projects for democracy, citizenship and nationalism. But, unlike the colonial administration, they preferred a uniform code of control to be formulated by the central bureaucracy and exercised by the CBFC. The reconstituted Regional Censor Boards, subordinate to the CBFC and with considerably reduced power, were but an insignificant concession to the concept of federalism. The Cinematograph (Censorship) Rules 1951 were consequently framed, setting out the modus operandi of the centralized Board.

Still, there were strong apprehensions in the government quarters that the Supreme Court would strike down the film censorship provisions contained in the Cinematograph Act 1918, which was still in force. In fact, the Supreme Court, at that point, was striking down censorship provisions relating to other media not restricted to grounds specified in Article 19(2). In a prompt reaction, the government enacted the Constitution (First Amendment) Act 1951, in June. It fundamentally altered the spirit and scope of the original Article 19(2). The amended Article 19(2) now provided for 'reasonable restrictions' on the exercise of rights conferred by Article 19(1), including the right to freedom of speech and expression [Article 19(1)(a)]. This First Amendment saved the Cinematograph Act 1918 containing pre-censorship provisions.

In July 1952, a more elaborate Indian Cinematograph Act 1952 came into effect, repealing the Indian Cinematograph Act 1918. It also revalidated the Cinematograph (Censorship) Rules of 1951 for these to continue to govern the operations of the CBFC. Also, a four-page document was prepared and published. Titled 'Directive to Examining Committees regarding the principles to be observed in determining whether a film is or is not suitable for public exhibition', it contained a detailed list of objectionable matters in films. The nomenclature of this 'Directive' was eventually changed to 'Guidelines'. This paved the way for a three-pronged strategy under the umbrella document of the Cinematograph Act 1952.

It is significant that the basic framework for this machinery was finalized even before parliamentary democracy started functioning properly in independent India. The First General Elections, based on universal adult franchise, were held between October 1951 and February 1952. The first session of the newly constituted Indian Parliament was convened on 17 April 1952. By then, the Indian Cinematograph Act 1952 had already received presidential assent on 21 March 1952.

Remarkably, not only did the citizenry not resent the continuation of film censorship in a postcolonial democratic India, but they also felt secure in this arrangement. The society by and large accepted the State-projection of this arrangement as the best method for neutralizing the pulls and pressures that the postcolonial Indian cinema was being subjected to. Perhaps we can even suggest that the censorship regime offered them a mechanism by which to defend themselves against cinema's supposed attack on their moral and ethical universe. Different interest groups discovered elements of merit or virtue within the censorship machinery for their respective constituencies. The State, on its part, started acting as an arbiter, and also a manipulator, of popular perception of cinema.

This was a paradigm shift. Film censorship in the colonial era represented a unidirectional act of coercion devised by the State. Post-independence, it was quite perceptibly transformed into a more diversified and multilateral, power-relation. It began to revolve around an antagonism between the limits of freedom of expression aspired by a technological medium driven by modernism and the exercise of power defined by class, sector or group perceptions and interests. Seen from the perspective of the State, this exercise of power started manifesting a particular brand of teleology couched in legal and administrative jargon. The citizenry, on the other hand, participated in this exercise of power armed with a different brand of teleology full of value-loaded moral or ethical terms.

Film censorship regime in postcolonial India thus turned out to be not quite an arrangement through which the State imposed repression overriding popular dissent. It rather came to reflect certain ideological compromises reached between social forces in an epoch of transition. It was indicative of the relative power and authority of different segments of society, including elements of the State machinery. More importantly, it gave rise to a terrain for power play that would start creating and recreating rules, evolving parameters of debate, categories, and subjects. Thus, it inaugurated a discourse of censorship, reconciling its apparently incongruous cohabitation with the constitutionally sanctioned right to freedom of speech and expression by teleological arguments.

This reconciliation was given the stamp of constitutionality in 1959. In the most significant amendment to the Cinematograph Act 1952 to date, the State incorporated certain guiding principles for the certification of films. It read:

> *A film shall not be certified for public exhibition if, in the opinion of the authority competent to grant the certificate, the film or any part of it is against the interests of the security of the State, friendly relations with foreign States, public order, decency or morality, or involves defamation or contempt of court or is likely to incite the commission of any offence.*

Significantly, it replicates the 'reasonable restriction' clause of the amended Article 19(2) almost word for word to prepare the ground for the prevention of the exhibition of 'objectionable' films. Once such arguments began to emerge and be accepted, it created opportunities for camouflaging the political essence of film censorship in postcolonial India.

The State's position was vindicated by a landmark judgement of the Supreme Court in 1970. Giving the verdict on a petition challenging the constitutional validity of pre-censorship of films, then Hon'ble Chief Justice M. Hidayatullah on behalf of J. M. Shelat, G. K. Mitter, C. A. Vaidyialingam and A. N. Ray JJ, observed:

> (C)ensorship in India (and pre-censorship is not different in quality) has full justification in the field of exhibition of cinema films. We need not generalize about other forms of speech and expression here for each such fundamental right has a different content and importance. The censorship imposed on the making and exhibition of films is in the interests of society.[2]

This judgement overlooked that the Enquiry Committee on Film Censorship (1968) had observed in its Report that many prevalent 'Censorship Guidelines' transgressed the legal standard of 'Reasonableness'.[3]

Despite such safeguards, the state ensured that within the polemics relating to Indian film censorship, the political undertone of film censorship was seldom brought to the foreground.

But that does not mean an absence of political narrative around film censorship. Between November 1952 and February 1963, the films *Fall of Berlin* (1949, dir. Mikheil Chiaureli) and *Nine Hours to Rama* (1963, dir. Mark Robson) were prevented by the Indian State from being exhibited on political grounds, despite being cleared by the CBFC. In the case of the former, the depiction of the role of the USSR army from an American point of view was deemed unpalatable to the Indian government. The latter film was alleged to have shown disrespect to Gandhi, the martyred political icon of Nehru's India. Indian films also faced government wrath, though not to the same extent as the foreign ones. During the same period, the Sovereign Democratic Republic of India under Jawaharlal Nehru was trying to befriend both the Union of Socialist Soviet Republics under Joseph Stalin/Nikita Khrushchev and the Peoples' Republic of China under Mao Tse-tung. Although professedly this was not to be at the expense of friendship with the United Kingdom (which was the leader of the British Commonwealth) or the United States of America, the Indian political leaders were careful not to appear to have even slightly encouraged any anti-Communist propaganda emanating from these countries. Thus, many American films were purged of any critical reference to Communist regimes. But such indulgence, at least towards the Chinese, was abandoned after the India–China border conflict in 1962. The jingoist anti-Chinese film *Haqeeqat* (1964, dir. Chetan Anand) palpably attracted state patronage for its propagation, while *Neel Akasher Nichey* (1959, dir. Mrinal Sen) was slapped with a temporary ban for promoting Indo-Chinese fraternity.

Even the torchbearers of New Wave Cinema often came into conflict with the CBFC. One such film was *Samskara* (1970, dir. Pattabhi Rama Reddy, Kannada). It was a film about Brahminical rituals and prejudices of earlier decades. But the CBFC promptly banned it for being revolutionary and anti-religious. This decision evoked a strong protest from the intelligentsia and was ultimately reversed.

Film censorship also affected documentaries or shorts produced or procured (through purchase or donation) by the government-owned Films Division (henceforth FD), which had almost monopolistic control over documentary films. FD primarily dealt with films made by In-house Producers and Empanelled Producers; it also procured (either through purchase or donation) films from Independent Producers. But the authorities of FD were much more careful in their choice of subjects so as not to offend the parent ministry's bureaucrats, which often translated into following the writ of politicians. The sentiment has been summed up well in the reminiscences of an ex-employee:

> In a live democracy like ours, government departments have to abide by the party in power and its dictates. (Mohan 1990, 128)

However, the Indian State has never officially acknowledged the political purpose of either the Indian Cinematograph Act 1952 or the resultant film censorship machinery. It has rather foisted a false narrative foregrounding 'moral' and 'ethical' issues to justify film censorship.

Political narrative brought to fore

The 'White Paper' is an exceptional document, being the only instance so far in which political narratives around film censorship have been brought to the surface in a government document.

It informs us that within two months after the Emergency was declared, the Minister-in-charge, Ministry of Information and Broadcasting (henceforth MIC, I & B), advised the journalists to frame a code of self-regulation with the help of the chairman of the CBFC and the newly installed Chief Press Censor. This was on 14 August 1975.

But the State was not prepared to leave everything to the non-State actors. On 6 September, the MIC, I & B informed the film industry that new and more rigid censorship rules would replace an earlier set introduced in 1961.[4] The Minister's forceful assertion stemmed from an unusual communication (dated 18 August) that he had received from the then chairman, CBFC. In that communication, the CBFC chairman had literally pleaded for the firm support of the government in CBFC's fight against violence-ridden films. Significantly, he had noted that at the meeting of 14 August, the film journalists had cited two Hindi films, *Dharma* (1973, dir. Chand) and *Pran Jaye Par Vachan Na Jaye* (1973, dir. Ali Raza), which the CBFC had wanted to ban for showing excessive violence, but the government subsequently cleared it with 'A' certificates.[5] More interesting was his allusion to the film *Sholay* (1975, dir. Ramesh Sippy), which the journalists felt was passed with a 'U' certificate despite excessive depiction of violence, simply due to the influence of one of the stars in the film.[6]

However, during the entire course of the Emergency, the proposed 'new and more rigid censorship rules' did not materialize. Contrarily, the government was bothered more about reference or even allusion to political phenomena on screen than the depiction of violence. And to put a political leash on the film medium in India, the existing censorship rules were sufficient.

The film *Aandhi* (1975, dir. Gulzar), which had woven into a tale of marital discord the story of a woman's political ambition, was one that went through much difficulty during the period in question. The film was initially given a 'U' certificate by the CBFC in January 1975 and was a reasonable success. But after the imposition of Emergency, the government suspended the film's certificate under section 6 of the Cinematograph Act, citing similarities between the reel-life female protagonist's characterization and the real-life Mrs Gandhi. After the film had suffered two months' compulsory hibernation, it was eligible for release once again. The State then communicated to the producer that the film could be banned for bringing the system of election by universal adult franchise into disrepute. While this was grossly untrue, the government had left the producer with no other recourse than to voluntarily restructure the film. He did so and got his 'revised' film 'certified' again in March 1976.[7]

More bizarre was the case of *Aandolan* (1975, dir. Lekh Tandon). It was given a 'U' certificate on 27 May 1975. The CBFC also classified it as predominantly educational (PE) because it depicted the Quit India movement of 1942. However, before the film was released, Emergency was proclaimed, and the government recalled it using its discretionary powers. Then, after prolonged deliberations, the producer was asked to carry out several drastic cuts. All these related to revolutionary and political activities of the Quit India movement. But the government construed that even these anachronistic and out-of-context scenes would incite commission of offence leading to disturbance of public order.[8]

The nadir of government activism involving cinema during Emergency centred on the film *Kissa Kursi Ka* (1975, dir. Amrit Nahata). It satirically depicted the desperate, unscrupulous and corrupt practices adopted by politicians to usurp power and then cling to it. Remarkably, the director was a parliamentarian of the ruling party, although out of sync with its prevalent posture. The CBFC examined the film twice just before the declaration of the Emergency. Both times, the majority decision was in favour of 'U' certificate subject to drastic cuts. Ignoring these recommendations, the CBFC referred it to the government under section 25(1) of the Cinematograph Censorship Rules, 1961 for necessary action.

Mr Nahata promptly filed a writ petition in the Supreme Court on 12 May 1975, praying that the apex court should direct the government to issue a 'U' certificate to his film based on CBFC deliberations. But the Emergency preceded any judicial order. And on 5 July 1975, the Ministry of Information and Broadcasting (MIC) ordered that 'all prints of the film be taken possession of and kept in careful custody irrespective of the course of the Court's proceedings'. On 14 July, the government declared the film undesirable and therefore forfeited the print, negative, sound negative, even stills and publicity material relating to the film, under the DISIR. Unable to get a stay on this order from the Supreme Court, Mr Nahata was forced to part with the material. The court, however, directed the government to preserve the material in proper condition until the disposal of the writ petition.

After three months, Mr Nahata approached the apex court requesting it to see the film in order to ascertain whether the confiscated material had been properly preserved. The government pleaded its helplessness to show the film on account of some 'mix-up'. Finally, on 22 March 1976, the government requested the Supreme Court to decide the matter on merit without insisting on the film's exhibition. This was an admission that the materials under government custody had been destroyed. Providing a further twist to the whole incident, Mr Nahata withdrew his petition without even asking for costs on 13 July.[9] One is not sure whether he did it willingly or under duress.

The regime's sensitivity affected foreign films also. The political thriller, *All the President's Men* (1976, dir. Alan J. Pakula), was based on the product of investigative journalism by two Washington Post journalists, Bob Woodward and Carl Bernstein. The duo had unearthed the Watergate scandal involving the re-election campaign of the Republican president Richard Nixon in 1974, which finally led to his resignation, was also frowned upon and blocked.[10]

Manipulation of documentary cinema was done more crudely through blatant misuse of the FD and its established norms. It is needless to iterate that the In-house Producers of the Films Division, entrusted with producing 'propagatory' documentary films and Indian Newsreels, were simply instructed under pains of disciplinary action and dismissal from service to focus on 'propaganda'. Empanelled Producers were given commissions to produce 'propaganda' films. And Independent Producers, having clout with the ruling party, had a field day with their dealings with FD.

It is on record that for commissioned films made by Empanelled Producers, the prevalent norms were frequently overlooked and certain filmmakers constantly patronized. One such filmmaker was S. Sukhdev. During the Nehru era, he was busy critiquing the inequities of Indian society, still steeped in feudal values. After Nehru's death, his stance became vociferously strident and radicalized in films like *And Miles to Go . . .* (1965), a bitter appraisal of the state's neglect of the poor, and *India '67*, portraying the cinematic pilgrimage of a young postcolonial nation in a stifled pursuit of its aspirations.

Sukhdev soon shifted his position by making *Nine Months to Freedom* (1972), during the independence war in Bangladesh in 1971. In it, he portrayed Mrs Gandhi as a saviour. Soon he was seen championing her political cause during a period of anti-Indira sentiments sweeping the country in 1974. He came out with such films as *Behind the Breadline, A Few More Questions, Violence: What Price? Who pays?* or *Voice of the People*, thus becoming one of her blue-eyed boys. Such was his clout that 'he never followed the system and got decisions approved directly in Delhi (where the Ministry of Information & Broadcasting is located) . . . and always managed to get enough raw stock (the government imposed raw stock quotas in those days)'.[11] And as a logical conclusion to this development, he was commissioned to make four films simultaneously justifying the Emergency. These films were *After the Silence, Thunder of Freedom, For What You Are Voting* and *Bonded Labour*.

Besides these, Sukhdev persuaded the FD to entrust Independent Producers with a series of documentaries praising Mrs Gandhi's 20-Point Economic Programme.[12]

The FD also succumbed to direct political pressure from Mrs Gandhi's party cadres or party units in accommodating films made or sponsored by them.[13]

Ironically, the mood within the FD in response to such manipulation was one of acquiescence, rather than one of fait accompli. That most insiders had learnt to fall in line with the government's directives came out vividly in the following statement:

Fortunately, the dictates were not '*diktats*' nor dictatorial in nature. (Mohan 1990, 128)

Hence, as far as the FD is concerned, the proclamation of Internal Emergency, and its subsequent operation, was neither an earth-shaking nor a temporary experience. The FD people did not wake up in the morning of 26 May 1975 to find a paradigm shift in the FD's style of functioning. It was business as usual at FD.

Thus, the 'White Paper' quite elaborately reveals that the Emergency led to a palpable overdrive in activism on the part of the State, especially the bureaucrats, and sometimes personal interference from the MIC, I & B, acting as 'Super Censor'. Under normal circumstances, they would have refrained from this. But emboldened by the extraordinary 'powers' vested in them during the Emergency, they transformed themselves into virtual plenipotentiaries, if not full-fledged dictators.

Interestingly, there were at least three significant episodes of politically biased decisions to control films during the same period that do not find mention in the 'White Paper'.

One instance relates to the Telugu film *Telugunadu* (1975, dir. B R Rao). Its storyline also had a political movement as the backdrop. However, this reference was to a more recent happening, the violent agitation for the partition of Andhra Pradesh from 1969 through 1972. The film was refused a certificate on 23 May 1975. The CBFC reasoned that the film could foment social unrest or discontent to such an extent as to incite people to commit crimes and could also promote disorder, violence, a breach of law, disaffection or resistance to government. Interestingly, the director himself was a Congress MP, who had lost an eye in the violent agitation during the movement. So now he was ostensibly arguing against violence and pleading for unity. However, he failed to make any impression on the corridors of power. Even his offer to change the name of the film and undertake modifications as per government advice did not break the ice. The MIB thought that the film contravened public order, decency and morality and was likely to incite the commission of an offence. One cannot discount the possibility of the internal politics of Congress playing a significant part in this episode. The Emergency, however, was a convenient camouflage. After trying in vain for seventeen months to secure CBFC's certificate, the producer B Narayanamurthy was forced to seek judicial intervention for the film's release.[14]

In 1975, Pattabhi Rama Reddy, who had earlier faced CBFC's wrath after making *Samskara* (1970), planned a film, *Chanda Marutha* (Wild West), intending to explore the prevalent fascination of the urban youth for armed revolutionary activity. He based it on a play (*Kranthi Bantu Kranthi*) by P Lankesh, one of the torchbearers of the Kannada *Navya* (modern) movement. Lankesh had subtly compared the armed and violent means of revolution with peaceful, non-violent means. During shooting, Reddy's wife, Snehalata, was arrested for participating in anti-government demonstrations and allegedly concealing the whereabouts of George Fernandes, an important person in such activities. An asthma patient, her condition deteriorated dramatically while in custody for want of proper medical care. The government was forced to release her, but she died within days thereafter. Meanwhile, Emergency had also been proclaimed. Devastated and short of money, Reddy postponed the post-production works. But his tribulations were not over yet. He had to suffer visits by government officials demanding to see the 'film'. With great difficulty, he thwarted the prowling officers' effort to seize the rushes. Reddy could proceed with the post-production of his film only after the Emergency was lifted.[15]

But the most significant instance involved Satyajit Ray. In 1971 he had made a documentary, *Sikkim*, on the life and culture of the then sovereign Himalayan kingdom. But after India annexed the kingdom in 1976, the film fell afoul of the official version about the new possession and was not cleared for public exhibition till 2010.[16]

The 'White Paper' is indeed a useful reference, giving us an insight into the political narratives emerging within the government system around the film medium during the Emergency. Yet, it remains at best a selective, if not a tendentious, one.

Post-Emergency camouflage

Post-Emergency, the government changed the nomenclature of the Central Board of Film *Censors* to the Central Board of Film *Certification* (but CBFC, both). A concomitant change was brought about in the form of *new* Cinematograph (Certification) Rules. All this was in 1983. The government offered no explanation for such a modification, let alone highlight the qualitative difference between 'censorship' and 'certification'. Certification classifies a film's content with reference to certain parameters, such as the age of the viewer, its sexual orientation, its violence-content, its moral or ethical implication and so on. It is more like a piece of information relating an audience to the content of a film than anything else. It therefore satisfies a desire on the part of an audience to be informed in advance if their act of watching a film would end up displeasing or offending them. But in the Indian context, the change of nomenclature from censorship to certification has simply been a cosmetic one, meant for public consumption as if to underline a more tolerant attitude of the government. Nothing really changed within the government's perception. The word 'certification' remains, for all practical purposes, a euphemism for 'censorship'. While certification puts emphasis on sensitizing the audience regarding the content of a film, the focus in censorship is on sanitizing. The former prepares the audience for a film, and the latter prepares the film for an audience within certain parameters of 'public interest'. In certification, therefore, the right to receive information accentuates the right to freedom of expression, the right to freedom of reception and the right to even refuse reception. But censorship is a different ball game, mired in regimentation and moderation, if not curtailment, of freedom of expression/reception. However much as the Indian State machinery wants us to believe that the CBFC carries out certification, in truth, it still indulges in censorship in the classical sense. Even as late as in 2002, a government communication to this author used the word 'censorship' to indicate the nature of the Indian government's principal engagement with, and activity vis-à-vis, the film medium. The very nature of film certification makes it a transparent practice primarily because it involves the dissemination of information. But film censorship in the Indian context is more in the nature of a restrictive or prescriptive practice and also shuns transparency by withholding information. The replacement of 'Censorship' by 'Certification' just created another degree of falsehood in the film censorship narrative.

Meanwhile, the political narrative continued to evolve post-Emergency in myriad ways.

The film *Kissa Kursi Ka* was remade with much fanfare in 1977 after the withdrawal of Emergency. When it was submitted for examination, the CBFC, then working under a new dispensation, again demanded many cuts. Finally, it was cleared by the MIB, with a single cut, underlining the political game around it. (Ramnath 2015)

But it was the documentary filmmakers who were made to suffer for their enthusiasm. A classic case is the treatment meted out to Anand Patwardhan regarding his film *Prisoners of Conscience* (1978). This B/W documentary was originally an important historical record of the process of political victimization during the Emergency. It was for all practical purposes an underground film, made under very trying circumstances when the Emergency was in full swing. The rushes were hastily edited under primitive conditions and smuggled out of the country to evade confiscation and eventual persecution of the filmmaker. Proper post-production was done abroad, and the film was shown to diverse groups to garner support for Indian people's fight for civil liberties and political rights. After the Janata Party government came to power, the film was brought back to India. Patwardhan, quite naively, expected his film to be allowed for public exhibition. But such an expectation was quickly belied. Significantly, the Janata Party government had gone back on its poll pledge for the unconditional release of political prisoners throughout the country. Frustrated, and perhaps angry too, Patwardhan put an epilogue to the film saying that although the Emergency had ended and many prisoners were released, political prisoners existed before it and they continued to exist even after it was formally over. Patwardhan secured the release of his film after much difficulty.[17]

Almost the same fate awaited another similar documentary, *Mukti Chai* (1977, dir. Utpalendu Chakrabarty). Utpalendu had been a radical political activist in the late 1960s and early 1970s, besides being a schoolteacher and short-story writer. His foray into filmmaking began with this documentary on the tradition of 'preventive detention' (actually, detention on political grounds). It was given a censor certificate, but surprisingly refused permission (by the CBFC itself) for a journey abroad, apparently without any cogent reason. It had been invited to the Oberhausen Film Festival in (then West) Germany. The regional panel of the CBFC, which examined the film in Calcutta, merely 'found it unsuitable for any international festival'. Interestingly, the panel took special note of the film's 'poor quality', and the film's journey abroad stalled.[18] Significantly, the film was also not 'allowed to be shown' at the 7th International Film Festival of India (January 1979).[19]

Another documentary in the vein of *Prisoners of Conscience* and *Mukti Chai*, titled *An Indian Story* (1981, dir. Tapan Bose), dealt with the infamous blinding of the inmates at Bhagalpur Jail (Bihar) in 1979. The CBFC refused the film a certificate. This decision was challenged in the Bombay High Court (per Writ Petition no. 293 of 1982). The court asked for a few deletions, to which the producers acceded.[20]

In 1984, Anand Patwardhan's documentary film, *Bombay Hamara Shahar*, was detained by the CBFC. His fault was that he had focused on the suffering heaped on the tenement-dwellers in Bombay by the city corporation's drive to beautify the metropolis. The resultant public uproar caused the CBFC to clear it.[21]

In 1985, Suhasini Mulay and Tapan Bose made a documentary on the gas leak tragedy in the Bhopal plant of Union Carbide that happened on 3 December 1984. Titled *Beyond Genocide*, it castigated both the dubious business policies of an MNC, showing an utter lack of concern for environmental questions, and the lackadaisical response of the government to the tragedy, acting hand in glove with the perpetrator. Much like their *An Indian Story*, this film was also refused a certificate by the CBFC. Once again, they nullified the CBFC's action by moving the Bombay High Court. However, there was no chance of the state-controlled FD patronizing it for theatrical release. Their offer to Doordarshan to telecast it on the National Network was also spurned. This time the duo moved the Delhi High Court. After two years, the court ordered in their favour and the film was telecast on the fourth anniversary of the tragedy.[22]

In 1987, the duo began another probing film on the Khalistan movement to secure a separate homeland for the Sikhs. It was completed in 1989 and called *From Behind the Barricade*. This film provoked the CBFC to demand all visuals of damage wreaked on the Golden Temple at Amritsar by the Indian Army during its Operation Bluestar. The Board felt that the film would undermine the nation's integrity and arouse communal passion. This time, however, the filmmakers' appeal to the Delhi High Court did not produce the desired result.[23]

On 6 October 1994, a Division Bench of the High Court at Madras passed an order prohibiting the exhibition of a Tamil feature film *Kuttra Pathirikai* (meaning 'Chargesheet'). It depicted the assassination of the then former prime minister Rajiv Gandhi. The court directed the revocation of a censor certificate issued to the film by the CBFC because of a directive from the Film Certification Appellate Tribunal (FCAT).[24] The CBFC had twice refused to issue a certificate to the film for two reasons. First, the film contained some very brutal scenes. Second, its exhibition might prejudice the ongoing trial of some accused in the specially designated court and the proceedings of various commissions of enquiry looking into the assassination. But the FCAT overruled the CBFC and directed that the film be issued an 'A' certificate after certain deletions. The CBFC had to oblige but also filed a writ petition in the High Court challenging the Tribunal's directive.

After viewing the film and hearing extensive arguments from the respective counsels, the court held that the film not only projected but also eulogized the objectives and activities of an outlawed outfit. The Bench held that the FCAT had failed to consider a vital question – whether the film (or, for that matter, any film) could portray the activities of a banned outfit.

Rejecting the defence that the film would affect the producer's freedom of expression, the Bench said that no film could be permitted to project the activities and commissions of crime by a banned outfit, and still insist on protection under Article 19(1)(a). The film was likely to influence the public and encourage the banned outfit's sympathizers, the Bench added. The Bench also rejected the oral request on behalf of the producer for leave to appeal in the Supreme Court.[25]

Mahesh Bhatt's film *Zakhm* (1998) was refused a certificate on grounds that it would provoke communal disharmony. This autobiographical film was based on memories of growing up with a Hindu father and a Muslim mother. It even won the national award for the best feature film on national integration. But to secure its public exhibition, Bhatt had to digitally alter a scene of the sixteenth-century Babri mosque being destroyed by Hindu extremists, turning their saffron arm- and headbands to grey.[26]

In fact, throughout the 1990s, independent documentary filmmakers played a significant role in unearthing the political narrative underlying film censorship. They subjected the heightened activities of the Hindu extremists during this period to regular scrutiny. And, as a result, they regularly came into conflict with the CBFC. Suma Josson's film on the Mumbai riots of 1992–3, *Bombay's Blood Yatra*, took two years before it was finally cleared without any cuts by the FCAT.[27] Even a film, titled *Aftershocks* (dir. Rakesh Sharma) or *Chords on the Richter Scale* (dir. Shyam Rajnakar) had some trouble getting a censor certificate because it suggested a bias against the minority Muslims when aid was being distributed after the catastrophic Gujarat earthquake in 2001.[28] The Gujarat riots (2002) generated quite a few documentaries, the more important ones being *Aakrosh* (dir. Ramesh Pimple) and *Final*

Solution (dir. Rakesh Sharma). Both these films were stalled by the CBFC. While Pimple won his case in the Bombay High Court,[29] Sharma's film was passed by the CBFC after public protests.[30] Anand Patwardhan had to seek judicial intervention against the CBFC for questioning the nuclear politics of both India and Pakistan and preaching a rational, pacifist approach in his documentary *Jung aur Aman* (2001).[31]

Another major element in the political narrative around film censorship was pandering to films promoting 'nationalism'. This has already been evident in earlier eras with films like *Haqeeqat* (1964), *Hindustan Ki Kasam* (1973, dir. Chetan Anand), *Upkaar* (1967, dir. Manoj Kumar) and *Lalkaar* (1972, dir. Ramanand Sagar). But the trend acquired a new dimension in the 1990s. A form of neo-nationalism began to weigh down Indian cinema with clockwork regularity, conveniently enmeshing and contraposing religious patriotism/nationalism with its 'other', namely its subversion in the name of a different religion. The country was told many times, and in no uncertain terms, that she faced a clear and present danger from Pakistan. An accompanying, and not-so-subtle subtext was that the Muslims of India were part of a fifth column. This has given rise to a series of jingoist films like *Roja* (1992, dir. Mani Ratnam), *Border* (1997, dir. J. P. Dutta), *Sarfarosh* (1999, dir. John Matthew Matthan), *Hindustan Ki Kasam* (1999, dir. Veeru Devgan), *Mission Kashmir* (2000, dir. Vidhu Vinod Chopra), *Maa Tujhe Salaam* (2001, dir. Tinu Verma), *Gadar – Ek Prem Katha* (2001, dir. Anil Sharma), *Indian* (2001, dir. N Maharajan), *Bharat Bhagya Vidhata* (2002, dir. Osho Raja) and *LOC Kargil* (2003, dir. J. P. Dutta).

A medium under siege

The operation of film censorship in our country boils down to a delicate, and often complex, contest between the authorial rights of the communicator and the spectatorial rights of the receiver. This contest is mediated by the State through CBFC, which is an 'attached and subordinate organization' of MIB. At times the judiciary also joins as arbiter, for better or for worse. In many instances, these actions, either autonomous or concerted, are guided by political considerations, taking film censorship beyond the popularly perceived realms of the moral and ethical universe. The Emergency has perhaps witnessed intense politically motivated actions within a short time span. But there are numerous comparable evidences of the Indian State's sustained, and almost antagonistic, political engagement with the film medium through film censorship – spread across eras and cutting across the ideological leanings of governments. Political manipulation of film censorship encompasses not simply the refusal/withholding of a censor certificate to 'objectionable' film(s) but deliberate promotion of 'favourable' films. And as we have amply demonstrated above, such actions have been perpetrated by successive regimes irrespective of their ideological traits, to be supplemented by popular/media support or apathy.

In 2016, the MIB constituted a committee to suggest reforms for the much-maligned film censorship practices with the renowned filmmaker Shyam Benegal as Chairperson. Its brief was to examine the film censorship mechanism and help evolve broad guidelines/procedures within the ambit of the Cinematograph Act 1952 and Cinematograph (Certification) Rules 1991. Many were hopeful, if not elated, in anticipation of a set of proposals for substantial change given Benegal's well-known position regarding film censorship as practised in India. The Benegal Committee's exercise was supposed to supplement the efforts of an earlier entity, the Justice Mudgal Committee, which was mandated to hold a full review of Indian Cinematograph Act 1952. The Mudgal Committee Report, submitted in September 2013, had an appendix in the form of a draft Cinematograph Act; but it also recommended that the central government should issue suitable directions guiding the CBFC regarding the sanctioning of films for public exhibition. Mr Benegal and his august compatriots were specifically asked to frame these directions.

The Benegal Committee submitted their report proposing certification of cinematic content appropriate for different age groups to replace mandatory pre-censorship. It recommended pre-censorship only in some special cases where film content transgresses one or more of the 'reasonable restrictions' on the constitutionally guaranteed right to freedom of speech and expression. It also recommended a revamping of the CBFC, proposing major reforms in its constitution. These are prima facie positive developments indeed. But nothing has so far come out of the Committee's exercise.[32]

Actor-director Amol Palekar had filed a writ petition before the Supreme Court in April 2017, submitting that certain provisions of the entire set of cinematography laws infringed on the fundamental rights of both the artists and the audience. He particularly wanted the CBFC's power to carry out excisions in films be scrapped. He also asked for the implementation of the recommendations made by the Shyam Benegal Committee. The case (Civil no. 187 of 2017) is still undecided.[33]

Film censorship in India remains a siege on the political rights of Indian cinephiles, under the pretext of societal interest, even when there is no threat of external aggression or public disorder, the constitutionally sanctioned reasons for declaring Emergency. During Emergency (1975–7), the State suspended the operation of Article 19 across media. But, Emergency or no Emergency, the Special Powers conferred on the State by Section 5B (1) of the Cinematograph Act 1952 practically override Article 19(1)(a). The film medium is kept under constant State surveillance and a dark shadow reminiscent of those nineteen months.

State

A patron and a tyrant: Indian film society movement in 'Emergency' times

Amrit Gangar

A photograph by way of a prologue

The College Street Coffee House or the India Coffee House in Calcutta/Kolkata has been an 'adda' place which thrived during the 1970s. Leading filmmakers such as Satyajit Ray, Mrinal Sen, Ritwik Ghatak and many other intellectuals, thinkers, artists, artistes and poets met up here and informally conversed about global and local politics and the possibilities of their artistic/literary practices over cups of tea or coffee and bundles of bidis or packs of cigarettes (Das 2002; Mukerjee and Silliman 2020).[1] The filmmakers mentioned here, among many others, were also part of the Calcutta Film Society established in 1947 by Satyajit Ray and his friends. In the decade preceding the turbulent 1970s, the Coffee House had become the intellectual battleground of the famous literary and cultural movement called the 'Hungry Generation'. The brother-duo poets Malay Roy Choudhury and Samir Roychoudhury, who pioneered this movement, were arrested and persecuted by the powers that ruled. Undeclared Emergency prevailed, and it continues. Several literary magazines owe their origins to the inspiration from the adda sessions of this Coffee House. Many new film societies were born during this time, which was creatively high time across the globe.

In the year of the Emergency, Ray had made the film *Jana Aranya* (The Middle Man, 1975), which is considered to be the last of his Calcutta trilogy, including *Pratidwandi* (The Adversary, 1970) and *Seemabaddha* (Company

Limited, 1971). Mrinal Sen comprehended the city unrest in his *Interview* (1971), *Calcutta 71* (1972) and *Padatik* (The Guerilla Fighter, 1973). Ritwik Ghatak's 1970s oeuvre included *Amar Lenin* (1970), *Titas Ekti Nadir Naam* (1973) and *Jukti, Takko aar Gappo* (1974). Were the echoes from West Bengal bouncing off the nation's wall? Were they apprehending the state of Emergency? Perhaps the Coffee House Adda knew the secrets!

My story of an iconic photograph goes back to a Coffee House but now to the capital city of New Delhi and to Mrs Indira Gandhi, the Prime Minister of India, who was to clamp the draconian Internal Emergency across India. The Delhi Coffee House had started in 1957, just two years prior to the structured formation of the Federation of Film Societies of India (FFSI), of which once Mrs Gandhi happened to be the Vice President along with Satyajit Ray being the President.

Well, instead of the photograph, let me attempt to create a word-image through a brief description: India Coffee House's Delhi branch was shut when Indira Gandhi declared Emergency during 1975–7. Clad in her white saree, she had shown the basic sagacity in visiting this Coffee House before clamping the Emergency and taking a photograph with the staff of the India Coffee House Workers' Cooperative Society's Head Office in Delhi. This photograph is part of Kristin Victoria Magistrelli Plys's book *Brewing Resistance: Indian Coffee House and the Emergency in Postcolonial India* (Cambridge University Press. 2020).

'Students holding a range of political viewpoints from different universities across Delhi met in the India Coffee House at New Delhi's Connaught Place to launch a movement against the Emergency and then continued organizing that movement from behind bars as political prisoners' (Magistrelli Plys 2020b). Kristin Plys writes,

> A range of activities took place in Delhi's vibrant urban spaces including rumour spreading, the dissemination of pamphlets and poetry, postering, formulating organizing strategies, forming cross-party alliances, recruiting, and even compiling bomb making materials and dynamite for use against public property. Not only did certain urban spaces facilitate collective action against the state, but they also facilitated surprising alliances between groups of different political persuasions. (Kristin Plys 2020a: 170)

Interestingly, Plys titles one of her chapters, 'The Coffee House Movement'. Can film societies drive a 'movement' of any sort? This is a puzzling question in both political and cultural sense. Plys, however, offers a clarification within her context, 'The major theoretical and political problem of totalitarian rule is that it is difficult to create a mass movement against a totalitarian regime given severe repression of dissent.' (170)

In 1975, post the declaration of the Emergency, Sanjay Gandhi took it upon himself to get rid of the Delhi Coffee House, since he believed it to be the hub of anti-government activities (shades of JNU today). And thus the legendary Delhi eatery and the rendezvous 'adda' was demolished to make way for what later became Palika Bazaar.

Movement: Film society, Emergency and echoes of time

Agreeably, film societies can never claim to be a mass movement (mainly because they operate on cultural firmament and not political), if so, what was their role in and response to the Emergency of 1975–7, a nationwide repressive regime foisted upon by the government at the top? This 'temporary' regime had a deep impact on cultural activities too, film societies not excluded, no matter they were not outside the parentheses of rules and regulations stipulated by the State.

Film society, a formal, legal entity and troubling ramifications

Dictionnaire du Cinéma, compiled and edited by Jean-Loup Passek, defines a film society or a film club thus: 'Legal association, of institutions and people, aiming to introduce its members to cinematographic culture', this is a gist of his long and elaborate entry (Passek 2001, 258).

The word 'legal association' is significant as far as the Indian situation is concerned. At a formal level, every film society has to register itself with the Charity Commissioner and the Registrar of Societies before affiliating it to the apex body, the FFSI. By virtue of it being a registered body, every film society has to follow certain rules and regulations, namely, holding general body and executive committee meetings, recording the proceedings in minutes books, getting its annual accounts audited and approved by a chartered accountant and so on. This becomes quite a cumbersome procedure for a film society which has no office space of its own and cannot afford to pay the professional fees to a chartered accountant and all that. Most of the activists dedicated to the film society movements are working-class people (largely doing nine-to-five jobs in government or private offices for their living) and besides all the mentioned stipulated work of being a registered (legal) body, they had to get the film cans released from railway stations, being celluloid films, they would be heavy cans in numbers 12–13 (35mm) or 2–4 (16mm) either coming from the National Film Archive of India, Pune or any other producers or distributors. They had to be carried manually or bear the expenses of carriage.

Screen Unit, a personal experiential example

I can cite my own example of Screen Unit, a film society that was established soon after the Emergency ended in 1978, by Manilal Gala in a far-off central railway suburb of Mulund in Mumbai. I was with him right from day one and took over the secretarial, programming and curatorial (the word was not much in vogue then) mantle after he started working with Ketan Mehta on the production of the Gujarati film *Bhavni Bhavai* (released in 1980). This is what I wrote in my Ruminations of Screen Unit:

> We would meet every Sunday evening to discuss cinematography and issues enveloping it; someone would read an article or a passage from a book that he or she had found significant. We had just begun to understand the vocabulary akin to cinematography, its aesthetics. Grappling were we to find tools of criticism that would be as original as possible! There were fights between tempers and wave-lengths. We would walk up and down the streets of Mulund, fighting, fighting and fighting; sit in parks to hold executive committee meetings. Thank God, there were parks in Mulund! And the police to drive us away!! Minutes writing was the most horrifying task. (Gangar 1986)

To this paragraph in my fairly long Ruminations published in the brochure titled *Celebrating Poesy of Cinematography* as an accompaniment to Screen Unit's retrospective of Alexander Dovzhenko's films at the House of Soviet Culture, Mumbai between 11 and 16 September 1989. It was India's first such retrospective of Dovzhenko's films, some were even without English subtitles, but that would not deter us from screening and seeing the masterly work that had influenced Andrei Tarkovsky. Well, to the above paragraph, I had footnoted some facts that are reiterated again in the footnote here. We cannot escape the utopia of complete freedom, the Moksha. I always call Television the Tyrannical Tube. It has intensified its tyrannical terror over time through lies, through dumbing the spectators' senses, through beating the drums for the rulers. Emergency remains perpetual in many senses of the term, so does the nature of resistance, though its nature changed with the technological means of communication and broadcasting. How did film societies resist the Emergency of 1975, or did they?

Films: Production, distribution and exhibition, an act of resistance

The day when the shoot of the Malayalam film *Kabani Nadi Chuvannappol* (*When the River Kabani Went Red*) commenced in Bangalore, Emergency was declared in India. Strict warnings were given by the Government against any act that supported extremist activities. Amidst harassment, the director P. A. Backer managed to complete the shoot. Backer, producer Pavithran and actor T. V. Chandran were arrested and imprisoned sans any case registered against them. At the level of censoring, more than 1,500 feet of what they had shot was cut and removed; the reason given was Naxalism. When it was being screened in Thiruvananthapuram (the capital city of Kerala), the police stormed the theatre. The reason they gave was that they received complaints against the film. They found a group dance sequence in the film where the dancers wearing masks was found 'objectionable' (Figure 3.1). Against all odds, film societies in Kerala showed this film in cities, towns and villages. The film was screened at several film festivals in 1975, though it was not given the censor certificate for over a year. It was even released in theatres in Kerala during the Emergency period, on 16 July 1976. The film also won several state awards.

Anand Patwardhan and his film *Kranti ki Tarange* aka *Waves of Revolution* (1975) provide yet another example of how a filmmaker rose to resist the state of Emergency and repression. The film was completed in secret in 1975 using outdated film stock and makeshift equipment. A part of it was shot in Super 8 which was then projected onto a screen and re-filmed with a 16mm camera. Processing took place in various laboratories for fear of discovery. The

Figure 3.1 Mask dance in *Kabani Nadi Chuvannappol* which was found 'objectionable' by the Censor Board.

sound was almost entirely recorded on a consumer cassette recorder. The film documents the Bihar movement led by the veteran Gandhian Socialist leader Jayaprakash Narayan (JP) with students' and peasants' struggles to overcome years of corruption and state-sponsored repression.

Clandestine screenings of the film took place in India during the Emergency. In September 1975, a print was cut into segments, smuggled abroad, reassembled and circulated by non-resident Indian organizations and individuals concerned with exposing the growing repression in India. Today, the film serves as a reminder of the spirit of a people who fought for the right to democracy (Figure 3.2).[2]

In its very first year of formation in 1978, Screen Unit, a Mumbai-based film society, was one of the first to screen this film along with another anti-Emergency film by Anand Patwardhan, *Zameer ke Bandi,* aka *Prisoners of Conscience* (1978), focusing on the state of Emergency (June 1975 to March 1977). Through this film, Patwardhan presents a first-hand account of the appalling brutality of prison procedures and holding political prisoners without trial (Figure 3.3). During the Emergency, the media was muzzled, over 100,000 people were arrested without charge, and imprisoned without trial. But political prisoners existed before the Emergency, and they continue to exist even after it is over.

Figure 3.2 A scene from *Waves of Revolution.*

Figure 3.3 A scene from *Prisoners of Conscience.*

Screen Unit's festival and symposium: Sociopolitical cinema, 1980

As a post-Emergency study, Screen Unit organized a four-day (21–24 February 1980) festival of sociopolitical cinema at Xavier Institute of Communication, St. Xavier's College, Mumbai. The screening of films: *Jukti Takko Aar Gappo* (Ritwik Ghatak), *Fire in the Belly* (Kumar Shahani), *Ek Adhuri Kahani* (Mrinal Sen), *India '67* (S. Sukhdev), *Moving Perspectives* (Mrinal Sen), *Gaman* (Muzaffar Ali), *Burning Stone* (Loksen Lalvani) and *Nine Months to Freedom* (S. Sukhdev) was organized. The festival was accompanied by a symposium on 'Political Trends in Indian Cinema', which was participated by Saeed Mirza, Kumar Shahani, Arun Khopkar, Vinayak Purohit, Inashu Thalak, Joseph Pinto, Ramesh Patkar and moderated by Kumud Mehta. This event was comprehended in a brochure that carried an editorial by Manilal and Amrit Gangar and an introductory essay by the scholar-activist Sudhir Sonalkar, and an interview with the Bengali filmmaker Buddhadeb Dasgupta taken by Screen Unit's I. Shanmgha Das.

Unfortunately, this significant event by Screen Unit, was not recorded (those times were not so easier as the present ones), but the thoughts that transpired by the participating thinkers and practitioners were of utmost importance and relevance. This event was attended by many students, teachers, filmmakers, thinkers and political activists (Figure 3.4).

Democratic despotism: A paradoxical possibility

Film societies had not been working in a vacuum, and since they were largely helmed and run by honorary activists, they had their own freedom as well as constraints towards developing a homogenous, broad-based movement as such, but by and large, they were anti-establishment, no matter they got patronage from the state – some grants-in-aid, censorship reliefs and so on. The Constitution of India devolves legislative powers under three heads: (1) Centre, (2) State, and (3) Concurrent. While the Centre has retained the weapon of 'censorship' under its control, cinema, in general (particularly the entertainment tax, etc.) is under the State list. The idea is also to see how a modern parliamentary democracy could lead to despotism even within the constitutional contours. In his study, Harry C. Hart calls it a 'constitutional

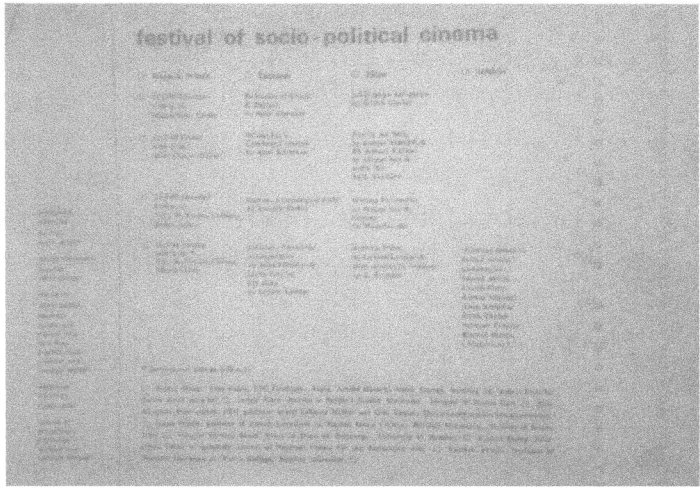

Figure 3.4 Programme schedule published in Screen Unit's brochure edited by Manilal and Amrit Gangar, February 1980, which discussed Emergency and authoritarian tendencies in parliamentary democracy.

dictatorship' or what I call 'democratic despotism', though it is a contradictory term as such, but not without eventual possibilities. The political history of India keeps proving them. Film societies cannot escape them.

The 1970s was the peak time for the film society movement in India, but it was concentrated mainly in two states – West Bengal and Kerala. During Emergency times, West Bengal was under the Congress chief ministership of Siddhartha Shankar Ray but as soon as the Emergency was lifted, in the ensuing assembly elections in 1977, the Left Front gained majority and came to power. Kerala was led by the Communist Party of India under C. Achutha Menon during the Emergency time. Film society movement was gaining much popularity among artists, filmmakers and students in this state, which had a much wider non-urban network compared to West Bengal, not to mention other state which had a negligible presence of film societies.

Emergence of film societies: A global centenary (1920–2020)

Recently, the world celebrated the centenary of the film society movement, as the first film society was launched in 1920 in Paris at the Cinema Pepiniere near the Gare St. Lazare. The Federation Francaise des Cine Clubs was formed in 1930 by Germaine Dulac, a noted experimental filmmaker; it was the first national film organization of its kind in the world. As movies were not going to be confined to France alone, neither were film societies. A film society was formed in Britain in 1925. Associated with the film society movement were some of the finest intellectuals of the time – Bernard Shaw, Julian Huxley, Clive Bell and J. B. S Haldane. Gradually, film societies were formed in different parts of the world.

In his extremely insightful study, *Film Societies in Germany and Austria 1910–1933, Tracing the Social Life of Cinema,* Michael Cowan draws our attention to phenomena such as film as mass media and the film society movement becoming a mass movement, besides drawing the historiographies of film societies and media at large in the German-speaking world where we saw the emergence of the Nazis under the dictator Adolf Hitler later. Though Cowan's study stops at the year 1933, he does refer to certain advertisements and letters from readers in the media with references to the rising Hitler with his anti-Semitic, dastardly ideology. Cowan writes:

> The phony 'letters' – signed with names like 'Sonnenkind 1929' (Sun Child 1929) and 'Unschuld vom Lande' (Innocent One from the Country) – posed typical star-struck questions (with one writer asking if he could acquire Werner Fütterer's false moustache) and offered an occasion for satirical answers with jibes at the film industry (e.g. 'It's true. Adolf Hitler has just acquired the Munich censorship bureau' [Es stimmt, Adolf Hitler ist Besitzer der Münchener Filmprüfstelle geworden]). Presaging Siegfried Kracauer's similar critique of letter columns from a few years later, the 'Unser Briefkasten' column demonstrates the VFV's deep suspicion of the industry's power to distract audiences from their real conditions through the encouragement of dreamy star gazing. (p.227) VFV or 'Volks-Film-Verbände' (National Federation of People's Film Associations) was an interesting collective move with reference to the question of scale. Unlike most of the film societies, the VFV set out from the start to create a nation-wide network of film associations. In fact, the very word Verband (association, federation), rather than Klub or Gemeinde (community), was meant to emphasize that this would be a mass organization, not tied to any given locality. (199)

The Indian scenario

To my mind, this was not only a cultural but also a political move, and this never happened amidst the film society movement in India, though just two years after Mrs Gandhi met the workers running the India Coffee House at Connaught Place in New Delhi, the apex body Federation of Film Societies of India was formed when a small gathering of Delhi, Patna, Roorkee, Bombay, Madras and Calcutta Film Societies met in New Delhi and decided to form such a body, whose president became Satyajit Ray. The date was 13 December 1959 (see the following chart).

Historically, film societies were formed much before the formation of this federal body or even the Calcutta Film Society in 1947. The first two film societies were the Amateur Cine Society and the Bombay Film Society, founded in 1937 and 1942, respectively. The lead to starting these film societies was affiliation to the FFSI would enable film societies to avail film supplies from foreign embassies and participate in the festivals and screening programmes held by the collective body. Public screening of films would invite legal actions without such registrations and affiliations. Democracy accompanies these drudgeries and burdens even for a public service someone desires to do selflessly, and s/he is often at the mercy of bureaucracy.

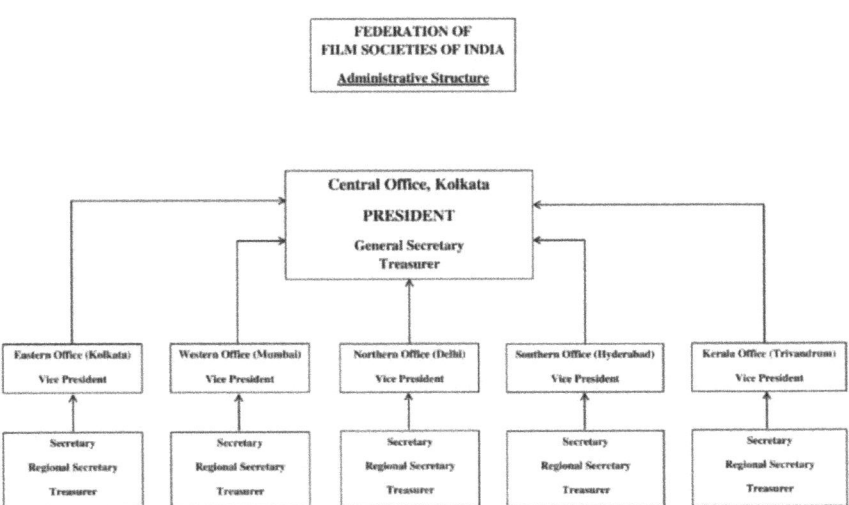

Patronage

Mrs Indira Gandhi was one of the vice presidents of the FFSI and continued to be so for a short while even after she became the I&B Minister (1964–6). She became the PM from 1966 to March 1977 and again from 1980 to 1984. Political and financial patronage continued. Mr I. K. Gujral, who became the twelfth prime minister of India between April 1997 and March 1998, was also an office bearer of the FFSI in the initial years.

GoI's grant-in-aid to the FFSI

Initially started under GoI's plan head, from Rs. 50,000, the amount rose up to Rs. 600,000 per annum. It stopped as soon as Bharatiya Janata Party (BJP) came into power in 2014.

GoI also exempted film societies from censorship restrictions with conditions attached. There were other restrictions continuing the legacy of the British Raj (Figure 3.5).

Ambiguities of patronage: Films, filmmakers and fascism

Someone like Roberto Rossellini had previously made three propaganda films for the fascist army with the assistance of Michelangelo Antonioni and in collaboration with Benito Mussolini's son Vittorio. Chadwick Jenkins very penetratingly writes about the guilt and exculpation in Roberto Rossellini's 'war trilogy'. He says, 'The War Trilogy' is just as propagandistic as any film from the Mussolini period; the difference is most of us want to believe this propaganda. Roberto Rossellini, one of the brightest luminaries of post-war Italian cinema, revered by directors and critics alike, and generally lauded as the true father of neorealism – began his career in this fascist context. He was close friends with Vittorio Mussolini, and it was through the latter's influence that Rossellini was able to direct his first three notable films: *The White Ship* (1941), *A Pilot Returns* (1942) and *The Man with a Cross* (1943). Often dubbed the 'Fascist Trilogy', these are propaganda films. The first was funded by the

Figure 3.5 FFSI delegation led by Mrinal Sen meeting Mrs Indira Gandhi, the then minister of information and broadcasting, on her left is seen Mrs Vijaya Mulay (Akka), pc IFSON, FFSI Western Region, edited by Amrit Gangar and V. K. Dharamsey on behalf of the Western Region of the FFSI, Mumbai.

Minister of the Navy, the second was sponsored by the Air Force, and the third which rewrites the then prevailing history to depict an Italian defeat at the hands of the Russians as a victory (Chadwick Jenkins, *Pop Matters*, 31 July 2017).

In India, even the so-called avant-garde could camouflage and become a collaborator, for example, the original voices such as S. N. S. Sastry's were recruited into smoke and mirrors exercises, for example, his 1975 Films Division film, *We Have Promises to Keep*.

S. Sukhdev's films produced during the Emergency made an interesting shift from his previous works, which were far cries from the patronizing, didactic quality of the typical FD productions.

Often the Patron and the Tyrant go hand in hand, masked or unmasked or masked and unmasked. This could be a deceptive paradox enveloped in the garb of historicity, and the critique is often post-facto. How was media treated during the Emergency (1975–7) in India?

Emergency and the media

On 26 July, the PM laid down the broad policy in respect of the media:

1. Press Council abolished.
2. Seventy publications, including dailies the *Indian Express*, the *Statesman*, *Mainstream*, *Seminar* and so on, denied any government advertising.
3. Government-controlled Akashvani, Doordarshan, Films Division became peddlers of a personality cult.
4. Refusal to toe the government line could invite reprisals, harassment, even arrest under the dreaded Maintenance of Internal Security Act (MISA).

1970s and film societies in India

The peak time for the film society 'movement' was in the 1970s, but its role in political resistance remained largely negligible except on minor individual levels. Film societies – a small cog in the entire political movement's wheel; their number largely in the states of Kerala and West Bengal – 300–400, the total number of members around 150,000.

In his book, *Indian Cinema in the Time of Celluloid*, Ashish Rajadhyaksha devotes a whole chapter to the Indian Emergency and briefly contextualizes the role of film society movement, 'which was then at its height' (242). He refers to the Bombay societies, Film Forum and Screen Unit. Rajadhyaksha's recent book, *Kumar Shahani: The Shock of Desire and Other Essays*, begins with a long chapter, 'Bazaar Realism: The Emergency Essays', incorporating Shahani's essays, including four essays written during the Emergency years (1975–7) (100–155).

Early on, Shahani was an active member of the Anandam Film Society in Bombay. The special number of IFSON published on the occasion of twenty-five years of Film Society Movement, edited by V. K. Dharamsey and myself, begins with our interview with Kumar Shahani, in which he talks about the role of the film society movement. By the mid-1970s, most of the independent cinema was ranged in united opposition to the Emergency. A large section of the film society movement had helped amplify the voice of resistance.

Post-Emergency 1980s and the exposure of film society movement

Based on my personal experience, I witnessed how the edifice of membership of Mumbai film societies collapsed once Doordarshan began to beam the epic series based on the *Ramayana* and *Mahabharata*. Members of film societies who treated films as a medium of entertainment or middle-class snobbishness at large chose to sit at home in front of television sets to watch these series. Gradually, viewership/membership began to dwindle. It is such people's preferences and popularity that dictators use as a weapon to divert general attention from political realities. Film societies, by and large, had been anti-intellectual that failed to deepen sensitivities strong enough. India as a nation spent thousands of man-hours around debates on the binaries of art-house and commercial cinema/films. But in this scenario, there were committed film societies with their enlightened activists that kept on sharpening their aesthetic and political edges. Times of āpātkāl remain as perpetual as people's resistance, which went on softening with the rise of the aspirational young middle class.

The state of Emergency (आपात / आपत्काल), like a Ward in a hospital, is a part of human life as it is lived, individually or collectively with the State being a governing organ. It is a perennial state of being that human society keeps resisting. With no resources at hand, Screen Unit had to constantly rage against the dying of the light. Its cyclostyled programme notes still stand witness to those times of stress and emergent temporal changes. Everyday was an 'apatkaal', and everyday was an act of resistance, political, apolitical, non-political, new grammatical syntaxes we were in search of.

The Emergency, FFC/NFDC and New Cinema in India (1970s)

Sudha Tiwari

Introduction

Indira Gandhi, as the Union Minister for Information and Broadcasting, government of India, had played a key role in the growth of the 'non-conformist' cinema in the 1960s. While delivering the convocation address at the Film and Television Institute of India (FTII) in Pune, she stressed the need for 'encouragement of the non-conformist'. She said, 'There is an element of risk for he (non-conformist) may turn out to be a crank but it is equally possible that he may be a genius' (*Screen* 1964, 2). She pointed out that high-budget films and big stars did not assure a great impact of a film. She urged the students of the Institute 'to improve the level of the industry and to infuse new ideas in it'. Putting an emphasis on picking up stories from India in films, she said, 'when the changing order of society has brought to the surface all kinds of challenging questions of adjustment, every town, every section of the country has its own store of rich film material' (*Screen* 1964, 2). At a reception given to her in 1965 by the South Indian Film Chamber, she assured that the government had no intention of interfering with the creative role of filmmaking or of bringing about regimentation of film production (*Screen* 1965, 15). She, once again, openly supported the newcomers by saying that the biggest works of art were turned out by newcomers, that not all newcomers to the field were opportunists or adventurers. On another occasion, Indira Gandhi restated her earlier conviction that the film medium should be used 'to know ourselves and to show to others the many-sided personality of our country' (3). She also repeated her appeal to the film industry to open its doors to young talent, allowing it the opportunity of experimenting with original ideas and new interpretations. As Prime Minister (PM) in 1966, she clarified her stand on cinema at the presentation of State Awards for Films, 'The cinema plays a great role in education but I am not one of those who value it only for its educational potentialities. I believe that entertainment is in itself a legitimate purpose' (*Screen* 1966, 13). She believed that films have contributed, in numerous ways, to fostering a sense of oneness in our country.

The Internal Emergency, Media and Censorship (1975)

The Internal Emergency imposed by Indira Gandhi in 1975 is widely regarded as a dark phase in India's democratic journey.[1] The extensive use of communication mediums to legitimize Emergency and create consent in its favour is extensively recorded. According to Rajagopal, the Emergency demonstrated that coercion was intimately joined with consent in state-led

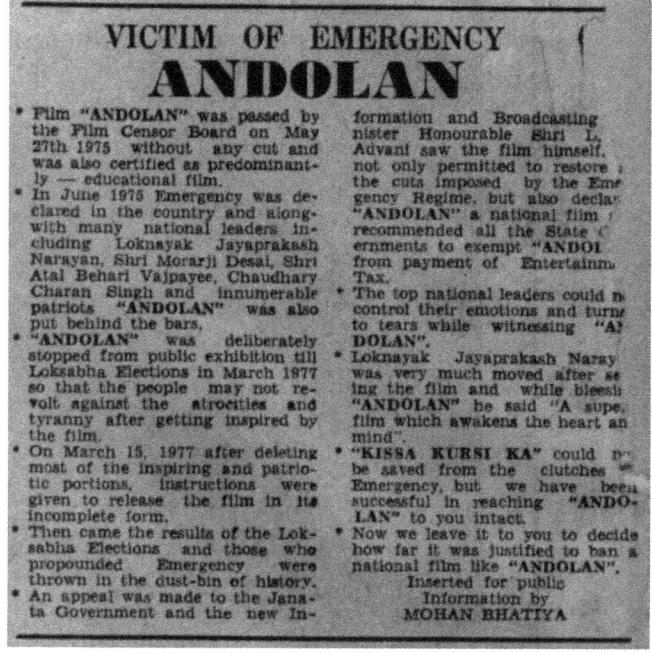

Figure 4.1 Source: *Screen*, 2 September 1977, p. 12.

development and led to a heavy reliance on practices of communication to redefine coercion and to stage popular consent (Rajagopal 2011, 1004). Government expenditure increased on propaganda, mostly through the Directorate of Audio-Visual Publicity (DAVP) (Report 1975–76). Films Division (FD) was making films relating to the declaration of the Emergency and its benefits (133).

The film industry was severely affected by Emergency-induced censorship rules. New instructions were issued for feature films, not to permit scenes showing degradation of women and violence (10). It was assumed, 'As the new outlook gradually permeates the film industry and the instructions are strictly enforced by the Central Board of Film Censors, a new trend would be set for healthy and purposive entertainment' (10). Central Board of Film Certification (CBFC) actually went ahead and banned nineteen films, eleven Indian and eight foreign films (*Screen* 1976, 1). Some of these films were banned for diverse and uneven reasons, including showing 'student indiscipline'. The censors pointed out, 'In all future films fight scenes would be reduced to a flash unless they were historicals or mythologicals in which the story demanded detailed depiction' (*Screen* 1976, 1). Shreeram Bohra, Vice President of the All India Film Producers' Council (AIFPC), pointed out the flip side of this strict censorship. Many producers did not submit their films for certification until the situation became clearer, 'preferring to postpone the releases', 'putting the industry to heavy loss' (*Screen* 1976, 1). He pleaded with the censors to make a distinction between 'violence' and 'valour' (*Screen* 1975, 10). V. C. Shukla, the Minister for Information and Broadcasting, told producers in Bombay that the government was serious about curbing violence and sex in Indian films. He was speaking at a meeting with representatives of the AIFPC in Bombay. When producers asked for a definition of 'violence', Mr Shukla was credited to have stated that 'there was no ambiguity about such things as sex and violence and these were well defined in the Indian Penal Code. These were well understood by everybody and, therefore, he advised filmmakers to remove such features from their films on their own' (*Screen* 1976, 1). Feature films based on social themes topped the chart constantly from 1973 (305 films) to 1977 (420 feature films) ('Thematic Classification of Feature Films Made during the Last Five Years' 1978, 7). It was followed by crime-based films, which showed a constant decline, too, mostly due to strict censorship rules ('Thematic Classification of Feature Films Made during the Last Five

Years' 1978, 7).[2] Legendary, mythological and devotional were other important themes many Indian feature films were based on ('Thematic Classification of Feature Films Made during the Last Five Years' 1978, 7).[3] There was only one feature film classified as political in the list in 1977 ('Thematic Classification of Feature Films Made during the Last Five Years' 1978, 7). The sources noted a considerable rise in the number of 'A' (Adult Only) films produced in Hindi in 1978 as compared to 1977. In 1978, nineteen films were certified as 'A', whereas the figures were six in 1977 and three in 1976 (*Bulletin on Film* 1979, 2). It was said that Sanjay Gandhi personally demanded substantial cash 'contributions' in return for permission to premiere new films in the capital (Mazzarella and Kaur 2009). Vasudev justly noted,

> The application of censorship under the Emergency lost all semblance of rationale and logic. It was used as a stick to beat the industry with, and the fear that a censor certificate would be withheld was enough to overcome the strongest reluctance to comply with the Ministry's most outrageous demands. At the same time, whenever a censorship certificate was not the issue, producers, directors, actors and musicians always had hanging over them the threat of retribution, or charges of income tax evasion to ensure that they toed the line (Vasudev 1978, 149).[4]

The enquiry committee formed by the Janata government collected and investigated complaints regarding instances of misuse of mass media and other related matters (*White Paper on Misuse of Mass Media* 1977). The Committee received eight complaints claiming irregularities in issuing censor certificates for films. The complaints, by and large, referred to delays in matters of censorship or the application of rigid and non-uniform standards in imposing cuts before certifying the film as fit for public exhibition. There were two complaints which called upon the Committee to look into the political motives behind the censorship of certain films like *Aandhi* (1975), *Andolan* (1975)[5] and *Kissa Kursi Ka (KKK)* (1978).[6] According to the *White Paper*, the Ministry of Information and Broadcasting (MIB), in one of the Coordination Committee meetings held under Shukla on 5 July 1975, ordered to immediately take possession of and keep in careful custody the exposed negatives and all prints of *KKK*, irrespective of the court proceedings (*White Paper on Misuse of Mass Media* 1977, 10). In another meeting, held on 8 August 1975, a decision was taken to extend the period of the ban on *Aandhi*, 'and no publicity need be given to this order. AIR [All India Radio] should be informed so that songs of banned films are not relayed' (*White Paper on Misuse of Mass Media* 1977, 13).[7] About *KKK*, a Central Bureau of Investigation (CBI) enquiry concluded that the film as well as its negative had been stolen and subsequently destroyed (*White Paper on Misuse of Mass Media* 1977, 17).[8] Vasudev described the whole *KKK* incident as 'bizarre', reminiscent of 'intrigue, factual distortions, mysterious figures, hundreds of cans of vanished film', and displayed 'all the trappings of a ninteenth [*sic*] century melodrama' (Vasudev 1978, 172). Similarly, *Andolan* (Figure 4.1)[9] could not be released because the producer was ordered to cut all the portions dealing with the depiction of violence or the underground movement during the 1942 Quit India movement.

On the contrary, certain films were favoured and exempted from entertainment tax (*White Paper on Misuse of Mass Media* 1977, 7). *Mazdoor Zindabaad* (1976) was such a film. According to a blog written on the film, 'there is not one moment in this magnus [*sic*] opus of sycophancy that lets the audience forget the great leader, her twenty points and her's [*sic*] son's five points' ('Indira Jaap in Mazdoor Zindabaad (1976)' 2009). Praising Indira Gandhi and her 'noble' war against smuggling, inflation and poverty, and glorifying values of labour, industriousness and discipline, the various songs of this film show a populist celebration of Emergency.[10]

It was not a wonder that once the Emergency was lifted and fresh elections were announced, the Hindi film industry campaigned for the Janata Party. Dev Anand was at the forefront of this campaign. He, along with a few other actors, formed a political party called Cinema for Democracy (CFD) and supported the Janata Party.[11] In an election meeting of the Janata Party, Anand spoke 'of the utter humiliation to which film people were subjected and the "bossism" that ruled during emergency'. He was quoted to have said, 'We were badly treated. They spoke to us with a stick in hand like arrogant officials' (Desai 1977b). Shatrughan Sinha was reported to have said that he passed 'through hell like a slave during the emergency'. He further told,

> Since I am from Bihar, I knew Jayaprakash Narayan and Jagjivan Ram. During emergency I was not allowed to meet them despite the fact that I do not belong to any party. And, in a recent party, some official came and told me that, if I did not campaign for the Congress Party I would be implicated in the Baroda Dynamite Case. (Desai 1977b)

Jayaprakash Narayan and PM Morarji Desai had congratulated Anand and Sinha, and filmmaker Chetan Anand for 'the courageous stand taken by a large section of the film industry during the recent Lok Sabha elections' (Saari 1977). A group of businessmen and professionals, led by Dev Anand, also submitted a memorandum to the Members of Parliament, demanding repeal of all the Constitutional amendments from 38th to 44th. L. K. Advani, the new Union Minister for Information and Broadcasting in the Janata government, assured that the film medium would be developed in a healthy and vigorous manner. He stated that the new government was fully conscious of the vital role cinema had to play as a medium of mass education and entertainment.[12]

Emergency, New Cinema and the FFC/NFDC

The element of disciplining, regimentation, and corporatization espoused by the Emergency affected the two Corporations and New Cinema[13] in multiple ways. It was during the Emergency that the New Cinema and Film Finance Corporation (FFC)[14] faced their first major crisis, where it was asked to 'go commercial'. Financing of low-budget films had come to a virtual halt during the Emergency. A revised charter of functions was drawn by the MIB for FFC, where its contribution to the nation's economy was stressed. Appeal to a larger audience and entertainment entered the charter, pointing to major departures from the earlier aims and objectives of the FFC/New Cinema. Pursuit of 'New'-ness came to a halt, as the government indicated that it may not be able to financially support the Corporation beyond a point. The Emergency also shaped the political perception of many filmmakers who played a substantial role in the New Cinema movement and also worked with the National Film Development Corporation (NFDC) on socially and politically relevant films. The Emergency, unintentionally, emboldened these artistes to question the state and its system. It also gave them a mandate whereby they could focus liberally on the everyday lives and struggles of the common people, cornering the saga of the nation state in the process.[15]

How precisely did the Emergency affect the New Indian Cinema and FFC?

First, the aesthetics was affected. Underlining the Emergency's 'complicated presence' in the history of New Indian Cinema, Rajadhyaksha established that the Emergency influenced the form and aesthetics of the New Cinema movement, and called it 'aesthetics of state control' (Rajadhyaksha 2009, 231). According to Prasad, Emergency gave rise to a third segment of film aesthetics, namely 'developmental aesthetic' and 'was addressed to the citizen as an abstract, political figure. Rural India featured prominently in these films, but the rural audience was its subject matter not its addressee' (Prasad 1998, 143). He made a distinction between films like *Do Bigha Zamin* (1953) and *Mother India* (1957) and films of New Cinema, for example *Ankur* (1974) and *Manthan* (1976). Prasad discussed *Manthan* as 'the most consummate example' of developmental aesthetic, 'staging the ideology of the Indira Gandhi regime by using the dairy cooperative as the scene of action' (Prasad 1998, 144). While in the films celebrating the aesthetics of mobilization (the first segment of film aesthetics), the state is one of the two entities fighting against each other, in the middle-class cinema (the second segment), the state is absent. However, in the New Cinema, the third segment, according to Prasad, the state is,

> the frame of representation. The point of view provided to the spectator coincides with the point of view of the state. The spectator is positioned, as citizen, before spectacles of peasant rebellion or reform of feudal society. The spectator's position is thus detached from the spectacle, making him/ her a vicarious onlooker, identifying with the reform-minded bureaucracy. (Prasad 1998, 145)

Second, the New Cinema practitioners found themselves in the middle of a storm. Mrinal Sen faced an 'uncomfortable' situation during a question and answer session after the screening of his film *Chorus* (1974) at the Berlin Film Festival just a week after the Emergency was declared (Sen 2006, 122).[16] A young woman asked him how he would relate his film *Chorus* to the state of Emergency imposed in India. Sen 'composed' himself and spoke with pauses between the lines,

> 'to be honest, I am not aware of the legality of Emergency. So, I do not know when, at what point, I cross the boundary of law. Under the circumstances, I prefer to keep mum and not answer your question'. I repeated, 'Sorry, no answer from me, not a word'. The hall was silent for a few moments. I did not know how it happened, but it did happen and I got a bit emboldened and said, 'Got my answer? Have you? I shall not answer. I hope I am clear'. (Sen 2006, 124)

Kumar Shahani shared his memory of the Emergency in a personal conversation, 'During the Emergency I was invited maximum to Delhi by the universities ... both Delhi University and Jawaharlal Nehru University (JNU).

And almost every time I would be surrounded by my body guards' (Personal Interview with Kumar Shahani 2016). He remembered to have addressed the protesting students, talked about films with them. John Abraham was invited to address the students during the Emergency, at a place Shahani referred to as 'freedom square', an open space in the then JNU (Personal Interview with Kumar Shahani, New Delhi, 3 May 2016). Saeed Akhtar Mirza's sister-in-law was arrested and imprisoned for supporting a strike. She was a school teacher and taught music and piano to students (Personal Interview with Saeed Akhtar Mirza 2018). Barnouw and Krishnaswamy narrate an important incident from the Karnataka New Cinema industry.

> Snehalata Reddy, the leading actress in *Samskara* and wife of its director Pattabhi Rama Reddy, was accused of concealing information about the whereabouts of George Fernandes, a trade union leader whose arrest had been ordered in the Emergency roundup. She was known to be a friend of the Fernandeses. She denied knowledge of his whereabouts and was jailed and questioned for eight months. An asthmatic deprived of needed medicines, she fell seriously ill, and was released only when near death. She died in January, 1977 – five days after her release.[17]

Shyam Benegal's *Nishant* (1975) ran into trouble due to the censor's rigidities. The film could not be shown at the Chicago Film Festival in November 1976 because of the MIB and government of India's suspicion that the film would harm India's image abroad. According to Vasudev,

> It seems extraordinary that over-zealous authorities could not see that allowing sensitive and intelligent criticism through films like this could only bring prestige and credibility to India's image. Pretending that there are no problems was not going to make the problems vanish. With this sort of attitude, it is not surprising that film makers by and large preferred to remain detached from political and even social comment. (Vasudev 1978, 178)

Third, FFC's autonomy was bypassed, and New Cinema's aesthetic spirit, as patronized by the FFC, had to pass the test of its contribution to the national treasury. The burden of financial disciplining, utilitarian approach to institutions and misuse of power by ministers concerned altered the course of the New Cinema movement and the nature and objectives of FFC. These alterations led, first, to a mass resignation of FFC chairperson B. K. Karanjia, along with other important Directors. Second, the Emergency gifted FFC with the recommendations of the Seventy-Ninth Report of the Committee on Public Undertakings (CPU) (1975–6) (discussed below).

Protesting against constant interference in FFC by state functionaries, several Board members, including Chairman B. K. Karanjia and Hrishikesh Mukherjee, resigned in 1976. The Indian Film Directors' Association (IFDA) passed a resolution, expressing its shock at the resignation of the FFC chairman ('Continue the Revolution' 1976, 35). Stating that FFC had led the crusade for art cinema, the resolution said, 'It is shocking to add that the entire movement has been nipped in the bud' ('Continue the Revolution' 1976, 35). The Association urged the government to 'Continue the revolution that was started by Mr. B. K. Karanjia and the then directors of the Film Finance Corporation' ('Continue the Revolution' 1976, 35).[18] Vasudev called this whole affair as 'one of the early casualties of the Emergency' (1978, 158). Karanjia's meeting with Indira Gandhi and her promise to look into 'these developments' failed to improve the situation; instead, 'petty humiliating acts of vengeance against the FFC followed' (Vasudev 1978, 158). Shukla did not leave a single chance to humiliate, demean and defame Karanjia and FFC. This included giving out press statements saying how the experience of his Ministry with FFC had not been a happy one, and providing factual errors relating to its functioning, not acknowledging the letter of clarification sent to Shukla by Karanjia, ignoring FFC at the IFFI held in January 1976, and replacing Karanjia at the eleventh hour with G. P. Sippy, 'known to be a close friend of the Minister's', as the chairman of the Festival Managing Committee. Shukla also tried to influence FFC's autonomous decision-making power by writing to an official of the Corporation directing him to sanction a loan for a film that the well-known novelist Rajinder Singh Bedi wanted to make. His application had already been turned down by the Board of Directors. This was the first time during Karanjia's tenure that the Ministry sought to influence FFC's discretion in granting loans. Immediately after the mass resignation, the first thing the Corporation did, in violation of the resolution of the Board, was to sanction a loan for Bedi (Vasudev 1978, 158). Vasudev reasonably alleged, amidst all this feud, the FFC 'lost sight of its uniquely inspiring ambition to raise cinematic sensibilities in both filmmakers and audiences' (1978, 160).

In April 1977, when the Emergency was called off and elections were announced, Karanjia wrote a detailed editorial in *Filmfare*, discussing how difficult it was to work with Shukla and other related concerns. According to him, due to the Emergency, more 'incalculable harm' was done to the film trade than to other spheres of national life because the film trade had to deal with

> a weird assortment of characters, ex-police officials and others, whose ignorance about film matters was matched only by their arrogance. They were blinded by the arrogance of power and resorted to bluff, bluster, terror tactics like midnight phone calls and even blackmail to achieve their often devious ends. ('For the Film Industry a New Dawn' 1977, 10)

Clarifying the reasons behind their resignation, he wrote,

> We had worked under four distinguished Ministers each of whom has gone on record praising the work of the Corporation. But Mr. Shukla was the fifth Minister with whom we had to deal and the very first with whom, in spite of our best efforts, we failed to establish any communication whatsoever ('For the Film Industry a New Dawn' (1977).[19]

He claimed that the circumstances in which he and other directors were 'compelled' to resign were 'sordid enough'. It took the Ministry more than seven months to accept their resignations and even before they received official intimation of the acceptance of these resignations,

> the Ministry took steps, for reasons which should be obvious, to censor the news in all dailies. The manner in which one of the resigned Directors became Chairman of the Corporation, without withdrawing his letter of resignation to us, added a touch of slapstick to the entire sorry episode ('For the Film Industry a New Dawn' 1977, 10).

In the post-Emergency period, Karanjia demanded that an atmosphere of freedom, self-respect and dignity had to be restored in the film industry. He demanded that FFC be taken back to its promotional objective, 'to be a trend-setter, a catalyst in the film industry'. Karanjia also blamed Shukla for shelving the NFDC proposal (discussed below), which was 'drafted, thoroughly discussed and, we learn on reliable authority, even approved by the Cabinet' ('For the Film Industry a New Dawn' 1977, 11).[20]

The Seventy-Ninth Report on the FFC of the CPU (1975–6): An Emergency Document

While these resignations and the Ministry's constant interference in the FFC undermined the reputation of the Corporation, the Seventy-Ninth Report on the FFC of the CPU (1975–6) and its recommendations regulated the nature and objectives of FFC and New Cinema, eventually paving the way for FFC's merger with NFDC.

The Committee gave recommendations to improve the financial position of the Corporation, streamline the procedure for granting loans and bring about an all-round efficiency in working of the Corporation. It noted that the Corporation's criteria for granting loans needed some essential changes (*Committee on Public Undertakings* 1976, 16). The Committee recommended that the Corporation should take a 'balanced view' of the films for which loans are sought and, before sanctioning loans, 'satisfy itself in all possible ways that the films would, in all probability, be not only artistic but also have a reasonable prospect of being *commercially successful*' (emphasis added), because the Committee believed, 'it neither serves the film industry nor the purpose for which the Corporation has been set up if the Corporation helps any entrepreneur in the production of a film, however artistic, which does not attract the public' (*Committee on Public Undertakings* 1976, 16). The Committee was informed that the Corporation had not produced many films on workers' problems, though there were films dealing with village life and social problems. The Committee recommended that the Corporation should encourage filmmakers to make films on family planning, on themes of generating and highlighting fellow-feeling for weaker sections of society, unity and diversity in the country and scientific knowledge. (*Committee on Public Undertakings* 1976, 17).[21] It decided to encourage films on early Indian subjects and historical figures. Names of figures like emperors Asoka, Chandragupta, Vikramaditya and Samudragupta were taken as examples. The MIB suggested to the FFC to see if it could interest filmmakers in such projects (Saari 1976, 1).

The Corporation was advised to thoroughly scrutinize film projects of persons without previous experience as producers or directors 'to satisfy itself that these are of high standards and . . . take all possible precautions to ensure that the public funds will be put to fruitful use and achieve the purposes for which they are intended' (*Committee on Public Undertakings* 1976, 17). Pointing out to cases where Corporation sanctioned fresh loans to producers who had not repaid the earlier loans borrowed from the Corporation, the Committee strongly criticized 'the lack of elementary commercial prudence' shown by the Corporation in such cases and recommended that all such cases – pre- and post-1969 – must be investigated with a view to 'fix responsibility'

(*Committee on Public Undertakings* 1976, 56). The Committee pointed out that the 'prime responsibility and concern' of the Corporation should be 'to recover the outstanding loans in time' (*Committee on Public Undertakings* 1976, 57).[22] The Committee also wanted the Corporation to reconstitute its Script Committee with 'imaginative persons' with 'proven standing in the film production', 'eminent men of letters' and 'representing the youth organisations', last criteria in accordance with the fact that most of the cinema-goers were young women and men, and mostly the films dealt with the lives and problems of young people (*Committee on Public Undertakings* 1976, 68). The Committee warned the FFC of any sense of complacency about the quality of films it produced just because they had won awards or recognition, and emphasized upon public acceptability. The Committee was concerned to find that a large number of the FFC-sponsored films had failed this test (*Committee on Public Undertakings* 1976, 83). It wanted the Corporation/Ministry to go deeper into factors accounting for the failure of its films to ensure better public acceptability. The Committee also advised the Corporation against entering the production of films at that juncture, as the Corporation was not ready for such a complex task like the production of films (*Committee on Public Undertakings* 1976, 93).

This report has to be read as an Emergency document. The recommendations clearly reflect the Emergency's agenda of controlling and marking the value of an institution on its financial usefulness. The suggestion to make films on workers and weaker sections, family planning, unity in diversity and themes promoting scientific knowledge clearly reflects the impact of the 20-Point Programme, the pet project of the Emergency. The (vague) pursuit of a 'balanced view', commercial success and 'fruitful use of public funds' were given more prominence. A thorough scrutiny of loan applications by persons without previous experience hindered the chances of young filmmakers, who had benefitted the most from FFC. The Committee entirely neglected the twin issues of distribution and exhibition, which were the monopoly of private agencies, and it was very difficult for FFC to intrude this space.

The Committee's effort to turn the FFC into another profit-seeking filmmaking organization was criticized. An anonymous write-up in the *Times of India* (TOI) found CPU choosing to assess FFC's record in purely economic terms as 'most unfair', as FFC was primarily promotional in its role ('FFC's Role' 1976). B. K. Karanjia, still the FFC chairman, in his editorial written for *Filmfare*, questioned the premise on which these recommendations were based. He believed that the Committee, competent enough to advise FFC on how to manage its resources, was not capable of laying down what ingredients should go into the making of a good film ('A Kind of Cinema Culture' 1976). The Committee also avoided the Corporation's promotional nature as per the Articles of Association while assessing its record and rather assessed it in purely economic terms, which was a contradiction. The *Screen* editor, S. S. Pillai, however, congratulated CPU for presenting 'a masterly 222-page report' on FFC, 'which should form the basis for any new steps to be taken for streamlining the working of the Corporation, which, despite its weak foundation, could form a sturdy national asset' ('What F.F.C. Should Do' 1976). The editor particularly praised one suggestion of the Committee, namely, Corporation satisfying itself before sanctioning loans about the artistic as well as reasonable commercial prospects of the film, with a capacity to attract the public.

The experimenters, led by Mani Kaul, Kumar Shahani, Mrinal Sen and others, were disappointed with the changing attitude. They felt that the FFC should encourage experimentation without insisting on profit-making devices. Kumar Shahani had said in 1975, as if foreseeing the future,

> If indeed the FFC succumbs to the dictates of the market or those . . . for whom the market is the new sacred institution, it will sooner or later stop performing the function for which it was set up. It may, in fact, like many other banking institutions in our country, do exactly the opposite – it may end up offering reasonable rates of interest to people whose main concern, however camouflaged, has been to extract as much capital as possible for their own benefit, not for general cultural upliftment. (Shahani 2015)

In the background of the Committee's various recommendations and the discussion that followed, the Ministry drew up a revised charter of functions for the Corporation in 1978. One of the key decisions was, 'The Corporation will now finance not only experimental and serious films but also films which could be considered as good from the aesthetic, intellectual and social view-points and which have *an appeal to wider audiences*' (*Report 1977-78* 1978) (Emphasis added). Yashodhara Dalmia rightly claimed, 'much of the FFC's piecemeal approach towards cinema is formulated by the government. Thus the government has asked the FFC to promote good cinema without trying to create a climate for it' (Dalmia 1976, 13). It was pointed out how two of 'the most promising film-makers' the FFC had financed earlier – Mani Kaul and

Kumar Shahani – were making films independent of it at that time. Mani Kaul, along with fourteen other film technicians, had formed a co-operative which was working on a film based on Vijay Tendulkar's play *Ghashiram Kotwal*. The members of the co-operative, Saeed Akhtar Mirza being one of them, contributed towards the share capital. They took a bank loan at fifteen per cent interest under the scheme for self-employed graduates. The FTII gave them equipment and recording facilities on deferred payment (Dalmia 1976, 13). While *Ghashiram Kotwal* (1976) saw the light of day, Kumar Shahani's two independent ventures could not succeed. And he could make *Tarang* (1984) only after twelve years of *Maya Darpan* (1972), with FFC help. The FFC, as it had practically ceased to function after the mass resignation by Karanjia and other directors in 1976, eventually gave in to the desire to generate revenue 'by supporting films that would have wider audiences and thus recover their costs', along the way losing sight of 'its uniquely inspiring ambition to raise cinematic sensibilities in both filmmakers and audiences' (Vasudev 1978, 159–60). Between April and December 1975, out of twenty-six applications for loans, the Corporation sanctioned only six with loans amounting to Rs. 4,73,258 (*Annual Report 1975–76* 1976, 36). The Corporation's annual general meeting, scheduled to be held in December 1975, was also adjourned and held only in July 1976 (*Annual Report & Accounts 1974–75* 1976, 2).[23]

FFC's performance during Emergency

Laxmishwar Dayal, Joint Secretary in charge of films in the MIB, in a briefing to newsmen in Bombay, said that the granting of loans for making off-beat, low-budget and regional films through the FFC would be continued and there was no change in the policy ('No Let Up in Censorship, Says Dayal' 1976, 1 and 4). But, while the Corporation had already done 'good work, much more needed to be done. And the Government had been considering different measures to step up' the activities of the FFC ('No Let Up in Censorship, Says Dayal' 1976, 4). On shelving the plan for starting the NFDC, he said,

> instead of creating a new body whose functions might overlap with the functions of the FFC and IMPEC, the Government was contemplating to provide both these bodies with more funds so that they could function like any other public sector undertaking. Both would be asked to set up their

offices in Delhi so that they could directly tackle problems with other Ministries from time to time. ('No Let Up in Censorship, Says Dayal' 1976, 4)

However, the Emergency's insistence on the economic usefulness of an institution, CPU's recommendations to have a 'balanced' approach to filmmaking, with a clear firmness on audience acceptability, and the new chairman's managerial skills deeply affected the functioning of FFC, altering the course of the New Cinema movement in India.

When FFC resumed proper operations with a new chairman, its tone was changed.[24] In an exclusive interview, Jagdish Parikh, the new FFC chairman, said that the objectives of the Corporation were not vague and that it wanted to remain in the centre of activities of national cinema, instead of remaining on the periphery. He said, 'We don't believe in parallel cinema because parallel lines never meet' (Desai 1976, 1). In another interview, Parikh said the question of financing only the cinema it had till now specialized in – meaning experimental cinema – had to be viewed in perspective. 'Today the thrust is towards good films, which are entertaining as well' (Mohamed 1976, 7). The promotion of the alternative cinema would continue, but the concentration would be on '*light and wholesome films*' (emphasis added). On another occasion, explaining FFC's expansion plans, Parikh spoke on how FFC's activities were at a standstill when he took over in 1976. The government was asking for a refund of sanctioned loans of Rs. 84 lakhs.[25] The production activities were zero, since there were no fund for financing films as the producers who had got loans earlier could not repay ('FFC Infra-structure Strengthened, Says Its Chairman, Expansion Plans' 1977, 1 and 14). Also, the subvention granted to FFC by the central government since 1970–1 to set off the loss arising out of financing activity partially was stopped altogether during 1976–7. Though the government wanted to influence the type of films FFC should make, it did not want to support it financially anymore.

A separate Director's Report addressing the shareholders informed about the restructuring and controlling of FFC in the background of events in 1975–6. Not citing the 'variety of reasons', the Report regretted that the main activity of the Corporation, namely financing low-budget artistic films, had come to a virtual halt in 1975–6, as not a single new feature film could be financed during that year. A complete review was undertaken in April 1976 to bring about a revival in FFC activities (*Annual Report 1976–77* 1977, 5). The Report duly noted two different standpoints that had emerged, namely, one, 'F.F.C. is a promotional body and even if it loses money, Government should subsidise this movement' (*Annual Report 1976–77* 1977, 5), and two, 'F.F.C. is using public money and it should not waste such funds in activities which are for the benefit of only a very small segment of the population. F.F.C. should, therefore, finance only films which are popular and recover its investments' (*Annual Report 1976–77* 1977, 5). Keeping in mind these conflicting views, the Directors, from April 1976, evolved a two-way strategy aiming at an incorporation of activities bringing about an all-round growth and development of good cinema in India, and also ensuring revenue generation, which could be recycled into developmental work (*Annual Report 1976–77* 1977, 5). Due to these major administrative and outlook level changes, FFC's focus shifted towards developmental aspects of the film industry, and 'changing the taste of Indian audience' took a back seat. New Cinema movement was on its way to get corporatized, as FFC had to integrate multiple activities from 1977. To signify this changed approach and create a 'corporate image', a symbol was designed (Figure 4.2), a special brochure published, and its objectives were elucidated (Figure 4.3). Of the five key activities, the developmental activities were more extensive.

NEW SYMBOL OF FFC

Reflecting a new, dynamic approach to films

FFC's symbol is a graphic representation of the main activities of the Corporation. The four spools, forming the roundels of the two initials, represent financing, importing, distributing and exhibiting of films that are realistic, possess artistic merit, and combine social purpose with healthy entertainment.

These activities culminate in the film frame forming the symbol's centre, which is also representative of the silver screen.

Embodying the grace and fluidity which is inherent in Indian art, the free-flowing lines of the symbol express FFC's commitment to raise cinema to an art, by giving film producers the freedom to experiment with form, content and technique.

You'll be seeing this symbol frequently. This is the symbol that stands for good cinema.

Figure 4.2 Source: *Annual Report 1976–7*, Annexure I, p. 11.

Objective: To promote the growth of good cinema in India in all possible ways

ACTIVITIES

I	II	III	IV	V
Financing	Importing	Distributing	Exhibiting	Developmental Activities

Feature Films | Short Films | Equipment | Row Stock | Films | Imported Films | FFC Sponsored Indian Films | Akashvani Bombay | Shakuntalam Delhi | Other Theatres elsewhere

Low Cost 16 mm Theatres (Rural Areas) | Mini Theatres (Major Cities) | Non-commercial Circuit | Festivals in India and abroad | Facilitating Co-productions | FFC Film Club, Seminars, Film Appreciation Courses, Publications, etc..

Universities | Industrial Welfare Centres | Film Societies

Figure 4.3 Source: *Annual Report 1976–7*, Annexure II, p. 12.

The Seventeenth Annual Report claimed that the FFC operations during 1976–7 resulted in a net profit of Rs. 2.73 lakhs, not enough to support its financing activities (*Annual Report 1976–77* 1977, 5). The Corporation faced issues like, 'Inevitable delays in revival of activities due to shortage of staff, particularly at senior levels, clearing arrears and introduction of new systems, disputes in connection with distribution of foreign films, involvement in International Film Festival without benefit in revenues etc' (*Annual Report 1976–77* 1977, 6). Compared to fifty-nine in 1971–2 and twenty-nine in 1975–6, the Corporation received only sixteen new applications during 1976–7, and sanctioned loans to three of these (*Annual Report 1976–77* 1977, 7). FFC also failed to obtain Shakuntalam Theatre in Delhi from the Trade Fair Authority to exhibit its films. Earlier, the Akashvani cinema 'which had gained considerable popularity', had to be closed down under orders of the Ministry in June 1975 for 'security reasons', another major casualty caused by the Emergency (*Annual Report & Accounts 1974–75* 1976, 7). The operations of Akashvani cinema had also resulted in a loss of Rs. 35,997.50, including the 'embezzlement' of Rs. 22,936.17 (*Annual Report & Accounts 1974–75* 1976, 7).[26] A case of misappropriation was reported to the police for necessary action. During 1977–8, the Corporation continued to face constraints such as a lack of adequate financial resources, sufficient and experienced human resources and unavoidable delays in dealing with a multitude of authorities at the local, state and central levels (*Annual Report 1977–78* 1978, 5). The main challenge continued to be how to create a balance between the Corporation's dual role as a financier and as a developer.

However, the Annual Report (1978) acknowledged the role of *'greater professional management and financial disciplines'* (emphasis added) introduced during 1977–8 in helping the Corporation not only generate higher revenues but also finance a record number of films (seventeen films, including eleven feature films) in one single year since its inception (*Annual Report 1977–78* 1978, 6). After providing for depreciation and interest on loans taken from the government, the operating profit of the Corporation came to Rs. 15.19 lakhs, as compared to mere Rs. 2.73 lakhs of previous year (*Annual Report 1977–78* 1978, 6). Of the twenty-seven new applications for feature films, eleven were sanctioned (*Annual Report 1977–78* 1978, 6). This was particularly noteworthy in view of a downward trend in financing activity during the past few years, reaching a situation in 1975–6 when not a single feature film was financed.

National Film Development Corporation

The setting up of an NFDC was recommended by two Study Teams appointed by the government of India to consider grievances of the West Bengal film industry and examine the possibility of reorganizing particular aspects of the Indian film industry as a whole ('The Proposed Film Corporation' 1972). The Team suggested that a comprehensive film corporation should be set up, which should be largely self-financing and could generate sufficient resources within itself from profits of the import and export trade. It was not to be entirely dependent on the limited resources that the government placed at its disposal. Intensive work was being done in the Union Ministries of Information and Broadcasting and of Commerce to commission the Corporation by October 1973.[27] An announcement to have an autonomous corporation was to be made during the budget session of Parliament in February 1974 (Saari 1973, 1). The formal announcement of the corporation was expected in October 1974. The entire blueprint was designed on the instructions of the Prime Minister, who was also the Minister for Information and Broadcasting. The corporation was likely to have separate directorates for raw stock and equipment, film financing, distribution and exhibition of films, import and export of films, construction of theatres, art theatres and the promotion of art films. It was likely that once the corporation was established, the government could make a definite effort to restructure the financial network of the Indian film industry. The proposed corporation was also to control numerous activities of the Indian film industry, including censorship, and would be the overall governmental agency handling film subjects. It was also to co-ordinate the activities of various state film corporations in India (Saari 1974, 1).

The Union Cabinet approved the establishment of this corporation in July 1974, and the NFDC came to be finally set up in 1975 ('Cabinet Okays Plan for Film Corpn. [*sic*]' 1974). The Corporation was to have an authorized capital of Rs. 3 crores[28] and a working capital of Rs. one crore. The broad objective was to plan, promote and organize an integrated and efficient development of the Indian film industry *in accordance with the national economic policy and objectives laid down by the Government* (emphasis added).[29] A political figure, instead of a film expert or a technocrat, was proposed as the chairman of the new Corporation. It was learnt that the chairman may also be given ministerial status. The members of the Board of Directors, with a three-year term, were to be appointed by the President of India. These directives indicated a significant change in the government's approach, particularly towards the 'promotion of quality films', which may or may not include financial help. NFDC was also required to generate its own resources and be less dependent, unlike FFC, on the government, and was expected to run along the lines of a 'financial' agency. The insertion of the word 'development' was intentional – development of the national economy via the film industry.

Interestingly, the NFDC did not function from 1975 to 1980, one of the many casualties of the Emergency. It was revived after Indian Motion Picture Export Corporation (IMPEC) and FFC were officially merged with it in 1980. By the mid-1970s, with the formation of NFDC and the calculated attack during the Emergency on 'financially inadequate' organizations, the discussion on the amalgamation of FFC and IMPEC with NFDC reappeared. By June 1979, things were finalized for merger.[30] The government had decided to activate NFDC and merge FFC and IMPEC with it ('FFC and IMPEC merged with National Film Development Corporation' 1979, 1). The Cabinet approved the proposal on 1 June 1980.

From 1975, the Indian state was changing its gear from being a socialist, welfare state to a liberal economy. The imposition of the Emergency played a key role in this transition, politically and culturally, too. It severely affected the New Cinema movement and FFC.

Concluding remarks

The Internal Emergency declared in June 1975 was an attempt to discipline the nation. From Parliament to family, every unit of democracy was under scrutiny. Contribution to the national economy became an essential criteria to judge a unit's usefulness. This political and economic rigidity pushed many institutions to a sense of existential crisis: FFC being one such casualty of this era, as discussed above. Apart from narrating how the Emergency affected the functioning of FFC/NFDC and the New Cinema in general, this chapter also attempted to consider the possibility of New Cinema being a state enterprise. FFC, being a government of India enterprise, was responsible for it. This aspect was going to damage FFC's growth during this period when the state became too regimental and pulled away from socialism. While the Emergency had also burdened the New Cinema with revenue generation and audience acceptability. The state was capable of not only changing the New Cinema movement structurally (through its patron body FFC) but also suggesting changes in its form and content. The strict disciplining and regimentation released by the Emergency had an adverse impact on FFC's functioning. The practitioners of New Indian Cinema found themselves in the middle of a storm. The main activity of the Corporation, namely, financing of low-budget artistic films, came to a near halt in 1975–6, as not a single new feature film could be financed during that year. FFC's autonomy was bypassed, and New Cinema's aesthetic spirit had to pass a test of its contribution to the national economy. A revised charter of functions for FFC was drawn up by the Ministry, with a major focus on *an appeal to wider audiences*. The government was not ready to support the Corporation financially any longer. This led to FFC's major focus getting shifted towards developmental aspects of the film industry, and 'changing the taste of Indian audience' took a back seat. This possibly also indicated an end to the pursuit of 'New'-ness in Indian cinema. The New Cinema movement was on its way to get corporatized. The merger of FFC and IMPEC with NFDC and the formation of a working group on national film policy attempted some damage control, but one knew that all this rearrangement was being done to favour entertainment and generate monetary returns. The damage was already done.

Between a logo and a memo

State-sponsored documentary films during the Emergency

Ritika Kaushik

About two months after the newly elected Janata Party had formed the government, effectively ending the state of Emergency that began on 25 June 1975, a memo reached India's primary state institution of documentary films – Films Division of India (FD). The memo, marked as 'Most Immediate' (Govt. of India 1977a), enclosed copies of a questionnaire from *Media India*, New Delhi, for an exclusive interview with L. K. Advani, who had just replaced V. C. Shukla as Minister of Information and Broadcasting (I&B). The questionnaire included items on the overhauling of media institutions and existing policies and inquired about the Minister's plans for the same, including the following excerpt relevant for FD:

> There has been an all-round feeling that Films Division has sunk to new depths of stagnation and even degeneration both in professional and political grounds. There have been allegations of widespread corruption in hiring private producers by the Films Division. One instance is the production of short documentaries in the series 'Film 20' based on the 20-Point programme.

Faced with accusations of 'degeneration' and 'corrupt practices' under his reign during the Emergency years, FD's Chief Producer Mushir Ahmed found himself in a curious position of having to come up with an appropriate response justifying the practices of FD to the newly appointed Minister of I&B.

I take this memo as a starting point to examine state-sponsored film practice during this historical period. Highly coded in bureaucracy-speak that shrugs any responsibility of power, Ahmed's response acts as a microcosmic instance of the peculiar position FD found itself in around the time of the Emergency. I ascertain Ahmed's response as a statement about the nature of FD's institutional calibration with the I&B Ministry. The second part of his response reveals how one of the main topics of accusation, the 'Film 20' series on the Prime Minister's 20-point programme, was spearheaded in ideation by the independent filmmaker S. Sukhdev, complicating institutional filmmaking through the role of the intertwined power relations between independent filmmakers and the state. To avoid any association with FD or the government, the films were made under a new logo. This chapter discusses Ahmed's response by drawing from the anthropological studies of paperwork and bureaucracy, alongside a historical account of the production and reception of the 'Film 20' series, which was at the centre of the above controversy. Between this 'Film 20' logo and the questionnaire in the memo emerge microhistories of institutional filmmaking during a period of crisis, which allow us to see specific contours of the institutional matrix that governs the relation between film and the Indian state.

It is a widely circulated assertion that state-sponsored documentary film production in India gave into the demands of Indira Gandhi's regime during the Emergency era to 'demonize social unrest and show the Emergency as the only rational panacea of the ills of the country' (Jayasankar and Monteiro 2015,: 18). Founded in 1948, FD had a mandate of making films for informational, educational and publicity purposes about the government's efforts in developing India's economy and society and securing its integrity. However, during the Emergency, according to historian B. D. Garga, 'fear stalked its corridors' (2007, 186). FD's filmmakers had to toe the line as filmmaking was monitored closely by higher-level authorities beyond the film institution, and Garga saw FD reduced to the status of an 'impotent giant' (2007, 186).

Indeed, the period of the early 1970s saw the production of several types of short films from the government's publicity efforts, especially instigated in the period preceding and continuing into the Emergency. These included film campaigns against violence, film series on the 20-Point Economic Programme to boost public morale, and films for displaying the 'gains' of the Emergency, all produced by FD. By May 1976, FD had made 180 documentaries (Times of India 1976, 12) on the Prime Minister's 20-point programme. The period also saw an increase in ad hoc film assignments, a quicker turnaround time for films, a general sense of urgency, more supervision by authorities like ministers from the government, purchases of pro-Emergency films, regular top-level meetings that trickled down orders about films and overtly specific mandates that wanted to show the government's policies in a good light. None of these, however, signal a massive departure from earlier practices of control and administrative management of filmmaking at FD. A closer look at the production practices of this 'impotent giant', while affirming the prevalent historical narrative to an extent, throws into relief how the films were mandated, how different institutional actors and filmmakers negotiated the translation of mandates into films, and how the plethora of films produced during this time do not cohere into a simplistic view about control during the Emergency.

It is pertinent to note here that while the 'Emergency' primarily refers to the period from 1975–7 when a state of Internal Emergency was declared, it was in addition to the continuing external Emergency. In fact, emergencies have punctuated the post-independence history of India. A state of external Emergency was declared at the time of the Indo-Sino War of 1962, continued until 1968, and was declared again for the Indo-Pakistani War of 1971. In each instance, the official film institution produced films thought appropriate to the context. During the Sino-Indian War of 1962, FD was mobilized to make very short films called 'quickies' (Our Film Critic 1962), motivating people to donate gold, clothes, wool, inciting a feeling of national integration and so on. The year 1974 would again see a focus on producing 'quickies' on violence or other topical subjects. In fact, a film on holding the price line during Emergency situations was literally recycled from 1962 and was re-released with a few edited scenes in 1971. In a way, an impending state of Emergency seems to be wired into the film production system with its own default mode of functioning during a crisis. It is this aspect of FD's production practices and its institutional matrix mobilized during times of crisis that comes out in an exchange between the Ministry and FD with respect to an interview, as I discuss below.

FD's Chief Producer Mushir Ahmed's response to the memo from the I&B Ministry was to vehemently deny the charges of 'corruption' and 'degeneration' as being 'baseless', and declare that FD did exactly what it was mandated to do – making sure to highlight that this is a function of the many limitations posed by its very institutional structure. What caught my eye in the production file of the query by *Media India* is that it includes a draft response which was edited into the final text. That draft highlights FD's status as a '*subordinate* office with *limited powers* and *limited scope* for independent action (emphasis mine)'. It goes on to explain that FD has 'very little say' in the content of the film, which also dictates the form of the film. It further elaborates on the process of how FD also has 'no authority' in the selection of films in its annual programme, which is drawn at the behest of different ministries, and how films are made based on a pre-given Line of Approach. The small section finally ends with the following text:

> And like any other Department subordinate to the govt. [*sic*], in power and accountable to it, Films Division also *cannot claim immunity from political pressure* (emphasis mine). (Govt. of India 1977a)

On one hand, it seems obvious why the above text did not make it into the final statement – while it states facts, it makes FD a complicit partner with the regime, agreeing that it did succumb to the party's 'political pressure'. But, on the other hand, its existence as a draft gives us pause in considering the reason behind the change of tone in the final edited text. What made Ahmed steer away from a defensive tone and not dwell as much on FD's lack of autonomy – editing out phrases like 'no authority', 'limited powers', 'limited scope' and 'very little say'? For brevity? Or as a strategic choice to not come across as too defensive or guilty of the accusations? And what does this have to do with the accusations of corruption?

The letter's assertions also share a curious resonance with the findings of the Chanda Committee Report (Govt. of India 1966), which recommended the overhauling of FD's institutional practices of filmmaking. Indeed, filmmaking at FD was far from autonomous and continued to be so even into the 1970s. The process of deciding topics for films involved meetings with the different ministries, which had their own agendas and requirements that FD had to meet. Apart from assigning films to its in-house directors, FD would often commission films to Outside Producers (called OPs). The directors worked within deadlines and under the given budgets in tandem with not just producers but also 'Subject specialists' who would give feedback about the film's content and often also their form. FD films were also subject to approval by the Film Advisory Board (FAB), which not only mandated which films were approved for screening in the theatre circuit but often suggested changes in the films, acting as a proto-censor (Barnouw et al. 1963, 194–5).[1] Not only did FD's office function just like any other government office in the country, but the entire system was riddled with bureaucratic catacombs, like the 'tender-system' of assigning a film to the lowest bidder, leading to badly made productions.

Seeing a reproduction of these aspects, meant to rehaul FD's institutional structure, in a draft letter deployed against accusations of 'corruption' and 'degeneration' during the Emergency, forces us to question the operation of power in this institution. The changes from the draft version to the final text illustrate how the power relations between the head bureaucrat of FD and high-level ministers are carved on paper in the official file, and how the relationship between the institution and the state is negotiated at a critical moment. On paper, FD and its official head – the Chief Producer – are depicted as powerless under the tight grips of overseeing authorities and procedures.

But paper is more than 'a thing that bureaucrats work with', as Nayanika Mathur (2016, 5) has shown, thus indicating the importance of tracing the key and constitutive role paper plays in the 'composition, maintenance, and assemblage of the Indian state'. In fact, bureaucratic writing is constitutive of state action, as Akhil Gupta (2012, 188) has argued; and as Matthew Hull (2012) has illustrated, it participates in the dynamic formation of social relations in a bureaucratic organization, that is, it does not merely reflect them. By looking at the period of the Indian Emergency, Emma Tarlo has shown us how 'paper-truths' (2003) emerge from the official files of the government and challenge the roles of the bureaucrat as agent and the common man as victim, revealing them to be ambiguous and often in negotiation with each other. Drawing from these interventions, we can see Ahmed's response as the site where power relations are being staged, where the boundaries between state and non-state are charted and how the state is challenged as a top-down vertical institution into a horizontality of operation where various forces work in collision with one another.

The texts also mimic, I argue, a stark artificial divergence found in government media of the time, which divides the period of the Emergency from the period following it, to justify how its declaration was to the country's benefit. We see this in films like *We Have Promises to Keep* (1975), *A New Wave* (1976), *Wheels Move Faster* (1976), *Thunder of Freedom* (1976) and *Fanatics* (1976). All of the above include a montage of events that signals violence and unrest as chaotic and anarchic events of the recent past, as per the government's propaganda. christening them as threats to the nation's governance, unity and stability, thus creating a temporal bifurcation between the events of the Emergency and the ones preceding it. This bifurcation is critical in understanding the processes that govern film practice during the Emergency: it allows Mushir Ahmed to detach himself and the institution of FD from the Congress Party's agendas, maintaining his legitimacy as a bureaucrat and justifying FD's film production during the Emergency through an utter lack of its own agency.

Here, I would like to discuss the second part of Ahmed's response, which included details about the process through which the infamous series of 'morale-boosting' films – most accused of corruption during the Emergency – came into being (Govt of India 1977b).[2] While Ahmed presented the facts related to this 'Film 20' series, he calmly managed to shift the blame from FD's agency in making the films to the independent filmmaker S. Sukhdev – who came up with the idea to make these films. This reconfiguration shifts the direction of power from top-down control to a more discrete formation as I show below.

It was in June 1976 that S. Sukhdev approached the Deputy Minister of I&B, Dharam Bir Sinha, with a proposal that the current documentary film production did not meet the topical demands and that there was a need to produce 'morale-boosting films' to incite 'hope' and 'pride' among the people of India. He further recommended that independent filmmakers should make these films and, more importantly, the films should not bear the logo of Films Division to avoid their association with FD and therefore of being a 'Government product' (Govt. of India 1976b). Soon after, on 17 June, in a meeting presided by Sinha, fourteen subjects were drawn from the Prime Minister's 20-point programme. Eight of these were assigned to OPs on 'Negotiation basis', while the rest were assigned to FD's in-house filmmakers.[3]

However, unlike other films of the time, these above-mentioned films were to be released under a special new logo and not the Films Division of India's logo. Under the catchy and dramatic banner of 'Film 20', these films were soon under production on a 'top-priority basis' and were meant to be released from the beginning of October to November 1976 at an interval of every two weeks.[4]

Known for his fierce independent sense of filmic expression and rebellious attitude, Sukhdev had come into his own with films like *And Miles to Go* (1965), *India '67* (1967) and *Thoughts in a Museum* (1968). But in films like *Voice of the People* (1974) and *A Few More Questions* (1974), which he made on the railway strike of 1974, his pro-government stance started to take over. This was paticularly evident as he asked his interviewees leading questions about the harmful effects of the strike, which was one of the largest recorded industrial actions and was brutally suppressed by the Indira Gandhi regime. It is also pertinent to note that Sukhdev was assigned more than his share of films, in fact, this contention formed the main complaint about corrupt practices in assigning films to OPs.[5] Nevertheless, this did not translate to his own films not running into problems.

For the 'Film 20' series, Sukhdev made *After the Silence* (1976), a film on bonded labour which he shot in Bihar and Uttar Pradesh, throwing light on the practice of women sex workers who are caught in the cycle of bonded labour. The film is remarkable for its candid interviews with the women narrating their stories, albeit with a lot of leading questions and interferences from Sukhdev. Interestingly, the film, while passed by the Censor Board, faced some 'inexplicable' delays in its release, as discussed by film historian Jag Mohan in *Times of India* (1976, 8). This is not to say that the film was in any way critical of the Emergency; it wasn't, but it somehow managed to find itself in some prickly situations.

Similarly, the case of *For What Are You Voting* is telling – it was assigned to Sukhdev to be made expeditiously but ended up getting shelved after completion. It appears that Sukhdev did not show the film at any stage to FD and took it directly to the Central Board of Film Certification (CBFC), according to the 'White Paper on Misuse of Mass Media' (1977b). The CBFC gave it an 'Advertisement Certificate' making it impossible to show the film in the theatre circuit. Therefore, FD refused to accept it. Sukhdev appealed to the Ministry, but nothing seems to have come of it. All this, however, makes Sukhdev's role more complicated than simply being a benefactor of toeing the party line or reveling in the patronage of Mrs Gandhi (Kaushik 2017).

It is also critical at this point to account for the group of other Independent Producers who were assigned the films and attended a 28 July meeting at the Ministry of I&B (Govt. of India 1976b). These included the prominent filmmaker and historian B. D. Garga, the pioneer of the film society movement in India and prolific writer Chidananda Dasgupta as well as the young filmmaker Goutam Ghose, already known for his film *Hungry Autumn* (1974) on the Bengal famine made a few years ago. While the meeting itself was more functional about how the films would be produced and how much they would get paid, the focus of the films was defined to be as 'morale-boosting films in the context of the current situation in the country with a view to create an awareness among the people of the challenges they were facing and infuse among them a sense of hope and pride' (Govt. of India 1976b). During the meeting, several representatives from the Ministries briefed the individual directors about the essential points to include in the films.

Still, each producer interpreted the mandate in their own way. Dasgupta's *Zaroorat ki Poorti* on essential commodities and prices begins with panning and tilting shots of still photographs, taken by Aparna Sen (filmmaker and also Dasgupta's daughter), featuring the faces of farmers on fields and their children. The rest of the film, acting as a didactic fable, is entirely made up of staged and enacted dialogue sequences between a farmer and his young city-dweller brother who is studying at a college, played by Kalyan Chatterjee, known for his supporting roles in Bengali cinema. The dialogue continues with various activities over the span of a day, as the young brother narrates to his brother and the neighbours in the village how he is able to get essential commodities at reasonable prices.

In stark contrast to Dasgupta's style, Ghose's *Chains of Bondage* on rural indebtedness is a lyrical documentation of poverty and hunger afflicting India's farmers, with a focus on the practice of moneylending and murderous interests. While *Chains of Bondage* mentions the new act of abolishing rural indebtedness by the government, it critiques the limitations of the law on its own at several moments. It does, however, resort to exaggerating the benefits of rural banks in addressing this problem, another major party line by the government. But, it turns out that this was at the suggestion of the Ministry consultant, as he asked that the film should feature a section on how rural banking is helping farmers with the capital necessary to kickstart their own production. Furthermore, while all the films were assigned under a fixed bracket of Rs. 50,000–65,000, this did pose problems for filmmakers like Ghose, who had to shoot his film in three different states and, according to the film's production file, did not know this in advance. He had to finish the film using his own money.[6]

The film also ran into trouble with FD, and none other than Sukhdev had to vouch for the filmmaker. Ghose's version of events throws into relief this dynamic in operation:

> *Chains of Bondage* was about rural indebtedness in Bihar, Bengal and Orissa. The initial reaction of FD's approval committee was negative. Again, Sukhdev intervened. He argued for *my freedom of expression*. The FD wanted me to include the 20-point programme in the documentary somehow. My stand was, I have only shown *what is actually happening*. If they wanted to show how the government was trying to solve the issue of indebtedness, they would have to do it on their own. (Battaglia 2018, 100)

Not only did Sukhdev advocate for Ghose's 'freedom of expression', he did it for a series he had himself proposed to the Ministry on the policies of Mrs Gandhi's regime. This compels us to reflect that the relationship of independent filmmakers like Sukhdev and Ghose with FD, the approving bodies (like CBFC or FAB), and the Ministry existed on an ever-changing see-saw between control and agency.

However, even within the chambers of FD, its in-house filmmakers shared a complicated relationship with the Chief Producer, the approving authorities, as well as members from the I&B Ministry. Like Sukhdev, the period from 1965–7 saw an array of filmmakers and artists like Pramod Pati and S. N. S. Sastry, who emerged during this time and were given free rein to experiment with film form and content under the leadership of Jehangir Bhownagary. This led to films like Sastry's *I am 20* (1967), *Burning Sun* (1973), which questioned the government and its policies. But the same filmmakers continued to make films during the mid-1970s when India saw stricter mandates for the publicity of the government's measures during the period of the Emergency. Sastry's *We Have Promises to Keep* (1975), which declared the gains of the Emergency to the people, saw the intervention of the Director (Information), Ministry of Information at I&B Ministry, G. N. S. Raghavan, who found the film's fast-paced cinematic montage much too ambiguous and thus 'unsuitable' for rural audiences (Govt. of India 1976a). I recount these instances as they beg a re-examination of not just how intentions and mandates were being translated into actual films but also how they filtered through the complex matrix of different authorities, as well as state and non-state actors.

Before concluding, I add another institution to this matrix, even as the films from the 'Film 20' series were being shown in theatres, the Indian Institute of Mass Communication (1976) was mobilized to document audience feedback for them. In an audience reaction study of the Film 20 series, the film *Not a Bed of Feathers* by Sastry was found incomprehensible and did not seem to have much of an impact on the audience. Some found the film interesting, and a few liked it, yet people could not get the 'message' of the film. More interestingly, some people found Sukhdev's *After the Silence* to be 'merely government propaganda on the 20 point programme' (Indian Institute of Mass Communication 1976). It would be remiss to not add here that in many theatres, the films were screened only in parts, and in many cases, the audience did not see the film as they came in late, or they could not watch it as the film was playing while the theatre was still being filled. This failure at the level of infrastructure and the failure of the films to be effective propaganda shows that even in an authoritarian regime, state-sponsored films are much more than the sum of their parts and never seem to do exactly what they are supposed to do.

Throughout this chapter, I have charted the differing bureaucratic processes of cinematic exchange, from the logo to the memo, during and after the Emergency, as they appear through the complex institutional matrix of FD, the FAB and the Ministry of Information and Broadcasting alongside the shifting position of filmmakers within it. It is in this light we need to understand that those like Sukhdev, who started to display a pro-government stance with his films on the railway strike, enjoyed the patronage of Mrs Gandhi herself, and came up with an entire film series on her policies, would still face problems with getting their films passed for theatrical distribution, while simultaneously vouching for artistic agency in the work of others. And for those like Ghose, who had terrible experiences with the institutions, would vow not to try their hands on documentary films again (Battaglia 2018, 100). At the same time, if the 'Film 20' logo provided a way for the government to hide its marker and gain some credibility for its policies through the work of independent filmmakers, the same logo becomes a marker of the institution's corrupt practices of assigning films post-Emergency. This is evident through the case of Dasgupta's film *Zaroorat ki Poorti*, which was completed much later, but was only released in 1978, after the lifting of the Emergency, bearing none other than the logo 'Films Division Presents'. As the regime changed from one party to the other, the institution recalibrated its relationship to other power structures accordingly, leading to this curious paradox of a film on the Prime Minister Indira Gandhi's 20-point programme being released under the Janata Party rule. It is in this vein that we can see the memo with the *Media India* questionnaire not only revealing power dynamics in its textual content but actively constructing them, through the shadowy spaces of things unsaid or edited out, in its own circulatory life as a document of communication between the Ministry and FD, as well as the nationwide media project. This allows us to visualize the relationship between film and the state through discrete configurations, which operate through the dance between power and powerlessness, patronal networks, individual leaps of exercising control, infrastructural inefficiency, as well as shifting terms of artistic and political agency in state-sponsored documentary film practice.

Memories and mixed-media

The event and the archive

Vinayak Das Gupta and Ananya Juneja

Introduction

This chapter attempts to complicate the relationship between public memory and archival memory (if one can speak of such a thing) through the examination of the Indian Emergency (1975–7), one of the most difficult moments in the history of independent India. The larger narrative around this event is well known. The period of the Indian Emergency saw the curbing and flouting of constitutional rights, widespread censorship, and extensive civil and political unrest. This examination attempts to show that the archive fails at moments of great trauma and the reconstruction of such an event can only happen through the incorporation of multiple forms of objects – a collage of artefacts of various media to paint an incomplete (yet, the only possible) image.

Walter Benjamin, in his last great, posthumously published work 'Theses on the Philosophy of History', reflects upon a Paul Klee painting titled *Angelus Novus*, or the New Angel. Describing the angel in the painting, he writes,

> [h]is face is turned toward the past. Where we perceive a chain of events, he sees one single catastrophe which keeps piling wreckage upon wreckage and hurls it in front of his feet. The angel would like to stay, awaken the dead, and make whole what has been smashed. But a storm is blowing from Paradise; it has got caught in his wings with such violence that the angel can no longer close them. The storm irresistibly propels him into the future to which his back is turned, while the pile of debris before him grows skyward. The storm is what we call progress. (1968,: 257–8)

This storm called progress drives us relentlessly towards the future, leaving behind the detritus of the past. What he sees is pre-eminently the experience of modern living: to salvage debris, to hold on to fragments of a past that we know to be irretrievable. This is at the same time the image of memory and the image of the archive. How do we talk about this act of recovery? Does the little that can be salvaged become the domain of the archive? The archive exists to store material objects of social, historical, cultural and political significance; it strives to be comprehensive and hence powerful;[1] it collects all that is pertinent to its archival mission; the archive becomes a form of artificial memory. While the archive should be comprehensive, it is known that a selection is at the heart of archival practice. Swapan Chakravorty (2019, 89) illustrates how '[a]rchives "re-member" not simply by collecting but also by selecting and organizing them, so that each act of collecting and "re-collecting" is also at the same time an act of forgetting'. This act of selection is also indicative of what is to be preserved and, by consequence, what is to be forgotten. Ghaddar and Caswell propose that the power of the archive is to decide, 'what is and what is not a serious object of research, and, therefore, of mention or thought' (2019, 76). The archive, with its (supposed) comprehensive array of material, allows us to grasp the interconnections between the archived objects; these interconnections illuminate the historical conditions within which the object is produced, the impetus behind its production and the social affect in its use (to name a few). This is what the historian uses to piece together the past. However, these become less visible in a disjointed collection; we cannot make any certain claims about the past when only a fragmented array – by accident, compulsion or design – is made available to us.

Archives and the Emergency

Archives, in the colonies, have served as instruments of control; what perhaps started as projects of documentation inevitably transformed into key technologies of rule. This has been traced by several scholars, including Elizabeth Yale (2015), Swapan Chakravorty (2019), Jamila Ghaddar and Michelle Caswell (2019) among many others. Yale describes how the work of the archive begins as tension between political will and community identity and continues in the struggle between archival ambitions and archival realities.

Chakravorty's views on the emergence and function of archives attribute greater agency to political motivations:

> Archival 'clauses' of the 18th century, that allowed the transfer of records to annexing states, were sharply defined as imperial archives in European powers such as France and altered legal provisions and suppressed materials to suit imperial objectives. Serviceable archives were now deemed the major gauge of historical reasoning, and superseded cultures were in danger of losing control over their own stories (Aziz 2016). The latter were either silenced or selectively canonised. (2019, 94)

The advent of the archive has two effects germane to this discussion: in the first instance, an axiological imbalance between orality and materiality is created. Within the framework of the new state, oral testimony, oral history and the anecdote are treated with great suspicion as forms of evidence to history. It might occur to us that a very large part of the 'culture' of any peoples might be embedded within oral traditions. It has been argued by scholars such as Joan Schwartz and Terry Cook (2002), and Verne Harris and Sherry Hatang (2000) that the written culture of European bureaucracies was never appropriate for preserving the memories of oral cultures. Denied a place in the archive, oral forms cannot bear witness to history in the way the colonial archive is designed. Orality, then, appears to stand in competition with the material evidence of the physical archive for a claim to history (which it always loses).[2] In the second instance, the advent of the archive signals the death of memory. Pierre Nora writes:

> Modern memory is, above all, archival. It relies entirely on the materiality of the trace, the immediacy of the recording, the visibility of the image. What began as writing ends as high fidelity and tape recording. The less memory is experienced from the inside the more it exists only through its exterior scaffolding and outward signs-hence the obsession with the archive that marks our age, attempting at once the complete conservation of the present as well as the total preservation of the past. Fear of a rapid and final disappearance combines with anxiety about the meaning of the present and uncertainty about the future to give even the most humble testimony, the most modest vestige, the potential dignity of the memorable. [. . .] Memory has been wholly absorbed by its meticulous reconstitution. Its new vocation is to record; delegating to the archive the responsibility of remembering, it sheds its signs upon depositing them there, as a snake sheds its skin. (1989, 13)

Archival records shape scholarship, memory and identity. Hedstrom (2010, 136) writes, '[a]rchival documents are not representatives of collective memory and archival institutions are no storehouses of collective memory. Rather archives are sources for the potential discovery or recovery of memories that have been lost.' Contemporary scholarship on archives has repeatedly questioned the role of memory in the activities of the archive. It is important to consider this aspect, as the disparate sources that will form the basis of the reconstruction of the Emergency must be related to the fundamental principles of the archive.

One might realize that archivists are acutely aware of the silences that are present in the archive. There has been a developing interest in the issue of silences and absences in archives in recent years, starting with Michel-Rolph Trouillot's *Silencing the Past: Power and the Production of History* (1995) to, more recently, David Thomas and Simon Fowler's edited volume titled *The Silence of the Archive* (2017a). Trouillot sees silences as inherent in the writing of history and in the creation of archives. Sometimes, they were the things left out, not deliberately but because they were not seen as important at the time. He argues (1995, 26) that silences are created at four central moments: the moment of fact creation (the making of sources), the moment of fact assembly (the making of archives), the moment of fact retrieval (the making of narratives) and the moment of retrospective significance (the making of history in the final instance). To understand the Emergency, one must, then, examine this troubled period of Indian history in the context of these four stages of silence creation. A second, fascinating approach, as suggested by Anne Gilliland and Michelle Caswell, is the use of imagination to fill in the gaps in the archive (2016). Drawing upon Arjun Appadurai's work on the social imaginary and Claudia Strauss's work on the imaginary in cultural studies, they suggest that archival imaginaries may work in 'situations where the archive and its hoped-for contents are absent or forever unattainable'. They write:

> These imaginings may be generated not only individually by scholars, filmmakers, novelists and artists, and grieving mothers of stillborn children (Douglas 2015), but also, more collectively by nationalists, fervent believers, Indigenous peoples whose history and memory has been obliterated through colonialism and Western information practices (Duarte and Belarde-Lewis 2015), and victims of state-sponsored crimes or bureaucratic violence among others. If instantiated, they may take various media forms, including fiction, film and performance. They can provide a trajectory to the future

out of a particular perspective on the past and may build upon either actual or imagined documentation and narratives. (2016)

Imposed in 1975 by President Fakhruddin Ali Ahmed on the advice of Prime Minister Indira Gandhi, the Emergency was a twenty-one-month period that bestowed upon the Prime Minister the power to rule by decree. Elections were cancelled, constitutional rights suspended, and the press censored. Citing internal and external threats to the country, the Emergency took away fundamental civil liberties, imprisoned Gandhi's opponents, and led to several human rights violations. If one were to view this as 'state-sponsored crimes or bureaucratic violations', one can see a path forward in terms of thinking of a new form of an archive where the records are in conversation with other forms of memory production 'including fiction, film and performance'.

Jaffrelot and Anil's recent, comprehensive work on the Emergency (2020) sheds light on the available sources for reconstruction. The authors reveal that the project remained unfeasible for a long period of time; between unreliable testimonies,[3] and sparse material evidence, the project had several false starts. It is only after the availability of the Shah Commission papers that the project could find solid ground. Of the official sources, the National Archives of India, New Delhi provide the majority of information pertaining to this period; the Ministry of Home Affairs Papers, the Prime Minister's Secretariat Papers, the Shah Commission of Inquiry Files and the All India Radio Files, housed within the National Archives, present an image of the Emergency.[4] Other records may include private papers, newspapers and journals. However, these records are neither exhaustive nor do they provide a clear picture.[5] The renewed interest in the Emergency in the past two decades has produced other substantive and significant works including P. N. Dhar's *Indira Gandhi, the 'Emergency', and Indian Democracy* (2000), Coomi Kapoor's *The Emergency: A Personal History* (2016) and Srirupa Roy's *The Long Emergency: Media and Democracy in India* (a web archive of oral history interviews documenting journalistic practices around the time of the Indian Emergency). These works, as Jaffrelot and Anil suggest, remain journalistic or autobiographical and not comparative or theoretical (2020, xxii). The need for a comprehensive picture of the Emergency must then incorporate various sources as evidence: from documentary evidence to exceptional, disparate records.

In May 1977, a committee was formed under Shri K. K. Dass to 'enquire and collect facts . . . regarding misuse of mass media during the Emergency'. In August 1977, the findings were published under the title, 'White Paper on the Misuse of Mass Media' and were to be presented to the Parliament. This document outlines the various allegations regarding the state's (mis)use of censorship provisions, harassment of journalists, manipulations regarding the certifications of films, manipulations of news agencies and other mass media outlets and other incidental matters. While this document outlines violations of law and policy, it also demonstrates the state's recognition of the power of mass media and its discomfort with it. The allegations in this document border on the bizarre; for instance, the 'White Paper' suggests that '[t]he film *Bobby* was telecast from the Delhi TV Centre on February 6, 1977 at 5.00 P.M. instead of the scheduled film *Waqt* at 6.00 P.M' (1977, 75). It is suspected that the change in schedule, replacing the film *Waqt* with *Bobby* – a very popular film at the time – was to entice people to stay at home instead of going to Jayaprakash Narayan's meeting at the Ramlila Grounds. The document goes on to describe the circumstances – a series of frantic phone calls from the Doordarshan management to the producers and distributors of the film – under which this change in scheduling took place:

> The private distributor who had the custody of the print was found reluctant to supply the same. However, during the course of the afternoon he was somehow persuaded to supply the same although it was in a bad shape and torn at many places. The technical staff of Doordarshan managed with great difficulty in splicing up the film and made it possible for telecasting just before the telecasting hour. In this process the print was not fully checked and it did not go through the Screening Committee as per rules. (1977, 75)

This curious case reveals the unsystematic and haphazard expression of political will through the cumbersome bureaucracy of Indian governance systems. Other allegations of coercion of film-industry personalities are common from this period. The well-known story of Kishore Kumar's refusal to cooperate with the state's agenda and the punitive measures taken against him are broadly within the anecdotal realm. The report describes the incident:

> [A] decision was taken that, with immediate effect, all songs of Shri Kishore Kumar on Radio and TV should be banned for three months. It was also decided that gramophone companies such as Columbia and HMV should

be asked to freeze all records of Shri Kishore Kumar, and no record of his songs should be sold . . . [t]his order was issued on 4th of May and withdrawn on June 18, 1976, when Shri Kishore Kumar decided to extend his full cooperation. (1977, 88)

The 'White Paper' also provides an insight into the manner in which censorship was used at this time. It points to allegations of corruption, unclear content guidelines, issues with the certification of films, and the lack of judicial recourse (87). The impact of the Emergency cannot be fully understood only through the state's interactions with the film industry. Rather, through what Michael Moss and David Thomas term 'critical reading' (2017b, 229) of a limited dataset[6] (in this case, the body of films produced by the Hindi film industry), we are able to produce a clearer image of this time. The examination of films produced at this time gives an overview of the prevailing sentiments of the public. If we were to follow Gilliland and Caswell's recommendations about the production of the imaginary within the archive (2016), the examination of cinema and their conditions of production would be critical to this project.

In *Bollywood's India*, Priya Joshi writes how while the issue of Emergency dominated the Indian mind during the decade of the 1970s, the silence about it has 'produced an elaborate mythology of the period but not much scholarly analysis' (2015, 30). Her examination of Indian cinema in the context of the Emergency situates the 'public fantasy' against the political and social upheaval of the period. She writes:

[N]ation and state embarked on very different destinies, at times inimical to each other despite their shared investment in the 'dreams' that Nehru invoked. It could be argued that the nation prospered exactly when – and perhaps because – the state descended into crisis, as it did before and during the 1975–1977 Emergency. During this period, popular cinema persistently pursued the cultural work of recalling the nation and retrieving its ideals. In retrospect, through the many crises confronting India, the blockbusters of Hindi cinema have remained one of the key places where the dueling desires fueling the nation's collective fantasies are indexed, shaped, and challenged. (2015, 4)

Amit Khanna, in *Words, Sounds, Images-The Emergency and Its Aftermath* (2019), talks about Indian cinema and its state during the decade of the Emergency. This period saw a surge in the refurbishment of old cinemas, while hundreds of new screens were also added. Almost 13,000 theatres were operating in the country, and box-office collections crossed a billion rupees annually for the first time (527). New directors like Ramesh Sippy, Manmohan Desai and Prakash Mehra in Bollywood, and Dasari Narayana Rao, K. Balachander and Bapu in the South came up with fresh ideas and themes. The 1970s were, Khanna writes, the 'decade of Rajesh Khanna, the phenomenon, and his eclipse but the angry young man, Amitabh Bachchan, as the king of Bollywood' (527). This was also the age of the collaboration between Salim Khan and Javed Akhtar, as they became Bollywood's most famous screenwriters. During the same time, the Government of India collaborated with the Motion Picture Export Association of America, allowing the import of Hollywood films into the country (528). This big boom in cinema in the country was, nevertheless, badly impacted by the Emergency. Khanna writes how 'absurd censorship rules', which edited out even images of liquor bottles and spots of blood, were implemented (529). The Central Board of Film Certification (CBFC), headed by 'government lackeys' like documentary filmmakers K. L. Khandpur and N. S. Thapa, rationed film negatives and told veteran directors how to re-edit their films. Films like *Aandhi* (*1975*), *Kissa Kursi Ka* and *Nasbandi* (*1978*) were banned as they directly critiqued the laws imposed by the ruling party during the Emergency. Other movies faced strict censorship. Satish Poduval, in his essay, 'The Affable Young Man', states that many serials that had initially been commissioned for delivering 'developmental messages', were 'forcefully driven by commercial sponsorships . . . creating a consumerist ethos that expanded the Indian market beyond recognition' (2014, 81). Nikita Doval, in 'Narrating Emergency: Bollywood's Silence', writes how, while filmmakers and writers have been known to use contemporary issues and events in their filmography, the 1970s observed a 'deafening silence on the Emergency, one of India's gravest constitutional crises' (2015). Even decades after the harrowing events that took place during this period, Bollywood deftly avoided this period. As print and films were censored, media scholarship observed the commercial shift in what was advocated in the country.

In 1971, Indira Gandhi's campaign slogan 'India is Indira, Indira is India' equated her with the motherland, making her both the mother and the nation. Joshi observes this comparison in a 1985 election poster that featured Indira Gandhi within the map of India (2015, 107). The decade of the 1970s saw a surge in films that dealt with themes of family, motherhood and a new kind of nationalism. Films like *Deewaar* and *Shakti* saw the role of the mother take on much more importance and depth, wherein she was equated with the nation. The mother was nation and nationality, and often the reason for the protagonist's downfall. While the mother represented the nation, it was also a direct allegory to Indira Gandhi, and the downfall of the protagonist represented the downfall of the nation and the common people. Ranjani Mazumdar (2007, 1) argues that '[a]nger, revenge, and urban subjectivity in popular Bombay cinema was perhaps most influential during the "angry man" phenomenon of the 1970s and 1980s'. Khanna describes this new persona as having the 'earthiness of the 1950s, mind of the 1970s, and a postmodern outlook' (2019). Instead of the social dramas, the focus shifted to the corrupt big city – especially the underbelly. The angst in the people's hearts was getting reflected on the screen more and more. Usually featuring a devoted son, brother or lover, this new archetype was different from the morally good protagonists seen before. Anjaria credits this inalterable change in Hindi cinema to the 'deep social angst of the time' (2014), a major shift from the soft romantic heroes of the 1960s. Joshi's examination of Amitabh Bachchan's character in *Deewaar* suggests that Bachchan becomes the embodiment of this prevailing sentiment (2015, 61). A society lacking faith gave birth to the gangster-like protagonist. The eradication of Nehruvian ideals during the 1970s and the rampant corruption and cynicism of the times led to the reformation of Indian cinema, which tried to question the Emergency while still ensuring to stay within the censorship reforms.

Sholay, the biggest film of the decade, was released two months after the Emergency was imposed. Ramesh Sippy's directorial debut was devoured by a starving audience, who enjoyed the film's gruesome depiction of violence set against the background of an unfair and corrupt social system. While the critics regarded it as a potboiler, filled with anger, nihilism and macabre devoid, perhaps, of any social significance, the audience accepted the morally dubious protagonists who used unfair means to win. Javed Akhtar credits the audience's liking to the current upheaval they were experiencing:

> If you considered the political mood of the country [in the 1970s], you'd find a lot of frustration. Social protest had begun. That was the time when Jayaprakash Narayan's socialist movement had begun. Hindi films are most widely seen in the Hindi belt and in that area, law and order was gradually breaking down. So the common man was experiencing upheaval. There was disillusionment with all the institutions, colleges, the police force. People

were disillusioned with the government. So it wasn't surprising that the morality of the day said that if you want justice, you have to fight for it yourself. No one will fight on your behalf. And if you didn't fight, you'll be crushed and finished off. [. . .] You can see that the hero who has developed between 1973–75 – the Emergency was declared in India in 1975 – reflected those times. (Kabir 1999, cited in Joshi 2015, 44)

The film was a direct attack on civic institutions and a critique of the government. However, Sippy was forced to change the climax as per the demands of the Censor Board. While he initially wanted Thakur to get his revenge by cutting off Gabbar's arms, the film ends as Gabbar is arrested by the police officials and taken away. The Censor Board felt that depicting an ex-police officer (Thakur) as a vigilante who took the law into his own hands would be a dangerous message for the audience. Joshi writes:

> What Sholay's public fantasy achieved is two things. In locating the nature of criminality beyond the individual and on social and political institutions, it helped articulate a growing public unease with a political and social system gone horribly wrong in the Emergency. (2015, 50)

Other films of the time, including *Deewaar* and *Roti Kapda Aur Makaan*, contained similar themes of injustice, broken political systems, and large-scale social unrest, leading to the creation of this persona of an angry protagonist who often uses illegal means to exact revenge.

While most of the changes to the production of films came through extreme censorship or banning, many film directors and actors were directly targeted by the government. Filmmakers and actors like Dev Anand, Feroz Khan, Amol Palekar and Atma Ram were, allegedly, harassed by officials and paraded around international delegates during International Film Festivals. Amidst all the turbulence, plagiarism became legitimate, and Hollywood movies were copied and mangled, remade into localized versions. New ideas and inventions were halted in fear of censorship, and potboilers became commonplace. Amit Khanna writes how the seventies normalized 'melodrama, hard-hitting dialogue, irrelevant comedy interludes, strange looking sets, funny costumes, gauche production designs, and elaborate dance numbers'.

What one might learn from the cinema of this period has implications for our understanding of the Emergency. However, to construe these as records would require a re-imagining of the archive and of archival purpose: from a site of power to a site of democratic knowledge.

Public memory and the Emergency

If material evidence can no longer bear witness to history, how are we to construct such a witness? Giorgio Agamben, in *Remnants of Auschwitz: The Witness and the Archive* (1999), reminds us of the two meanings of the word witness: the first is derived from *testis* (from which we get 'testimony') and etymologically signifies the person who, in a trial or lawsuit between two rival parties, is in the position of a third party. The second word, *superstes*, designates a person who has lived through something, who has experienced an event from beginning to end and can therefore bear witness to it. We are interested in the meaning attached to the second sense of the word: to the survivor and the witness whose account relates to us the full extent of the Emergency. Agamben writes, '[t]he witness usually testifies in the name of justice and truth and as such his or her speech draws consistency and fullness. Yet here the value of testimony lies precisely in what it lacks; at its centre it contains something that cannot be borne witness to and that discharges the survivors of authority'. True witnesses or complete witnesses are those who did not bear witness and could not bear witness. The survivors speak on their behalf, by proxy, as pseudo-witnesses; they bear witness to a missing testimony. Agamben argues that

> to speak here of a proxy makes no sense; the drowned have nothing to say, nor do they have instructions or memories to be transmitted . . . [w]hoever assumes the charge of bearing witness in their name knows that he or she must bear witness in the name of the impossibility of bearing witness. But this alters the value of testimony in a definitive way. (1999, 34)

This is the paradox of testimony. Agamben both argues against and builds on top of the Foucauldian construction of the archive and suggests that

> [i]n opposition to the archive, which designates the system of relations between the unsaid and the said, we give the name testimony to the system of relations between the inside and the outside of langue, between the sayable and the unsayable in every language – that is, between a potentiality

of speech and its existence, between a possibility and impossibility of speech. (145)

What he is drawing our attention to is the space between the potentiality and the impossibility of testimony and the subject's 'capacity to have or not to have language' (145–6). He attempts to place the subject at the heart of this new sense of the archive.

If even testimony, which bears the weight of evidence, appears sparse, this reconstruction might turn to the anecdote. Anecdotal accounts – different in spirit to the testimony – are the foundations of public memory. The archival record of the Emergency is a fragmentary remnant: recovered from the troubled time that saw its creation, materially unchanged, but inevitably repurposed and reimagined for a different kind of consumption. The anecdote, on the other hand, as Joel Fineman writes, is essentially disruptive. For him, the anecdote is the unique form that '*lets history happen* [italics in text] by virtue of the teleological, and therefore timeless, narration of beginning, middle and end. The anecdote produces the effect of the real, the occurrence of contingency, by establishing an event within and yet without the framing context of historical successivity' (1989, 61).[7] For Fineman the anecdote, in spite of its inherent literary character, is nevertheless 'directly pointed towards or rooted in the real', and it is this that 'allows us to think of the anecdote, given its formal if not its actual brevity, as a historeme, i.e. as the smallest minimal unit of the historiographic fact' (57). Both the anecdote and the testimony exist within the domain of orality; it is easy to mistake one for the other. The testimony might appear anecdotal, and the anecdote might pretend to bear witness to history; however, their functions in the reconstruction of the past are different. While testimony may be reliable or unreliable, the anecdote remains outside the realm of verification; in fact, the anecdote, if verified, becomes testimony, though it tries to evade this specificity. Much of what this article has explored has been gathered from anecdotal accounts. Should we ignore them if their veracity cannot be tested? Traditional scholarship would suggest that archives have no space for anecdotes while the inclusion of testimonies in archives is a contentious subject. There are some specific purpose-built archives and collections that record testimonies;[8] the traditional archive, however, is designed for the object – its materiality being that which is significant; content (on which testimony rests) is very often outside the purview of the physical archive. Here, we may see space (and a reason) for the growth of public history and public memory projects, and of digital collections. The popularity of digital projects on themes of public history and public memory might be seen in a twofold manner. In the first instance, the growth of these projects signals the limitations of traditional archives. These projects recognize the importance of the public in discourses surrounding an event that are often beyond the purview of the state's archival activities. These web-archives are able to collect documents that are often ignored by their traditional counterparts. Within the context of India, projects like *The 1947 Partition Archive*, the *Indian Memory Project* and – specific to this domain – *The Long Emergency* project are notable contributions. What brings each of these projects together is an evidential force produced through the recording of oral testimonies and anecdotes. In the second instance, these archives are manifestations of desire with the aid of technical systems. The World Wide Web has changed traditional models of publication and has created new avenues for self-publication and the creation of publicly accessible collections. It is accepted that these archives may be ephemeral and might not have the security and the stability of traditional archival models; however, these new archival efforts – to commit large resources to the World Wide Web – are negotiations between longevity and access. These projects provide access to material that wasn't available for inspection before. It is in this space that the explorations of the Emergency might bear fruit. With the paucity of material evidence, testimonies and anecdotes become central to the project of critical collecting and critical reading. With this, we may produce the best yet image of this troubled period.

'A unique Indian revolution'

S. Sukhdev, the Films Division and the Emergency

Vikrant Dadawala

This chapter reflects on the relationship between documentary cinema and the years of crisis that culminated in the Internal Emergency of 1975–7, focusing on the work of the acclaimed filmmaker S. Sukhdev (1933–1979). I analyze Sukhdev's short films from the 1960s to 1970s – especially *And Miles to Go* (1965), *Voice of the People* (1974), *Thunder of Freedom* (1976) and *After the Silence* (1977) – as a polyphonic visual archive of this period of rage, despair and complicity, placing documentary cinema in dialogue with economic policy, literature and popular cinema. What emerges from this exercise is an ambivalent montage of the Emergency as the final scene, the denouement, of the tragedy of Nehruvian socialism.

Born Sukhdev Singh Sandhu, the son of a farmer from Sahnewal (near Ludhiana), Sukhdev was not formally trained as a filmmaker, and learnt filmmaking via a lengthy apprenticeship with the German director Paul Zils. Sukhdev rose to prominence as an independent director with the award-winning *And Miles to Go* (1965), whose acquisition by the FD marked the beginning of a new era of boldness and experimentation within the otherwise bureaucratic institution.[1] An hour-long experimental feature in Eastmancolor, *India '67* (1967, later retitled *An Indian Day*) would bring Sukhdev even more fame, as well as the prestigious Padma Shri award. Once seen as a rebel, Sukhdev (or 'Sukh', as his friends knew him) became increasingly associated with Prime Minister Indira Gandhi's regime in the early 1970s. In the period of political turmoil that preceded the Emergency, Sukhdev's films for the FD included documentaries that celebrated the government's infrastructural plans (*A Village Smiles*, 1971), championed the Public Distribution System (*Behind the Breadline*, 1975), criticized anti-government violence (*Violence: What Price? Who Pays?* 1974; *Ma Ki Pukar*, 1975), and opposed the proposed railway strike of 1974 (*Voice of the People*, 1974); with Sukhdev often appearing in front of the camera himself, as the voice and face of the 'committed' intelligentsia. Besides these FD films, which ranged in length from a couple of minutes to about thirty minutes, Sukhdev also filmed a documentary on the 1971 war, *Nine Months to Freedom*, which was sponsored by the Indian Ministry of External Affairs and included images shot by Sukhdev and footage provided to him by Bengali guerrilla fighters. During the Emergency, Sukhdev became the most prominent face of a new 'Film-20' group which produced propaganda highlighting the revolutionary potential of Prime Minister Gandhi's 20-Point Programme (*Thunder of Freedom*, 1976; *After the Silence*, 1977). When the Emergency was lifted, Sukhdev's prominent support for the Emergency was criticized in unusually direct terms by the new government's *White Paper on the Misuse of Mass Media* (1977, 89–100). The former favourite of the Films Division was now an outsider. Sukhdev died in 1979, relatively young, after suffering a heart attack while editing a friend's film (he had struggled with alcoholism for much of his life).

As Srirupa Roy has observed, 'India after 1950 was a nation that was defined through the big dreams of its state' (Roy 2007, 38). Rather than relitigating debates about the degree of Sukhdev's complicity in the Emergency, this chapter takes a more sympathetic look at Sukhdev's oeuvre as a profound and tragic expression of the dreamworld of Indian socialism during the era of Five-Year Plans and import-substitution policies. It was the newsreels and documentaries of the Films Division, distributed across the nation under the terms of a compulsory exhibition policy, that interpolated spectators across the country into this dreamworld (Mohan 1990, 25; Roy 2007, 38).[2] Within the archives of the FD, the move towards a new 'Emergency' aesthetic of crisis and urgency did not begin in 1975, but as early as the mid-1960s, as filmmakers began responding to a debilitating sense of crisis that haunted Indian policymakers and intellectuals. Sukhdev's cinema of commitment thus challenges more recent accounts of the Emergency that see this period as a purely opportunist or 'Sultanist' moment in which the Indian government 'exchanged ideology for fear and nationalism'.[3] More broadly, I argue that the visual archives of the Emergency housed by the Films Division of India pull us towards a different set of questions than the policy documents, memoirs and print ephemera that have usually served as the basis of our histories of this period.

Consider, for instance, the following two sequences from *After the Silence* (1977), Sukhdev's celebration of the achievements of two years of the Emergency regime:

The first sequence: set in Delhi's G. B. Road, a notorious 'red-light district'. The soundtrack rattles off sociological observations about the exploitation that undergirds sex work in the national capital, in a dispassionate register: 'forced to submit to sexual intercourse as many as twenty to thirty times a day'; 'ten rupees for the use of a fan'. It is all quite sad and predictable, in the way life can be sad and predictable. A group of women sleep on the terrace of a house, in their blouses. (I say women, but they look like girls.) The camera zooms into the face of an unnamed sex worker. It is an invasive, melodramatic

Figure 7.1 The Emergency as an agrarian revolution? Stills from S. Sukhdev's *After the Silence* (1977), a remarkable contribution to the 'Film-20' series supporting Indira Gandhi's 20-Point Programme. *After the Silence*, directed by S. Sukhdev. Copyright: Films Division, Ministry of Information and Broadcasting, Government of India, 1977.

shot – the kind of aggressive zoom Sukhdev was famous for. The woman looks straight at the camera. She has scars or tattoos on her face; as we zoom into an unnatural close-up, her eyes look oddly bestial. From this close, it is the power of celluloid to carry an existential or indexical trace of reality that captivates us; we are face to face with an irreducibly real person, and not with a cliché or a symbol.

The second sequence: set in Bihar's Palamau district and celebrates the results of Emergency-era campaigns against debt bondage (Figure 7.1). During the 1970s and 1980s, undivided Palamau district, now in Jharkhand, had become a symbol of everything that had gone wrong in rural India since independence: Palamau was notorious for starvation deaths, for systems of bondage, and for the dispossession of tribal communities and the slow ecological degradation of forests. ('My Palamau', Mahasweta Devi would write, 'is a mirror of [tribal] India') (Devi 1998, vi).[4] 'It was only after the declaration of the Emergency that the abolition of bonded labour really became meaningful', says Sukhdev in the commentary track. 'Earlier, the states had denied the very existence of bonded labour but now they are vying with each other to free the largest number of people in bondage.' But the optimism expressed by the narration is undercut by the montage that accompanies it, depicting a group of former bonded labourers who represent, as Sukhdev puts it, in his warm Indian accent, the 'animal poverty of the rural poor'. A man and a woman stand by a river, their heads bowed as if they have committed a crime. Cut to a close-up of a middle-aged woman's brown hands, a ring gleaming on her finger. Cut to a close-up of a younger woman's face, looking straight at the camera. Cut to a young boy with wet hair, eyes fixed on something we cannot see. A middle-aged man, a *gamcha* on his head, looking to the bottom-left of the frame. An elderly man with thinning white hair who looks away from us, averting his gaze from the camera. The drums in the soundtrack are tense but restrained, we do not build towards a crescendo.

For a work of propaganda, all of this is remarkably sombre. An enthusiastic review of *After the Silence* in *Socialist India* (a Congress-I weekly) declared, hyperbolically, that a 'coating of nitro-glycerin' had been added to celluloid to produce this explosive film. 'This film', the review suggested, 'when released by the Films Division and when shown by the Field Publicity Directorate all over the country will stir the conscience of the nation' and 'put fright in the hearts of money-lenders and sahukars' (Mohan 1984, 83–4).[5] Perhaps. The available evidence on the impact of Emergency era attempts to abolish debt bondage is more mixed. While official sources claimed that more than 50,000 Indians had been liberated from conditions of bondage during the Emergency, the same sources estimated that as many as 600,000 to 700,000 others remained trapped in the condition despite the elevation of the issue to a policy priority through the 20-Point Programme (unofficial sources suggested an even higher figure, close to six million) (Jaffrelot and Anil 2020, 76).[6] In retrospect, it is easier to see *After the Silence* as a troubling record of the limitations and failures of the developmental state than as an explosive work of agitprop cinema that stirred the conscience of the nation.

But, as the briefest analysis of key sequences from the film suggests, these are questions that the film also asks of itself. Sukhdev's commentary track may echo the 20-Point Programme's rhetoric of urgency, discipline and development but his own montages undercut any sense of confidence the film may give us about the Emergency as a new era, a new beginning, or a new moment of commitment. The very title of Sukhdev's film (*After the Silence* in English and 'Khamoshi Ke Baad' in Hindi) underscores the enormity of the challenge; the 'silence' that haunts his film is the silence of a refractory land problem built on drudgery and desperation that had proved remarkably impervious to post-independence legislation. What we are left with is a profound suspicion of words and slogans.[7] The silent figures in Sukhdev's montages seem to suggest that we need to rethink the Emergency through images rather than words.

-1-

I have argued elsewhere that the newsreels and documentaries of the Films Division indelibly shaped the Indian public's encounter with the Five-Year Plans, as a romance that slowly curdled into indifference and disillusionment (Dadawala 2022, 220–35). From this broader, historical perspective, it would be impossible to overstate the significance of the mid-1960s as the start of an extended period of crisis for the developmental state in India. The years that followed Prime Minister Nehru's death in 1964 were marked by war, famine scares and political turmoil. The rupee was sharply devalued in 1966, partly in response to American pressure, shaking national self-confidence. Two successive conflicts with Pakistan (in 1965 and 1971) doomed any attempts to reduce military spending back to the relatively low levels of the 1950s. Persistent projections of food grain shortages lent a touch of hysteria to political debates in this period, particularly in the mid-1960s, after the monsoons failed for two years. As the *New York Times* put it: 'Indians will remember 1964 as the year Nehru died and the food shortage began.' (Brady 1965; Dadawala 2022) Even as fears about famine began to recede after the green revolution, they were replaced by a new concern about increasing inequality and waves of agrarian violence (Ministry of Home Affairs 1969; Frankel 1971; Desai 1986; Brady 1965). Successive reports commissioned by the Indian government suggested that two decades of economic planning had done little to improve the living conditions of those at the bottom of the pyramid, even as India's population continued to grow, prompting a Neo-Malthusian panic (Narayan 1961; Mahalanobis 1969; Eleyaperumal 1969; *The Causes and Nature of Current Agrarian Tensions* 1969; Frankel 1971; Desai 1986).[8] The Second and Third Five-Year Plans had failed to meet their most ambitious targets – and the mood within the Planning Commission was often as grim as the mood outside (Kudaisya 2015, 711–52). Public opinion surveys from the time also reveal a widespread loss of confidence about the future. For instance, a survey conducted in the latter months of 1966 in the four major metropolitan cities – Calcutta, Delhi, Madras and Bombay – revealed that six out of every ten persons interviewed, across income groups, anticipated that things would change for the worse in 1967 rather than for the better. Eight of ten expected prices to rise continuously, and more than two-thirds anticipated an increase in unemployment figures (IIPO 1966, 29–34).

This widespread and debilitating sense of post-Nehruvian disillusionment – often expressed in a populist register that could verge on the authoritarian – shaped Indian documentaries and popular Hindi cinema just as decisively as it shaped the vocabulary of political life.[9] I think it is instructive to think of this *mohabhang* (Hindi for 'disenchantment' or 'disillusionment', with connotations of a broken love) as a compelling example of what Raymond Williams calls a 'structure of feeling' – not an explicit genre or formal worldview but an inchoate and messy response to changing circumstances, whose patterns (residual, dominant and emergent) can only be understood retroactively (Williams 1977, 128–35). Thinking in terms of a dynamic 'structure of feeling' allows us to see distorted echoes of the same dilemma across texts that belong to entirely different genres and assume opposing political stances.

Consider, for instance, Manoj Kumar's *Roti Kapda Aur Makaan* ('Bread, Clothes, and a Home', 1974), one of the highest-grossing films in a year of unprecedented strikes and political turmoil. Kumar's film tracks the travails of 'Bharat', Kumar's patriotic everyman persona, first introduced to audiences in *Upkaar* ('Charity', 1967). The 'Bharat' of *Roti Kapda Aur Makaan* is a jaded and defeated character, framed in odd Dutch angles as he wanders about helplessly in search of a job, looking to support his large family consisting of a retired father, mother, two college-going brothers and a sister whose fiancé demands an extensive dowry. The opening sequences of the film establish its urgency through melodramatic vignettes that dissolve into a hypnotic, almost avant-garde montage representing the three basic human needs referenced in the film's title: *Roti* (bread), *Kapda* (clothes), *Makaan* (a home). All the elements of the political crisis of the time are baked into the film's plot: a mysterious man in a suit working on behalf of a foreign agency who offers Bharat's brother, Vijay (Amitabh Bachchan), a bribe to burn the university down; a war that leaves Vijay partly disabled; a ballad about *mehangai* (inflation) and its poisonous impact on working-class lives; and a secret plot to destroy India by crippling its railway infrastructure. *Roti Kapda Aur Makaan* concludes with a rousing, action-filled climax that eerily anticipates Emergency rhetoric. A coalition of patriots – characters representing the honest businessman, soldier, policeman and worker – come together to rescue the country from a corrupt businessman (played with great panache by Madan Puri). Stagnation, paralysis and *mohabhang* are replaced by ethical commitment and swift action. The future is saved.

In early foundational work on the entanglement of form and ideology in Indian cinema, M. Madhava Prasad has traced the origins of the new forms that emerged in the late 1960s – a popular cinema of mobilization, embodied in the new angry young man persona of Amitabh Bachchan; a developmentalist cinema, often funded by the Film Finance Corporation (later, the National Film Development Corporation); and a new middle cinema – to the political crises of the time.[10] An analogous argument can be made about the emergence of the cinema of *mohabhang* within the confines of the Films Division, through the work of pioneers like K. S. Chari, S. N. S. Sastry and S. Sukhdev. As the public face of the developmental state, closely associated with the mystique of Prime Minister Nehru, the Films Division was hardly immune to the growing crisis of legitimacy afflicting Indian planning, which had crystallized into three mutually reinforcing critiques: (1), a pessimism about the inevitability of state capture and corruption; (2), a demographic panic that anticipated a rate of population growth that would lead to worsening per capita food availability and possible conditions of famine in the near future; and, (3), a sense of radical scepticism about the ability of elites to implement the kind of land reforms that would substantially benefit the landless. In the words of Asok Mitra, then a key bureaucrat in the Ministry of Information and Broadcasting, 'the only plausible course for the official mass media in 1967 was to establish credibility with the citizen by first acknowledging that the worst that could have happened since Nehru's death had in fact happened, but all was not lost and "we shall overcome"' (Mohan 1984: 49). Indeed, as Rithika Kaushik, among others, has argued, Jean Bhownagary's appointment to the Films Division between 1965 and 1967 (during Indira Gandhi's tenure as Minister of Information and Broadcasting) can be seen as an early expression of Gandhi's proclivity towards working with a 'committed bureaucracy'.[11] Following Bhownagary's 'discovery' of *And Miles to Go* at the Third International Film Festival in Delhi in 1965, it was Sukhdev who increasingly became the face of a new kind of FD film, deeply touched by disenchantment (even as Sukhdev remained an outside producer and not an employee). The new FD documentary thus anticipated the growing closeness between India's Gandhi's Congress and sections of the Indian Left, even before the Congress entered into a formal alliance with the S. A. Dange-led Communist Party of India (CPI). Seen from this perspective, there is no real contradiction between the radical freshness we associate with S. Sukhdev's early work (*And Miles to Go; India '67; Thoughts in a Museum*, 1968) and the strident, even sycophantic, defence of Indira Gandhi's regime in later films (*Behind the Breadline, Thunder of Freedom, Voice of the People, After the Silence*), or between his delightful parody of the FD bureaucracy published in 1967 ('Mass Message Medium') and his rather formulaic (and vaguely Marxist) defence of 'social relevance' in a speech delivered at the height of the Emergency ('Film-maker's Purpose: "Personal Cinema" or "Social Relevance"') (Mohan 1984, 53–5 and 96–103).[12] Nor is there any real contradiction between the role of the FD as an institution that enabled critiques of the developmental state to reach an impossibly wide audience, even as it remained an institution committed to censorship – most notably, during the Emergency, when FD bureaucrats served as top officials of the Censor Board (Dadawala 2022, 224–9).

A struggle against the paralysis of *mohabhang* defines S. Sukhdev's award-winning breakout film, *And Miles to Go* (1965), which begins with a striking image of the sun, slightly obscured by a row of factories. In the low-angle shots that follow, people speak, but their voices are drowned out by a hypnotic soundtrack (drums, cymbals and cellos?). It doesn't matter, we know what they would say, the genius of this sequence consists in the juxtaposition of this sordid drama with a pitiless sun. As the camera zooms out, we discover that we are looking out at Marine Drive from inside a posh apartment. This is our first taste of the classic Sukhdev contrast between high and low, one that would later become its own kind of cliché. But, seen in 1965, the 'contrapuntal' images that Sukhdev used to puncture the FD dreamworld would have appeared impossibly fresh: a capitalist smoking a pipe, looking like one of Eisenstein's villains; a dog, vulture and kite; a long line at a Fair Price Shop; a large group of policemen warily watching a Communist procession, armed with *lathis*. Though *And Miles to Go* does not depict Nehru's death directly, its title recalls one of Nehru's favourite poems: we cannot but help think of the unfulfilled 'promises' that precede the phrase 'and miles to go' in Robert Frost's 'Stopping by Woods on a Snowy Evening'.[13]

And Miles to Go concludes with a rather ponderous monologue voiced by Zul Vellani, who unconvincingly switches pronouns midway through his commentary (from 'they' to 'we') when speaking of the 'people'. The final montage consists of still images: a 'rural' woman in a state of despair (cut to a close-up of her face buried in her hands), an 'urban' woman by a dressing table (cut to a close-up of her applying perfume to her nape), a row of cots in a slum (cut to a man who appears to be flagellating himself, followed by a cut to a close-up of a shocked child). The lack of any resolution makes all the action in the film appear like an elaborate ritual performed to relieve our sense of acute helplessness in the face of a tragedy we cannot avert. Indeed, *And Miles to Go* is transparent about its own incoherence, announced in the form of a prefatory statement (that Sukhdev was almost certainly arm-twisted into including): 'This film is dedicated to all forces of rational thought that are opposed to the path of violence and seeks to strengthen the hands of our government in its stupendous task of tackling the pressing problems facing our country.'

This formulaic insertion is only the most obvious mark of the power of the Ministry of Information and Broadcasting. The entire second half of the film, Sukhdev would later claim, 'was made by the censors' who 'virtually rewrote the commentary', made 'a number of cuts', and 'changed the title of the film' (Mohan 1984, 43).[14] In the interviews and obituaries published after Sukhdev's death, apocryphal stories emerged of an earlier cut of the film, a shadow documentary, that would never see the light of the day. As Sukhdev's old friend Jag Mohan described it, *And Miles to Go* had originated as a newsreel commissioned by the CPI to document its presentation of a million-signature petition against high prices and corruption (who remembers this petition today?). Sukhdev had managed to shoot 'tremendous coverage' of this event 'with high-key photography, unusual camera angles and dramatic cuts' (1984, 172). It was this raw material that he re-edited into *And Miles to Go*. The original film was subsequently lost, though Sukhdev was known to speculate that a copy could still exist 'in some vault in Moscow' (1984, 172). But until the day the vaults of Moscow decide to surrender all the secrets they hold, the FD's version will remain all we have.

In their recent monograph on the Emergency, Christophe Jaffrelot and Pratinav Anil argue against an exceptionalist interpretation of the Emergency as a uniquely authoritarian episode in the history of postcolonial India. The period between June 1975 and January 1977 was neither a 'parenthesis' nor a 'turning point', Jaffrelot and Anil argue, but a 'concentrate of a style of rule' that had characterized Indian political life since independence (2020, 20). Some of the features of what they describe as an Indian style of authoritarianism, already incipient in the 1950s and still with us today, include: 'a preference for corporatist government and a lack of ideological coherence', 'the liberal recourse to emergency powers [. . .] pilfered from colonial statute books' and a 'simultaneous evocation of rule in the name of the masses and their denigration' (20). In retrospect, Jaffrelot and Anil suggest, the difference between 'Indian democracy' and 'Indian authoritarianism', at least in the experience of the poor, has only been a difference of degree (454). A similar argument can be made about representations of the Emergency in the newsreels and documentaries of the Films Division – which drew on tropes and techniques that the FD had long used to envision development, the state and the people. Between the films that preceded the Emergency and the 'Film 20' series produced during the Emergency, there was only a difference of degree.

-2-

Looking through an archive of print ephemera from the Emergency – such as the documents compiled by Arun Limaye and currently housed at the Center for Research Libraries, Chicago – can be an experience more sobering than exhilarating (Documentation of Emergency Period in India). While the regime in power speaks loud and clear through radio, celluloid and newsprint, dissent is forced into more subdued mediums: cyclostyled newspapers or bulletins, private letters, postcards from jail, and clandestine political cartoons or the occasional poster. An anonymous, handwritten, single-page pamphlet titled 'Jhoote Prachar Ki Asliyat', or 'The Reality Behind the Propaganda', is a typical example of how the underground literature from the period conceptualized its role within the larger media ecology of the time.[15] The bottom-left corner of the pamphlet contains a simple cartoon that depicts a yeti-like beast (labelled 'Sankatkaal', or 'Emergency') standing over a dismembered human body (labelled 'lokatantra', or 'democracy'); the beast is being cheered on by a tiny figure holding a CPI flag. The bottom-right corner is even more direct. It consists of a single populist slogan aimed at the media: 'Hume chahiye jantavani, nahi chahiye sattavani' (We Want the Voice of the People, and not the Voice of Power).

Jantavani versus *sattavani* – the voice of the people versus the voice of power. At first glance, this appears like a binary that can be easily transposed onto the Indian documentary tradition, pitting the *sattavani* of the Films Division against the *jantavani* of Anand Patwardhan's early films (*Waves of Revolution*, 1975; *Prisoners of Conscience*, 1978). As Patwardhan would later recall, the original impetus behind the shooting of *Waves of Revolution* was simply to collect footage (using borrowed Super 8 and regular 8 cameras) to serve as a 'record of police violence against non-violent demonstrators' (Patwardhan 1989, 68). Ten rolls of film for the Super 8 camera were purchased at exorbitant black-market prices, and a cassette player was used to record sound. The climactic moment of the film emerged organically, with Patwardhan finding a place in Jayaprakash Narayan's overcrowded jeep during the famous Patna rally of 4 November. Perched perilously on this jeep, Patwardhan managed to capture sublime images of the crowds gathered in support of the movement, as well as the brutal police action used to suppress it. Finding themselves face to face with history in the making, Patwardhan and his collaborators now decided to borrow a 16mm camera and return to Bihar to turn their scraps of footage into a serious film, about thirty minutes long. The distribution of the film was also as different from FD newsreels as could be. 'We knew that the film would never get a censor certificate so did not show it openly but held limited screenings in people's homes', Patwardhan recalled. After the Emergency was declared, screenings became 'even more clandestine' with 'each person attending [. . .] personally vouched for by reliable colleagues' (72). Eventually, a print of the film was smuggled into North America, where it was screened at universities and in meetings of diasporic groups. It was only after the end of the Emergency that the film obtained a censor certificate and was broadcast on a few local television channels. Patwardhan's other Emergency-era film, on Naxalite political prisoners, titled *Prisoners of Conscience*, was shot in more favourable conditions. But its distribution remained equally clandestine, with most screenings privately organized by groups like the People's Union for Civil Liberties and Democratic Rights.

S. Sukhdev's Emergency-era documentaries, on the other hand, were distributed by the FD to its vast network of cinema theatres and seen by an audience of millions (even if this was an audience that was often bored and restless). Yet, in purely formal terms, pro- and anti-establishment cinema converged into a similar style – defined by short shots, an aggressive use of Soviet-style montages, rapid camera movements, direct-to-camera address and the use of drums in the soundtrack to build towards a revolutionary crescendo. The effect is overwhelming: the spectator is not allowed the privilege of apathy; we build towards a moment of crisis that demands partisan moral clarity.

Focusing on formal convergences, rather than the partisan debates of the time (which often mapped onto the divisions between the three major factions of the Indian Left), allows us to analyze the documentary cinema of the 1970s as an alternative visual archive, distinct from the bureaucratic-speak of sources like the Shah Commission Report (1978). The people of Bihar burst onto the screen in Patwardhan's *Waves of Revolution*. A mob becomes a movement in grainy, flickering images – Super 8 footage projected onto a screen and then recaptured on 16mm. The camera is surprisingly agile, we see the promise of a new beginning from behind Jayaprakash Narayan's shoulder. All questions about the ideological coherence of the Bihar movement – that brought together Left and Right, socialists and Hindu nationalists – are deferred to the future.[16] 'We will take what we want from Gandhi, what we want from Marx, and what we want from Mao', says an earnest activist, convincing himself more easily than the spectator. The 'people' are also the ultimate source of legitimacy for Sukhdev's *Voice of the People* (1974), except here, they are disaggregated into individuals, the subjects of *vox populi* style interviews. Sukhdev holds the mic himself and feeds his subjects leading questions about the upcoming railway strike. The editing is fast-paced, the tempo is urgent, there is little time for reflection. But no clear mandate against the strike emerges from their responses, the people are quicker to express apathy than anger, the only political emotion they seem confident about is the despair produced by runaway inflation. Meanwhile, the state continues to address citizens with easy bureaucratic condescension (in Partap Sharma's distinctive Indo-British accent) in Sukhdev's *Behind the Breadline* (also from 1974): 'Behind the breadline, a never-ending battle to reach food grains from one part of the country to another. A struggle to fight the vested interests who want to paralyze the movement of food and create more scarcity. Can the government alone combat this situation? Who is responsible for this paradox? This is the question behind the breadline.' The usual Sukhdev touches in this film – the contrast between rich and poor, its dramatic zoom-ins and zoom-outs, its juxtaposition of people waiting in a motionless line outside a Fair Price Shop and activists marching in a rally – feels tired and cliched. But its mood of nervous dread is very real (Figure 7.2).

The grandiose title of Sukhdev's *Thunder of Freedom* (1976) presents the Emergency as the renewal of a broken social contract. New homes will be built, the old apathy will end, the children of the working class will no longer live in slums and grow up playing in the dirt by worksites. 'Some of these workers have never heard about the Emergency', the narrator concedes. 'But their lives, and the lives of their coming generations, have been changed forever. The unscrupulous contractors have been banished and the government has taken over the mining operations. Thousands of people now hope to get a fair deal within their lifetimes.' A truck is loaded. The sky looks dull and grey. A man on a *charpai* addresses the camera; behind him are three women and a couple of children, their clothes dusty-pink against the ochre of the landscape. Everything on the screen – every human, every piece of equipment, the bareness of cots set up in the middle of nothing – seems to resist the dynamic rhetoric of change in the commentary, leaving us with a stubborn and static pessimism. It was only after the Emergency ended that the reality of what happened inside

Figure 7.2 Establishing the moral authority of the state in a year of unprecedented political crisis. Stills from S. Sukhdev's *Behind the Breadline* (Long Version, 1974). *Behind the Breadline*, directed by S. Sukhdev. Copyright: Films Division, Ministry of Information and Broadcasting, Government of India, 1974.

the prison was transposed from pamphlets and fact-finding reports onto the screen. In the final images of Patwardhan's *Prisoners of Conscience*, a group of citizens rally for democratic rights and civil liberties, as a popular Naxalite song from Bengal plays in the soundtrack. It is an uplifting moment, the flames of the *mashaal* serving as a sublime symbol of an unbroken radical tradition. But the final image takes us back to the prison. Viewed together, pro- and anti- Emergency documentaries have more in common than we may initially suspect — the visual archive of the Emergency is deeply scarred by a sense of the tragic, of a struggle against unbeatable odds.

-3-

A debilitating sense of disillusionment colours the otherwise dry analysis in the three volumes of Gunnar Myrdal's *Asian Drama*, perhaps the most influential work on post-independence India in its time, whose fatalistic title was a reference to Greek tragedy (Myrdal 1968). To Myrdal, in 1968, the future of India looked bleak, defined by a widening gap between 'the lofty aspirations of the leading actors' and the 'abysmal reality' of the living conditions in which the vast majority of people still lived. The 'air of optimism and confidence' that the Swedish economist had encountered during his initial visits to the country appeared to have completely vanished (1968, 134). Myrdal's diagnosis pointed to a number of deep-seated sociological constraints that had made a mockery of the Indian elite's attempts to jumpstart development through public-sector investment in heavy industries or to legislate away deep-rooted problems like caste. For Myrdal, the postcolonial Indian state had remained a 'soft state' incapable of enforcing the necessary fundamental reforms, vulnerable to corruption and misdirection. The root of most of India's problems, Myrdal suggested, could be traced to the colonial nature of the contract between state and society in the region, whose most glaring symptom was the lack of a robust tradition of social discipline.

Faced with the disappointments of post-independence India, Myrdal turned towards one of the most resilient aesthetic genres in the Western tradition to make sense of what he observed: tragedy. From tragedy, *Asian Drama* borrowed a sense of the hubris, grandeur and waste associated with a futile struggle against destiny, as well as a diminished and chastened view of human agency. Given its fatalistic tone and ominous invocations of 'discipline' (a keyword that would become ubiquitous during the Emergency), *Asian Drama* is no longer a touchstone text for students of the Indian state. Indeed, Myrdal's nebulous terms – soft state and social discipline – arguably anticipate the arguments that would later be used to justify the state's recourse to heavy-handed coercion and violence in the slum-demolition and forced sterilization campaigns. But I am nonetheless drawn to Myrdal's use of tragedy as a genre through which we can think about the dilemmas and disappointments of the Indian developmental state, especially as experienced through Sukhdev's cinema.

In the best art that emerged from the Emergency, our sense of disillusionment is rarely contained within the realm of formal, electoral politics, but threatens to coalesce into a more damaging kind of *anagnorisis* (or 'recognition') about the nature of postcolonial Indian democracy. I'm thinking, for instance, of the metastatic terror and paranoia of Nirmal Verma's novel *Raat Ka Reporter* (The Nocturnal Reporter); the nested nightmares of a man returning to India after a fictional military coup in Vilas Sarang's 'Return', walking down a dull corridor, convinced that he is still asleep; the suddenness with which the windows of an ordinary home begin to resemble the bars of a prison in Sarveshwar Dayal Saxena's poem 'Lal Cycle' (The Red Cycle) (Verma 1989); Sarang 2006, 177–89; Saxena 1976, 49). A similar kind of sinking realization colours some of the most extraordinary prison memoirs of the time: Mary Tyler's 1976 memoir, in which the spectral and anonymous figures in the women's wards of the Hazaribagh and Jamshedpur jails become representative of the abjection of ordinary citizens in the face of state power; or Joya Mitra's equally troubling Bengali memoir, *Hanyaman*, which places female revolutionaries in uneasy proximity with the mentally ill, and views the declaration of the Emergency as a non-event inside the penal system: 'The air in here is stagnant [and] for the blind there is no night or day' (Tyler 1977; Mitra 2004, 117).

S. Sukhdev's work for Films Division, in its best moments, also reaches for the same kind of *anagnorisis*, recreating the drama of the developmental state coming face to face with its failures in full view of the public inside the cinema theatre. By way of contrast, consider the *hubris* of the prison memoirs by the most significant political prisoners who were arrested during the Emergency. In the prison scrapbook of future deputy prime minister L. K. Advani, for instance, the Gandhian ability to learn from the hardship and humiliation of jail seems to have hardened into something more harsh and unyielding – neither his (nor future prime minister Morarji Desai's) embrace of an austere prison routine seems to be matched by Gandhi's capacity for introspection or reinvention (Advani 2002; Desai 1979, 124–38). Similarly, Jayaprakash Narayan's short prison diary, written from a hospital ward serving as a temporary prison, inadvertently reminds us of his advanced age, even as it occasionally descends into unconvincing Cold War paranoia about the 'Communist stooges' in the Congress who were allegedly in charge of implementing a secret 'Soviet plan' to transform India into a 'naked Communist democracy' (Narayan 1977, 3–6, 72). JP's obvious physical frailty and vulnerability, recorded in his own words, seem to mock the ambition of his vague and amorphous vision of 'Total Revolution' (indeed, JP would die of complications from his heart ailments and diabetes before the end of the decade).[17]

In interviews given during the height of the Emergency, as the most active member of the Film-20 group, Sukhdev would defend his support for the Emergency using a radical idiom:

> I see the Emergency as a unique Indian revolution. We have a genius for missing revolutions but can't afford to miss this one. People have been saying that Mrs. Gandhi has declared the Emergency just to keep herself in power. That may be part of the truth. But I don't care who is in power as long as they do something for this country. Now I believe and I want to believe that Mrs. Gandhi intends to do something for the people. Her Twenty Point Programme is not new but it provides us with a vision of India's future. (Mohan 1984, 73)

As it turned out, there would be no revolution in India: neither bottom-up nor top-down. For better or for worse, the postcolonial Indian state turned out to be more resilient, tougher to decolonize – and more capable of cruelty – than any of the would-be revolutionaries of the 1970s seem to have anticipated.

India's National Emergency and its media afterlife

Ranjani Mazumdar

In 1975, the then prime minister of India, Indira Gandhi, declared a National Emergency, citing a threat to internal security, resulting in the suspension of civil rights and public dissent for a period of twenty-one months. Opposition leaders were arrested, all forms of public protests disallowed, and a regime of stringent press censorship was instituted. The declaration of Emergency was followed by social engineering campaigns such as the forced sterilization of young men in the name of family planning and the removal of inner-city slums to peripheral resettlement colonies. At the time of the declaration, no one knew how long this would last or whether India would return to democracy again (Prakash 2018). Despite being a period of recognizable authoritarian rule, enormous political effort went into erasing 'the Emergency as a living memory' (Nandy 1995). This is powerfully argued by Emma Tarlo in her groundbreaking book *Unsettling Memories* (2003), where she asserts that the history of independent India remains a story of remembering and forgetting, with only certain individuals, situations and events standing out. The nature of public memory usually depends on the narration of an 'iconic' past alongside a rapidly fading sense of events. The Emergency, says Tarlo, has this faded form with its own texture. While the twenty-one-month suspension of democratic structures had affected large numbers of people, the primary analysis in most writings that followed placed the Emergency as an aberration and a political conspiracy that involved people in high places at a particular juncture in India's postcolonial history. This form of political analysis reduced the period to one of curtailment of free speech and fundamental rights, leaving out the range of experiences that ordinary people had of the Emergency. This is something that Tarlo's book tackles through her detailed archival and ethnographic work in Delhi.

It was a chance visit to the municipal archives of a resettlement colony named Welcome that accidentally led Tarlo to a pile of dusty files, opening a window into the everyday life of the Emergency. Thus began a process of investigation, resulting in a vivid account where readers find themselves immersed in an archaeology of political memory, a complex constellation of conversations, policy documents, legal rulings, land allotments and sterilization certificates. Fragmentary traces, anecdotes, polemical comments, bureaucratic accounts and personal thoughts are intertwined in a delicate balance that requires the reader to attend to the numerous tales rather than sift out a single thread. For those who imposed the Emergency, it was an 'exceptional moment' viewed as necessary action for the survival and persistence of a stable and normal world – a narrative that is strangely reified even in many critical writings of the Emergency. Tarlo, however, moves away from established modes of historical investigation and desire for a singular narrative of the time to encounter 'memories' of the Emergency. Tracing the historical moment in this approach is to ensure that the Emergency is not seen as a 'rupture', which is typically associated with revolutions, wars, natural disasters and genocide. Rather, Tarlo depicts the Emergency as a form that drew on the technologies of modernization to painstakingly establish some chilling connections between sterilization and the allotment of land to the urban poor.

If we take Tarlo's gambit seriously, reflecting on the movement of these memories becomes significant, especially when an 'undeclared emergency' today derives its power from a highly performative portrayal of 'normalcy'. Since 2014, when the Bharatiya Janata Party (BJP) came to power, we have seen how all the institutions of democracy have been mobilized to suppress dissent, target minority populations and expand Hindu majoritarianism (Chatterjee, Hansen and Jaffrelot 2019). Simultaneously, the state's public discourse on development and the performance of an anticorruption zeal are played out as 'normal and routine' measures required for good governance. This current context is, therefore, crucial to the way we must assess the Emergency as an event with an expanded media afterlife.

When Tarlo wrote her book, online activity and social media had still not taken the shape they have today.[1] As a period of authoritarian rule, the

Emergency is now part of a memory industry – a ubiquitous and swarming electronic presence in a rapidly expanding online world where archival documents have evolved into new media, and digital performance makes it possible to invoke an active archival sense. In what follows, I explore two important threads. The first is an analysis of the explosion of television programmes and other short videos on YouTube, presenting the Emergency as a political aberration that belongs to the past. The second is an approach to the Emergency in an essay film by Pallavi Paul, where the past is connected to the present. Common to both audiovisual productions is a sense of an online universe of rapidly circulating images and information. Through my discussion, I hope to reflect on the fragility of the relationship between political memory, the archive and the media today.

The Emergency online

The fortieth anniversary of the Emergency in 2015 coincided with one year of the BJP in power. With this, the official silence about this period was reversed, and today YouTube holds a large cluster of programmes on the Emergency. As a new media infrastructure, YouTube is one of the most popular video platforms with a large global following, and India has the highest number of users. This success and expansion of YouTube can be attributed largely to its user-friendly interface, since accessing one video displays a sidebar of comparable videos of related interest, and the viewer can navigate through an entire collection of other videos by moving with a click from one to the next. As an interactive form, this type of navigation provides a sense of 'seriality to the viewing experience' (Hilderbrand 2007, 49). Internet searches for well known or contentious events yield a swarm of related video clips, and their popularity is evident from user ratings and an active and endlessly generated set of comments. YouTube's ability to bypass television's real-time viewing requirements has helped to foster a culture of the clip and a new temporality of immediate access (49).

Since 2015, the Emergency has acquired a huge presence on YouTube with videos of television programmes and an array of short videos of varying lengths, recalling the events of the past. Some of these videos are amateur, and some are produced by television channels like Aaj Tak, ABP, Doordarshan, India

Figure 8.1　Sanjay Gandhi with his mother Indira Gandhi. Source: https://swarajyamag.com/blogs/the-emergency-of-1975-why-history-never-forgets-and-forgives.

Figure 8.2 Collage of newspaper headlines as the backdrop to Indira Gandhi's face. Source: https://newsroompost.com/opinion/how-indira-gandhi-led-congress-government-muzzled-media-during-emergency/.

Today and Business Today. How do we respond to the presence of this political memory in this new context of digital abundance? YouTube videos of the Emergency produced by powerful television channels display a visual rhetoric: anchors address the audience with what appear to be photographic and video images of the Emergency woven into their narratives. These can include shots of the Allahabad High Court where the historic judgement was delivered on

12 June 1975; images of Indira Gandhi alongside photographs and video footage of her son, Sanjay Gandhi (Fig. 8.1); a collage of newspaper headlines about the Emergency as a backdrop for Indira Gandhi (Fig. 8.2); and various political leaders addressing public gatherings.[2] These internet image traces float freely, as do archival traces from multiple Emergency shows aired by various television networks, which are now available on YouTube. In several of these videos, we can see news tickers with Narendra Modi's quotes on the Emergency. The anchors are placed against a backdrop of newspaper headlines, or just overlaid with archival footage. The most obvious element is the way their voices draw spectators into tales that sound like the unfolding of a dark and dramatic conspiracy with dates, radio announcements, micro-events, photographs of political leaders and music. While the anchors retain a voice-over style that suggests an exposé is underway, the archival gestures on screen are rather limited. What makes the cluster of these television videos significant is the way privately financed powerful channels are openly allied with the vision of the government in power, pointing to a reconfigured relationship between the state and the media landscape. In using the Emergency to frame public discourse through the media, the BJP has positioned itself as the force 'destined to uphold' democratic values. There is a clever sort of intimidation at work here – not simply a warning to the public about the Emergency and its ties to the opposing political party, but also a demonstration of their own influence over numerous

Figure 8.3 Jab Desh Me Lagi Thi Emergency (When Emergency was declared in the country – programme for Aaj Tak). Source: https://www.youtube.com/watch?v=8GBi71ekTn0&t=7s.

media outlets. With the official silence on the Emergency now lifted, we have transitioned to a noisy and conspiratorial style in which the everyday narratives that Emma Tarlo so vividly brought to life continue to remain obscured by a form of political retelling, with those in power portrayed as survivors and heroes of an aberrant past.

In a video programme produced by Aaj Tak, we see a woman anchor citing Arun Jaitley, a BJP politician's social media post, where he compares Indira Gandhi to Hitler (Figure 8.3). Photographs play in the background as she poses some questions, taking us to the Allahabad High Court and the announcement of the judgement. The voice changes to a man's; we see the court and again footage of Indira Gandhi and Sanjay Gandhi, a picture of the judge at the court, and finally the judge himself speaking about his order. The sonic registers persist with an overblown style of analysis meant to introduce the BJP as the political force that supposedly played the biggest role in fighting the Emergency. The internet now abounds with such commemorations of the Emergency, and this consolidation of narratives about a period unknown to large sections of the Indian citizenry today has acquired the quality of an ongoing media event that begins to provide fodder for our contemporary political context. As Laurence Scott has argued, 'a history of our era may one day be told through the hungry, wide-angle lens of YouTube, where hundreds of hours of footage are added every minute. YouTube captures the delirium of our times and shapes our modernity' (Scott 2019: 1). For younger generations, YouTube is the site to visit to access both news and entertainment, now available in fragments at all times of the day. Scott goes so far as to say that YouTube is the closest we have to a time machine since its channels can open out new routes back to the past (1).

The YouTube videos on the Emergency have a repetitive style; a heavy voice-over organizes the narratives with some images of leaders addressing political rallies, Indira Gandhi seen with her ministers, still frames of crowds during mass protests, abstract images of faces behind bars and so on (Figures 8.4 and 8.5). Beyond these fragments, there is literally no concrete archival material. Instead, using a high-pitched narrative style and seemingly historical traces, the Emergency is presented to us as an "exceptional event" of the recent past. This creates a new kind of hyper-visibility about the past, enabled by the infrastructure of memory that new media technologies have made possible. The 'Emergency Archive' is transforming into something like a

Figure 8.4 A sample of images that are used in several programmes on the Emergency.

Figure 8.5 A sample of images that are used in several programmes on the Emergency.

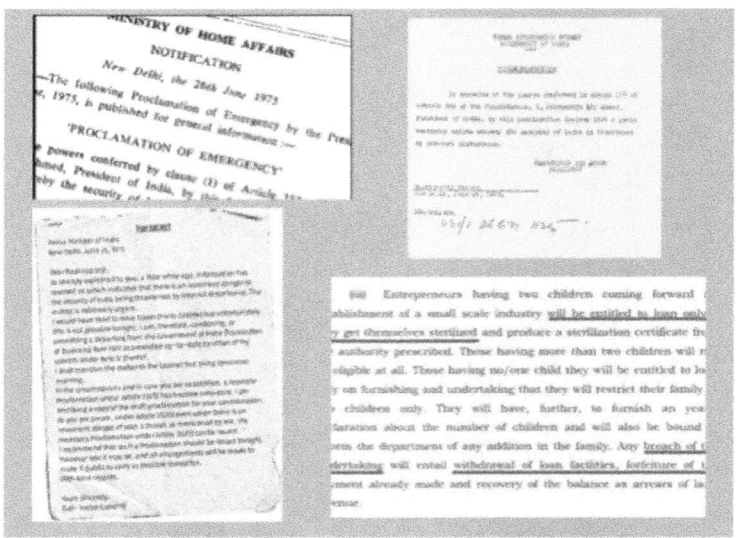

Figure 8.6 Emergency-related documents available online. Source: https://blog.ipleaders.in/impact-internal-emergency-india/; https://www.facebook.com/pibindia/photos/a.529751997164610/148063 3295409804/?type=3; https://www.business-standard.com/article/beyond-business/1975-shock-treatment-114121201235_1.html; https://homegrown.co.in/homegrown-explore/emergency-1975-chilling-documents-which-encapsulate-the-ind; https://www.reddit.com/r/india/comments/c572nt/declaration_of_emergency_june_26th_1975/; https://theleaflet.in/revisiting-the-emergency-a-primer/; https://thewire.in/history/emergency-free-press; https://odishabytes.com/indira-imposed-emergency-out-of-personal-political-vendetta-guv-ganeshi.

Figure 8.7 Emergency-related documents available online. Source: https://www.deccanherald.com/india/george-fernandes-rebel-715538.html.

scattered and forceful collection of scanned documents, photographs, and old videos. This kind of collection exudes a feeling that these items are sensitive but safe because digital paper does not disintegrate and the text will not fade. Therefore, we move from the notion of the archive as a storage depository of paper to that of an electronic signal.

Lisa Gitelman has drawn our attention to the performative power of paper documents as epistemic objects (2014). While Gitelman focuses on documents that have an all-pervasive presence in our daily interactions, such as identification, insurance, death certificates, licences, application forms and so on, I am interested in official documents that have never easily been available or accessible but now exist as a performative presence in digital territory (Figures 8.6 and 8.7). In the various programmes I came across on YouTube, this archive of paper documents is not only limited; it is highly generalized. We do not see any of the dusty files that Emma Tarlo encountered in the Municipal archive in Delhi (2003, 62–93).[3] The pattern we see here again is a structured collation of general images, with the voice-over providing an analytical frame. Old newspapers yellowed from time, some photographs with hazy resolution, typewritten orders, legal petitions and judgements, offer us a performance of the 'authentic'. The ban on a right-wing organization like the Rashtriya Swayam Sevak Sangh (RSS) is highlighted, black-and-white footage is constantly used as a loop, and the spectator is drawn into a movement between the past and present.

In one of these dramatic moments from the Aaj Tak programme referred to earlier, we see Indira Gandhi's face on one side and George Fernandes's shackled hands on the other (Figure 8.8). This photograph became one of the most iconic after the lifting of the Emergency, presenting Fernandes as a defiant figure even after his arrest. Fernandes was a trade unionist and socialist who took part in the 1974 railway strike, which disrupted train services throughout the country.[4] His role in the Baroda dynamite case, which sparked a series of explosions on government infrastructure, bolstered the underground movement during the Emergency (Reddy 2014). When Fernandes was eventually captured and imprisoned, he was chained, and photos of his arms raised with a slight smile on his face became iconic (Figure 8.9). In his later days as a politician, Fernandes, who was always a fierce critic of the RSS, ultimately allied with the same forces to form a government with the BJP against the Congress.

Figure 8.8 Jab Desh Me Lagi Thi Emergency (When Emergency was declared in the country – programme for Aaj Tak). Source: https://www.youtube.com/watch?v=8GBi71ekTn0&t=7s.

Figure 8.9 File photo of George Fernandes in *Deccan Herald*. Source: https://www.deccanherald.com/india/george-fernandes-rebel-715538.html.

The constant playing out of this iconic photograph in several television videos, as well as its circulation as an archival trace within a dense new media ecology, is significant for the way it becomes ensconced within a reconfigured visual culture of the Emergency. Catherine Russell (2018) describes archiveology as a practice in contemporary media culture where fragments of audiovisual material taken from an existing image bank are creatively remixed and recycled to generate alternative forms of historical memory. The productions she examines are primarily avant-garde and experimental videos where alternatives to hegemonic and official histories are invoked through personalized and subjective uses of archival traces. And yet, the most extensive appropriation of the online video archive can be seen in popular programmes for television and short videos created for random internet circulation. In the internet videos available on the Emergency, we do not see the creative 'counter history' that Russell talks about since her analysis is auteur-driven, reflecting on the work of artists. What we are seeing instead is a vast movement of these videos via platforms that not only allow for continual interactions but actively steer them.[5] With the increasing platformization of cultural production, the official projection of the Emergency has now expanded into an overwhelming assemblage of photographic and moving image 'indexical traces' in videos that are both televisual as well as user-generated digital objects. These highly verbose creations, providing details of time, announcements, events and a sense of liveness, are now part of the vast networking and sharing economy of internet users.

The archive effect and memory

Jaimie Baron suggests that the indexical is more prominent in the audiovisual form because there is noise, excess, ambiguity and disruptiveness—all of which make the form alluring (2014, 4). The power of the indexical sign is determined by the concrete ways in which the trace is deployed. The question, then, is to reflect on how the relationship between the archive and history has altered as audiovisual mediums have evolved and expanded. Baron contends that, while rare historical material can be seductive and enticing, the actual location of the repository is no longer permanent in the internet age. She says,

'The notion of an archive as a particular place and of archival documents as material objects stored at a particular location has ceased to reflect the complex apparatus that now constitutes our relation to the past through its photographic, filmic, audio, video, and digital traces' (7).

Baron recognizes a movement of archival sources away from storage to an experience of reception. This is the archive effect – a movement from the authority of place to the authority of experience. The internet is the site of several digital objects that float about and attach themselves to different narrative drives. How do we then look at these wildly circulating forms and their relationship to the archive? The audiovisual archive of photographs, films, videos and sound recordings is an unruly conglomeration that is constantly being moulded by filmmakers and internet users.

In a segment from another Aaj Tak documentary report on the Emergency, there is an attempt to depict power play and politics, pitting the political activist Jayprakash Narain addressing large crowds against Indira Gandhi and her coterie descending steps in slow motion (Figure 8.10).[6] The obvious staging of Indira Gandhi's hunger for power and desire to continue in office at all costs

Figure 8.10 1975 Emergency under Indira Gandhi: All you need to know. Source: Aaj Tak https://www.youtube.com/watch?v=dsdLJ0uEEMw&t=90s).

is presented through an extended loop containing two distinct sonic registers. The first is a fragment from Nehru's 'Tryst with Destiny' speech delivered on the eve of independence, and the second is Indira Gandhi's declaration of Emergency as a radio broadcast delivered on June 26 1975. In the first, Nehru's voice can be heard saying, 'At the stroke of the midnight hour, when the world sleeps, India will awake to life and freedom.' The second in Indira Gandhi's voice carries the words, 'The President has proclaimed Emergency. This is nothing to panic about.' Archival images of Nehru in Parliament and crowds in the streets play over his voice, while in the second, only the voice is played over a still image of Indira Gandhi. These two sonic traces play out historical memory as a fall from the dawn of independence, but within a melodramatic imagination, the daughter appears to lose her connection with what she had witnessed when her father took over as Prime Minister of India. This sound loop is also cleverly organized with the BJP leader, Lal Krishna Advani's interview placed in between Indira Gandhi's declaration – used twice to bookend the interview. Through this structure, the sonic trace of the authoritarian leader envelops the supposedly gentle musings of the BJP leader. The temporal sweep of this segment moves from 1947 to 1975, to the moment when the BJP is in power. This assemblage of audiovisual archival traces, using the original soundtrack belonging to the father and daughter, stages the Emergency as both a political and a familial crisis. Indeed, this kind of interpretation continues even in the way Sanjay Gandhi is presented in all the accounts of that period. There are several television programmes and short videos where we see a focus on the mother-son relationship, a strategy through which the fall from independence is amplified, since Sanjay Gandhi's role in the forced sterilization campaigns to control India's population and his personal involvement in several authoritarian actions are well known.[7] This familial discourse has a public presence that is potent and built through voice-over connections.

What we witness is the creation of a narrative that employs bits of photos and newsreel footage to simulate the archive effect. The photographic and filmic are braided together in this performative play using the structure of current televisual anchoring. Time, according to Mary Ann Doane, 'is television's basis, principle of structuration, and persistent reference' (269). If photography is about 'pastness', television is about 'presentness' (269). Doane classifies television's use of time into three basic categories: information, crisis and catastrophe. Information normally flows, but the catastrophic can abruptly consume time, spill over and persist. However, both tend to be subject-less. Crisis, on the other hand, condenses time by defining an event and then promising to resolve it within a specific time frame; it is dependent on human agency and hence tends to be political, such as hijackings, assassinations, political coups and so on. Crisis can also be traced back to a certain group, class, political party or individual (269–85). This temporal structuring proposed by Doane could never have worked for Indian television when it was entirely state-controlled. Television fare was usually educational, with some entertainment and news programming meant to support government propaganda. It was only in the 1990s that private networks started to broadcast for the first time. The BJP's triumph in 2014 prompted a review of what they perceived as the abuse of power in the past, as well as state television's silence on the subject. The result is the emergence of a mediatic political event at the intersection of newly acquired political power by a former opposition force and powerful television outlets.

Almost all broadcast programmes on the Emergency have a hyperbolic sense of urgency, overdramatic gestures and a conspiratorial presentation style, as if to instil a conviction that such a moment will not be tolerated again. This painstakingly crafted method is meant to distinguish the present from the past by splitting time between then and now using a presentist logic. When these television videos swarm the online world along with other fragmentary data on the Emergency, a new sense of the past and present is created. Wendy Chun has argued that new media works with a perpetual sense of crisis, focusing on the iconic and noteworthy and inviting people to engage in real time. This differs from photography, cinema and television's indexical promise since the online world requires quick responses, connections and feedback. This type of engagement exacerbates the feeling of crisis and gives us a perpetual impression of a never-ending present. Surfing, uploading, storing and repurposing information online is a response to the threat of disappearance, making us active players in new media's continual reliance on crisis (Chun 2011).

The use of crisis to reinvent the Emergency for a contemporary narrative is one of the ways in which media infrastructures have reshaped political memory. In the digital world, all these archival traces are now circulating as signals and codes and can be reused and reassembled for different kinds of objectives. Indeed, a quick look at all the programming shows how the same archival footage travels from one production to the next, though reassembled for different kinds of arguments. The digital archive available on the internet is now both a source and a venue for exhibition (Baron 2014). Search engines typically capture archival sources that circulate in digital form, offering an oblique connection to ideas about the past. The search engine is a pervasive presence in contemporary culture, making the user of history engage with material in complex ways. There is recognition that accessibility through interfaces leads us on a journey through documented texts and events we want to see and those we do not. Through this flood of electronic data and signals, new patterns and historical analyses emerge across digital territory. This context, according to Baron, transforms the reader of history into a user of historical documents, participating in a variety of narrative constructions.

It was during this kind of search from one link to the next that I stumbled upon a segment in part four of a Doordarshan series on the Emergency. In this segment, sterilization is introduced and discussed at length, but one of the locations where we spend considerable time accessing these stories is Muzaffarnagar. I want to suggest that the inclusion of Muzaffarnagar in a 2015 production as a location where the sterilization drive took a certain form in the

Figure 8.11 The Truth of Emergency Part IV DD News. Source: https://www.youtube.com/watch?v=kAYKRd1kGiw.

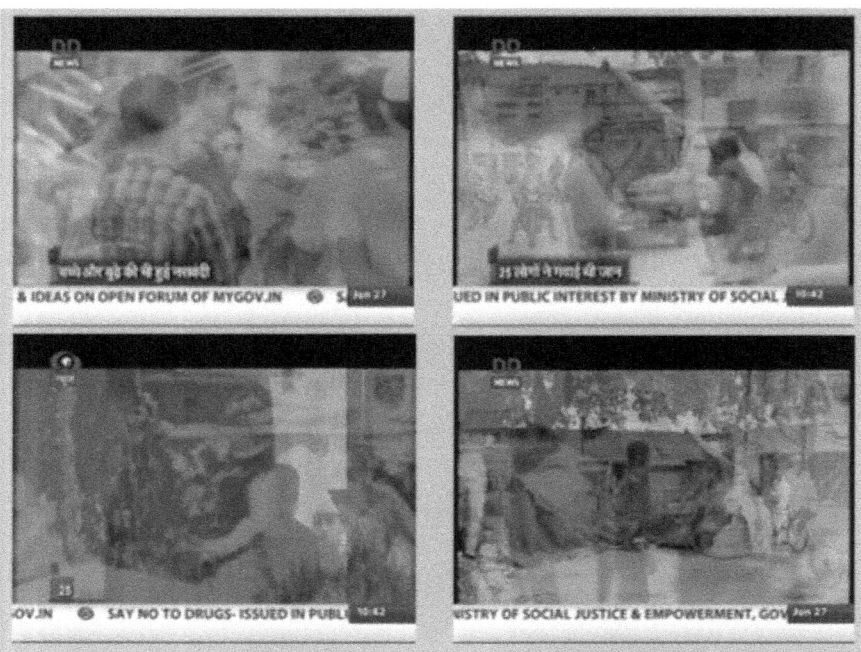

Figure 8.12 The Truth of Emergency Part IV DD News. Source: https://www.youtube.com/watch?v=kAYKRd1kGiw.

1970s was a technique deployed to erase the memory of the 2013 riots where many Muslims were killed.[8] The riots occurred before the 2014 elections, when the BJP came to power. In a sequence of the news report, we first see an Islamic world, introduced through the minarets and the clothing of the people (Fig. 8.11). We then see how the sound design, the narration and the visual layering invoke a violent imagination and memory that is very similar to the recall of a post-pogrom scene (Figure 8.12). The anchor connects sterilization to firing and violence. We hear of dates, time, bullets and the tragic deaths of innocents. The audiovisual layering introduces muffled screams as a sensation along with hyperbolic narration, making this moment appear both familiar and strange (Figure 8.12). In the aftermath of the 2013 riots, inquiries conducted by human rights groups and concerned citizens indicted the Samajwadi Party and the BJP for their role in polarizing the population.[9] The scale of the violence was reported by several journalists, along with a large production of video news and documentaries by television houses and independent filmmakers. On YouTube, we can see a full range of testimonies recounting the horror as well as precision-style clinical analyses of the reasons for the eruption of violence.

In layering what effectively appears to be a moment from 2013 in Muzaffarnagar with a narrative about forced sterilization during the Emergency period in the same location, we witness what Steve Goodman and Luciana Parisi refer to as the experience of déjà vu triggered by the immersive environments that digital networks have produced. This is a 'condition whereby images and sounds from the non-present can reappear in any place or time, producing a kind of technologically enhanced déjà vu' (2010, 352–3). Media technologies, according to Goodman and Parisi, are continuously reorganizing the gap between long-term and short-term memory. We incorrectly hear a familiar tone and believe we have uncovered previously unknown images. This machinic ecology of memory provides an experience in which the past persists as a potential of the present. We are confronted with an amplified form of memory – a sensation heightened by a sample-based new media culture (2010).

Political memory in *The Blind Rabbit*

It is as if, recognizing the fragility of the archival trace available online, filmmaker and artist Pallavi Paul's *The Blind Rabbit*, an essay film on violence past and present, problematizes both paper and visual documentation in an online world today. Paul's essay films are influenced by an immersive sense of our digital media environment and a belief that linear unfolding may not always capture the complex experiences of the world we live in. She responds to and draws on contemporary dimensions of media culture to frame her own essayistic interventions.[10] The essay film, as many have noted, has emerged as one form of non-fiction cinema that responds to the widespread changes introduced by digital technology since the 1990s.[11] Some have identified the form as a meeting ground between documentary as we know it and art videos. Nora Alter sees this as a distinctly contemporary and hybrid non-fiction practice that combines narrative, reportage, poetic visualization and other elements to have viewers contemplate the images (2019). The essay film is marked by a sense of indeterminacy, hybridity, openness and playfulness and is also a type of 'film philosophy', drawing inspiration from the cinematic experiments of the avant-garde (Alter 2019, 4–5). Timothy Corrigan views the essay film as a form that straddles fiction and non-fiction and poses an encounter between the self and the public domain, in the process exploring the 'limits and possibilities of each as a conceptual activity' (2011). Laura Rascaroli says this form has proliferated with digital technology and has combined the personal with the intellectual and the political. It is also a contrarian form of audiovisual expression moving against its own time with the camera as a new kind of pen (2017, 4–5). In a visually saturated contemporary context, the experimental work of the essay film is designed to make spectators think critically, merging the experience of distraction with that of contemplation. The form has seen its greatest expansion in the digital world with innovative uses of mobile cameras. Paul acquired her first digital camera in 2010. Her sense of joy with the camera was immense, and it was the internet that became a vast playground for her to glean, recycle and use images along with the camera's indexical promise.[12] Her shooting infrastructure became the camera in her backpack, along with a laptop. This artisanal mode has shaped all of Paul's video work until now.

The Blind Rabbit is an essay film in which the recall of the Emergency moves beyond the obvious and the known to engage with the inner workings of governance – details of the police's role that are now lost because the files have disappeared. The voice of a female member of the police force tells us how loitering children were picked up to meet a certain target of arrests (eighteen to twenty a day) from the streets every day. We only hear her voice and do not see her face as the screen is intercut between a fragmented and abstract collation of images and black frames. The children were taken away and marked as delinquents for their supposedly unruly behaviour. When the Emergency was lifted, the police were asked to return the children to their parents, but this was no easy task. Many of the children were now unable to recall where they lived; incarceration had affected their capacity to remember.

We also hear a policeman refer to the production of false documents to help them make the arrests. There was a standard format followed with minor variations, and when Paul asks if the police were indulging in 'creative writing', the policeman accepts with a laugh. The recounting of the procedures demonstrates the insidious ways in which power permeated the realm of everyday life and how policies were statistically performed through the daily ritual of work (the number of arrests). This is the interior life of governance: clinical, precise instructions that official functionaries needed to perform. Conjuring the voices without bodies becomes a very significant element here;

the persons providing the information are never identified; they must remain anonymous because the testimony is important, and keeping the identity hidden is a move that allows us to understand both the operations of power as well as the economy of evidence. In between the narratives provided by the female and male police is one child's story introduced as a lost file with text that goes as follows on black screen:

> File: 8 months have lapsed since his incarceration. He is now unable to recall his home address due to his young age. File: Delinquent only recalls a Peepal tree near his house. No break through so far. No breakthrough. Breakthrough.

> In the summer of 1977 political Emergency was winding down and democracy was set to return to India. Coinciding with this grand return were also a series of smaller returns. Hundreds of boys aged between 7-6 years, found 'loitering' in the streets were abducted by police patrols between 1975-77. They were labelled 'vagabond' and sent to prison as 'delinquents'. In the capital city of a newly re-democratized country these abducted children needed to be restored to their homes, there was just one problem – many kept in detention for about two years had forgotten their homes, they would supply only blurry details of what houses looked like in memory – a tree, a train, a drain. In one case there was even a blind rabbit. All documents related to this operation are now lost. We are here between memory and forgetting.

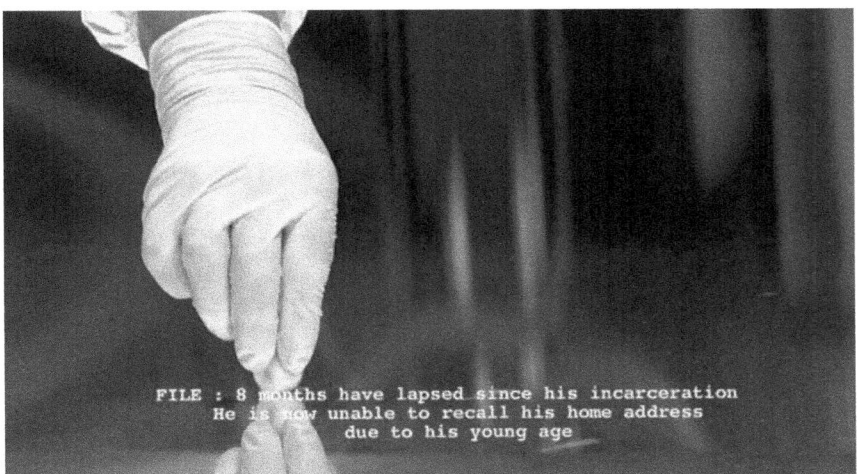

Figure 8.13 *The Blind Rabbit* (2021). Source: Courtesy Pallavi Paul.

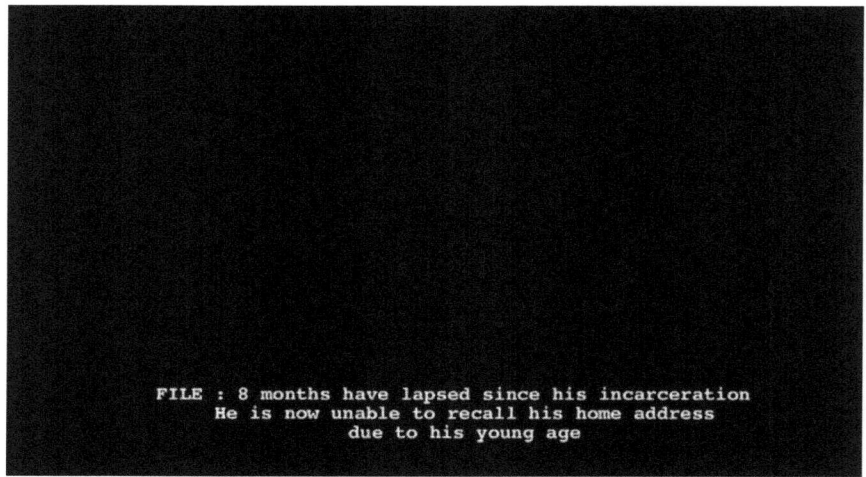

FILE : 8 months have lapsed since his incarceration
He is now unable to recall his home address
due to his young age

Figure 8.14 *The Blind Rabbit* (2021). Source: Courtesy Pallavi Paul.

Paul uses oral narratives gathered from the police to evoke what a lost file could have contained, interspersed with her own reflections. There is loss of memory as well as files that are now lost (Figures 8.13 and 8.14). There is forgetting, but there are traces and memories that can be brought together to situate the story of a boy's return, which depended so much on his ability to remember. The inclusion of this story here is presented as an audiovisual experimental trace where the audio track carries the sound of the republic (parade sound), while the delinquents story becomes an account of routine violence within the archaeology of the political event.

The Blind Rabbit, however, is also concerned with the explicit history of police violence such as the pogrom of Sikhs in 1984 after Indira Gandhi's assassination and police atrocities unleashed on protesters challenging the Citizenship Amendment Act (CAA) introduced by the Indian government to grant citizenship to persecuted minorities from neighbouring nations, except for Muslims. The deliberate convergence of different time zones of violence is part of Paul's approach. The violence against students opposing the Citizenship Amendment Act was overwhelmingly felt when some of the footage inside the Jamia University library in Delhi went viral. Paul combines recorded footage of the violence captured by a CCTV surveillance camera and the chaotic witnessing by other cell phones (Figure 8.15). We can see and hear the violence with a piercing force rendered through the soundtrack. The sonic

Figure 8.15 *The Blind Rabbit* (2021). Source: Courtesy Pallavi Paul.

and the imagistic are dislodged from easy connections; the violent hitting sound starts when the CCTV camera is smashed by the policeman and then is heard over black screen. This merges into a medley of angry voices against police brutality. What we see is a rendering of excessive and explicit violence – a moment that is spectacular in its performative enactment. This is different from the discussion of the absent file of a delinquent to stage the insidious everyday transactions that allow brutality to become routine via the language of social engineering and governance.

In their reflections on narratives of violence, Matthew Fuller and Eyal Weizman demonstrate how, in an evolving technological environment, the field of investigation has shifted due to the sheer volume of images from smartphones and streaming services now accessible online (2021). This means that an investigation must be conducted collaboratively, utilising networks of solidarity. For the authors, these networks can comprise individuals who have personally witnessed violence and documented it, self-taught journalists, filmmakers, and artists, as well as those who upload these images at great risk. This creates a new aesthetic space where creative intervention is shaped by "investigative commons," challenging the conventional expert style approach with a variety of viewpoints. The result is a technique of "investigative aesthetics" that assembles accounts and reports from disparate media sources, and serves as points of entry to make connections with other moments rather than as standalone pieces of evidence. Investigative aesthetics is therefore a form that facilitates navigation and the weaving together of dissimilar elements into a powerful intervention (Fuller and Weizman 2021). While the scale of investigative aesthetics is a vast terrain of evidence, what it opens out is an understanding of a field of conflicted testimonies. In *The Blind Rabbit*, Paul draws on this field of conflicted testimonies to suggest links between various violent contexts such as the anti-Sikh pogrom of 1984, The National Emergency of 1975-77, and the police violence unleashed during protests against the Citizenship Amendment Act (CAA). Her use of CCTV footage from Jamia University along with other witness testimonies to contextualise the violence is one of the film's most potent use of this 'scavenging' approach.

While Paul examines and follows the archival grain to encounter certain moments, especially from the past, she also includes in the investigation a desire to go against it to record what could not be archived. This is exemplified in the incident of a female security officer who was ordered to become Indira Gandhi's body double during the annual commemoration of India's independence. The female security guard was asked to dress up like the Prime Minister to divert any foreseeable attack. Paul sees this as a 'micro encounter with the life of power',[13] which the bodyguard conveys in a clear tone with no rancour. This is not a moment that could have been officially documented, yet in *The Blind Rabbit*, Indira Gandhi's newsreel footage appears with the body double's voice. She is never seen; we only hear her. The Independence Day ritual, as an iconic and unmistakable representation of the head of state, is thus punctured by the voice of the body double. Doubling is similar to slicing anything in half; this framing technique is also used intentionally to strip classic archival strains of their truth status and their sense of coherence and unity.

The Blind Rabbit is an essay on the archaeology of power and violence – sometimes visible, sometimes not; we are asked to sense, feel, hear and imagine the dynamic energies at work in these images. The Emergency does not emerge as an 'exceptional event' here, nor are its manifestations reduced to the work of a few individuals; rather, we are asked to reflect on the relationship between archiving, imagining and evidence in our times. The film does not split time and memory into the past and the future of the present. As a result, the past never passes but coexists with the present. Paul refuses to accept a static sense of the past and instead encounters non-linear temporalities where a highly mediatic environment taps the archive to invoke a sense of simultaneity. Memory here is not a stored phenomenon but a quality that attaches itself to current events to generate something different and not yet experienced. The lived present synthesizes the past as an extended duration in which distant memories replay themselves as a multiplicity of recollections. There is an attempt here to connect the extended feeling of being caught in a time loop of authoritarian culture with what has been separated out as an aberration limited to the past. In these attempts to connect the two moments, one a time-bound series of events and the other an ongoing situation with no sense of an end, we can see the difference between the way Emma Tarlo engaged with the Emergency and its landscape of memories in a climate of official silence and the current context where authoritarian narratives of the past proliferate alongside contemporary acts of violence.[14] The Emergency in its archival imagination as it circulates today is no longer about a past but is the present past, folded into an extended durational structure, facilitated by new media technologies.

In defence of a not-so-political cinema

Parichay Patra

Prologue

Why does political or not-so-political cinema need any defence? Or, for that matter, why would any cinema need defence? In an edited collection devoted to the Indian National Emergency of 1975–7 and its cine-politics, media politics, many afterlives, archiving, censorship, institutional histories and other issues, an essay on a film that predated the Emergency may seem somewhat anachronistic, somewhat removed from the cataclysmic event and its memory. This temporal gap might be considered as an unbridgeable one, something that can separate this chapter from the rest of the chapters.

However, contrary to such expectations, this chapter does not want to confine itself to the idea of explicit cine-political temporal associations. Instead, it wants to address many possibilities of cinema and politics that are not representational, that may not manifest through obvious textual-temporal alliances.

The idea of political cinema is not easily definable. This is not the only elusive term in cinema studies. As Paul Willemen addressed many such ambiguous cinematic concepts and terminologies in the 'film-critical vocabulary' as 'displacements' (1994, 226), political cinema often poses a challenge for the cinephile in terms of its *displacement*, its constant shifting of location and meaning. Ambiguity, however, might also be a necessary element in film criticism because, as Hoi Lun Law's recent work suggests, it is not only polysemy, multiplicity of meaning or the difficulty in meaning-making, it is a complex aesthetic choice (and reason) that invites the critic to inquire (2021, 9). While Hoi Lun Law reads specific shots in often classic, canonical and contemporary film-texts that offer difficulty for the critic, the idea of the ambiguous can surely be extended beyond the text, towards concepts that entangle, encircle cinema in myriad ways. Plurality and multitude, 'perplexity of style', all related to the domain of aesthetics, affect the film critic and may lead her to many destinations. Law covers a wide range of films with no temporal/auteurial connections between them, avoiding established and decisively ambiguous films and preferring specific shots/sequences in many films that may not seem suitable.

In the European long 1960s, film criticism, its functionalities and purposes, its categorizations of cinema underwent a metamorphosis from which cinema itself never 'recovered' fully. Without a recollection of that, the ethos of the period can never be grasped conclusively. It might be located unequivocally in the transitions and transformations of *Cahiers du Cinéma* (hereafter *Cahiers*), the maverick film magazine in France usually associated with the French New Wave in popular parlance. In the 1960s, *Cahiers* departed from its Bazinian (after André Bazin, the mentor of the young turks of the New Wave and one of the greatest film theorists in cinema history) mode of realist-idealist-auteurist criticism, moving towards Althusserian Marxism, Derridean deconstruction and Lacanian psychoanalysis that led to the formation of its Marxist-ideological stance, its invocation and exploration of apparatus theory, and, after May 1968, its more radical Maoist interventions that continued for a few years (1969–72/73). The Maoist phase saw the loss of a large readership before a role reversal, as with Serge Daney and Serge Toubiana at the helm, it went back to the more 'conventional' film criticism after 1973, reconnecting with the French New Wave auteurs (see de Baecque 1991; Fairfax 2021; Daney 2022, 13–28). *Cahiers*' writings, albeit selectively, appeared near-simultaneously in translation in *Screen*, having a profound impact on the development of cinema studies in the anglophone world. The long 1960s moment in film theory and criticism, especially after the 1968 cataclysm, was characterized by Jean Narboni and Jean-Louis Comolli's fiery 'Cinema/Ideology/Criticism' (Comolli 2015, 251–9), Jean-Pierre Oudart's 'La Suture'/'Cinema and Suture' (Oudart 1996, 45–57), Comolli's unfinished 'Technique and Ideology: Camera, Perspective, Depth of Field' (Comolli 2015, 147–244) and other iconic outbursts. The aura of radical cine-political-ideological criticism intermingled with the ambiguities that enshrouded the critics, with Jean-Pierre Oudart's overnight fame for 'La Suture' supplemented by his Parisian disappearance without a trace or reason.

Narboni and Comolli, while dividing cinema into several politico-ideological categories (unconsciously conformist cinema, cinema on explicitly political subject, cinema on political content but without any critique of their ideological system and so on), identified many roles for the critic including that of deciphering the ruptures/distortions/discrepancies within the apparently conventional cinema. But there might also be, as they pointed out, 'films in which the signified is not *explicitly* political, but, in some way, "becomes" so; that is, finds itself re-produced as such by the "formal" critical work on it. . . . For *Cahiers*, these films . . . are the essence of the cinema and make up the essence of the journal' (Comolli 2015, 256, emphasis original). Here, in this chapter, I am concerned mostly with such a film, helping it in its process of 'becoming' political through the formal critical work.

In the contemporary and in the wake of a renewed interest in the long 1960s, the problematic of cinema and politics, cine-politics,[1] the multimodal associations between cinematic and political thoughts are consistently being subjected to radical rethinking. While deploying French figuralism[2] in his most recent work on Italian political cinema in the aftermath of 1968, Mauro Resmini offers the contradictory, seemingly mutually exclusive continental philosophical thoughts on this. Resmini refers to Alain Badiou, who proposed a 'reciprocal autonomy' between cinema and politics, and to Jacques Ranciére, who contradicted Badiou's mode of theorization (2022, 265). Resmini focuses on several *figures* in Italian political cinema of the long 1960s (or, more specifically, in 1968 and after), and not all of them may have apparent associations with politics. The absence of an explicit association between cinema and politics of a turbulent period and a consideration of the respective and reciprocal autonomy may lead to a more nuanced understanding of many exchanges between these two concepts and public institutions.

Political scientists, while exploring the cine-ideological-political thinking and phenomena in the 1970s, offer an often synchronic consideration of the time. In his exploration of Stanley Cavell's iconic 1971 text *The World Viewed*, Davide Panagia recounts how the early 1970s seem significant for political theory itself, with John Rawls's *A Theory of Justice* published in 1971 and Hannah Arendt's *Lectures on Kant's Political Philosophy* delivered at the New School in 1970 (Panagia 2020, 81). Cavell's book was published in the same year and from the same publisher as Rawls's and his cinematic political thinking, extended beyond the idea of mere representation, exerted its influence on several American political theorists working on cinema and politics. The latter group includes William Connolly, Michael Shapiro, Joshua Foa Dienstag et al., with issues covered as diverse as neuropolitics, geopolitics, cinematic and political/democratic modes of representation, or cinema's multimodal engagement with democracy in general.[3]

In order to locate his 'political ontology of the *moving* image' (with an obvious reference to André Bazin's concern for the ontology of the photographic image), Panagia offers a far wider framework:

> I want to claim further that the world made thinkable by a cinematic mode of political reflection takes as a remarkable fact the transformative ontological possibilities of a medium – transformative, that is, of our aesthetic and political experiences. (2020, 106)

The idea of the transformative will be of help again, especially since I am exploring the formulation of the critical work that is needed in a film's process of becoming political.

The context

The long 1960s and its distinctive global cine-politics manifested itself across several Global South locations. The emergence of Third Cinema as a conceptual apparatus and a mode of new cinematic praxis,[4] the rise of the New Latin American Cinema across several countries battling dictatorships, the organization of Third Cinema conferences in the 1970s[5] and the formation of debates over political cinema's exhibition, cinema-events and movements between the Global North and the Global South contributed to the cine-political discourse of the time. However, in the Third Cinema conferences and cine-events, there was a visible non-presence of Asia[6] even though such a politically committed Indian auteur as Mrinal Sen engaged with his Latin American counterparts in multiple ways that featured within and outside the cinematic text.[7]

The long 1960s in the Indian cinematic context is marked by the emergence of the Indian New Wave/New Indian Cinema, a largely state-sponsored and occasionally collectively financed film movement scattered across multiple production centres. While Mrinal Sen and John Abraham made explicitly political films in their respective states of West Bengal and Kerala, Mani Kaul and Kumar Shahani's ambiguous, enigmatic cine-aesthetic experimentations hardly betray any apparent engagement with the radical politics of the time. But in the film society discourse, the increasingly left-leaning politics of film programming became pronounced.

As the global radical political movements in and after May 1968 sent shockwaves across the Global South and the Indian Maoist radicals, known locally as Naxalites, started a violent insurgency against the Indian state that led to unprecedented statist repression culminating in the National Emergency of 1975–7, the explicitness of political engagement manifested in theatre, film society movement, little magazine publications and transformations in art.[8] Rochona Majumdar's historical research on film societies in India and art cinema maps the evolution of the film society cine-exhibition model from a mere propagator of 'good cinema' to a committed left-wing curatorial venture (2021, 92–123). Moinak Biswas has shown how a pronounced Brechtian influence was discernible in independent/group theatre of Kolkata, the insertion of the political in the domain of the little magazine was apparent, the Marxist film society discourse in magazines such as *Chitrapat*, *Chitrabhas*, *Chitrabikshan*, *Chitrakalpa*, *Movie Montage* and *Frontier* included ideas of and debates on Engels, Plekhanov, Lenin, Christopher Caudwell, Ralph Fox and Mao Zedong, and theatre became an 'intuitive choice' for the 1970s filmmaker 'for a response to orchestrated violence, nightmare and fantasy' (Biswas 2020, 159).

But, as I have stated, there has always been cinema that *avoided* the immediacy and explicitness of the political experience. Writing on such cinema poses a greater challenge, perhaps, as they are not to be located within the visibly left-wing cine-events and film societies. The latter often remained confined to its engagement with European art cinema and Indian 'political' cinema, ignoring more formally experimental, avant-garde works of Kaul and Shahani (Biswas 2020, 140).

In an article on Shahani's *Tarang* (*Waves*, 1984), I have shown how Shahani's post-Emergency film, despite accommodating the tumultuous industrial city of Bombay, its labour unrest, radical left trade unionism, political and sexual violence, allows the insertion of the mythological (Patra 2021, 231–48). In a telephone conversation with me, Shahani addressed his own politics as *Kosambian*, named after his mentor Damodar Dharmananda

Kosambi (1907–66), the polymath who, apart from being a mathematician, is well known for being one of the pioneering figures of Marxist historiography in India. As Kosambi often read into the Hindu mythologies from the perspective of a Marxist historian, delving deep into the class structure and other civilizational intricacies, Shahani's *figures* in the cinema metamorphose into mythological beings, relocating his idea of the political on a different plane.

The aesthetic avant-gardism of Kaul and Shahani may not betray any signs of an apparent engagement with the 1970s politics (with, perhaps, the notable exception of *Tarang*), but that does not deter them from pursuing their own nuanced alleyways that lead to politics, *Kosambian* or otherwise. In his article on Mani Kaul's reading of Gilles Deleuze's film-philosophy and the development of Kaul's own cinematic thought-process, Moinak Biswas raises significant issues such as Kaul's distinctive aesthetics and use of interregnums/absences/breaks/gaps, his resistance to convergence in art and European Renaissance perspectivalism, his belief in an anti-representational cinema and the interval-principle prevalent in Hindustani classical musical forms. Through such formal experimentations, Biswas reaches at the question of politics towards the end:

> A significant point about politics can be derived from the aesthetic thought of Mani Kaul, whose cinema appears to be apolitical – it is the point about working with absence as yearning. (Biswas 2021, 92–3)

In their times, Kaul and Shahani's ambiguous responses to the long 1970s were not well-received in many quarters. State funding through FFC/NFDC[9] gradually waned, as debates over channelling state help through subsidy/loans and their inability to procure returns for the money invested pervaded film magazines of the time.[10] The apparently apolitical mode of representation/address did not receive many takers in the film society scene either.

Several decades later, in contemporary times, both Kaul and Shahani have attracted more scholarly and curatorial attention.[11] A more enthusiastic spectator group for their cinema has been located *elsewhere*, within the confines of the gallery space that can accommodate more experimental cinematic forms. Ashish Rajadhyaksha organized screenings of Kaul in international art galleries along with Ranbir Singh Kaleka's art, as different forms and mediums started having dialogues with each other (Rajadhyaksha 2012, 44–8).

The text

Mani Kaul's first two films were based on the works of Mohan Rakesh (1925–72) and the latter is widely regarded as one of the greatest figures in Hindi modernist literature, especially in new literature/*nai kahani*.[12] Kaul went on to engage with many modes of modernism in Hindi literature, adapting Vinod Kumar Shukla towards the end of his career[13] and making an experimental work on Gajanan Madhav Muktibodh[14] that earned the wrath and displeasure of the Hindi progressive circles for its alleged incomprehensibility and the lack of the political, the apparent loss of the agitprop ethos of Muktibodh.[15] These accusations will never cease to haunt Kaul and Shahani, as I already have shown here.

Kaul's second film, *Ashadh Ka Ek Din* (1971), is his reworking on Rakesh's unarguably the most well-known play that initiated a sharp break from the conventional dramaturgy and playwriting traditions in Hindi, from the older forms popularized by Jaishankar Prasad (1889–1937) et al. Unlike his predecessors who worked on literary, not-so-theatrical dramatic texts and history plays, Rakesh insisted on many forms of innovative experimentation in theatre. His debut play *Ashadh Ka Ek Din* appeared in 1958, and Rakesh followed it up with *Lahron Ke Rajhans* (1963) and *Aadhe Adhure* (1969). Rakesh translated classic Sanskrit plays including Kalidas's *Shakuntala* (1965). Despite *Ashadh Ka Ek Din* being regarded as the first of its kind in Hindi modernist literature, Rakesh remained unhappy with the 'excessive literariness' of his first two plays. During his European sojourn, Rakesh became acquainted with such experimental, absurdist works as Peter Handke's 1967 play *Kaspar*,[16] and it is reflected in his last completed play before his death, namely *Chhatriyan* (translated into English as *Mad Delight: A Scattering of Words, Sounds, and Visuals*), an experimental play with structural, thematic, even optical affinities with *Kaspar* (Dalmia 2008, 138, 147).

Ashadh Ka Ek Din has its distinctive and curious performance/production history associated with several careers in the theatre world of Delhi (and elsewhere) in the long 1960s. Shyamanand Jalan's pioneering 1960 Calcutta production, Ebrahim Alkazi's celebrated 1962 production for the National School of Drama (NSD) at the Kailash Colony Courtyard in New Delhi (Dave-Mukherji 2016, 315), Satyadev Dubey's Theatre Unit production in Bombay, several other performances in Jaipur, Sagar, Raipur, Udaipur, Dehradun and other tier 2 cities, later productions (in multiple languages) directed by such celebrated thespians as Amal Allana, Rajinder Nath, Ram Gopal Bajaj, Feisal Alkazi, B. R. Nagesh, K. V. Subbanna, Mohan Maharishi, Ratan Thiyam et al. have all been commented on (Dharwadker 2016, 38–46). The play-text's translation history is significant as well. The first English translation by Sarah Ensley has been performed and read for a long time even though it had its limitations. Then appeared Aparna Dharwadker's most recent translation with a detailed introduction and essays. Dharwadker has intended to draw her reader's attention to issues within and outside the play-text, as the performance/production history of the play sometimes reflects some of the major preoccupations of the latter.[17]

Mohan Rakesh's play-text borrows its title from the opening verses of *Meghadūta*, the canonical classical lyric poem by Kalidas (fourth–fifth century CE), the legendary Sanskrit poet whose life and times have been shrouded in mystery. The importance of Kalidas, especially for his *Abhigyan Shakuntalam* that earned the now-famous praise of Goethe and represented Sanskrit literary/dramatic traditions for the orientalists and indologists during the colonial period in the nineteenth century, should be remembered. Rakesh's play becomes controversial because of him resisting the process of canonization and presenting an ambiguous characterization of Kalidas that did not go well with the Sanskritic scholarly and literary establishment. Rakesh's Kalidas abandons his indigenous roots and rootedness for the sake of political patronage and social mobility offered by the Empire, leaving behind Mallika, his muse, whose ill-fated narrative forms the crux of the play. Mallika degenerates into prostitution, while Kalidas's pursuit of the ways of the world gradually resorts to the void where he finds himself in towards the end.

Rakesh's play creates a strong sense of a centre/margin binary that offers Mani Kaul the necessary space for his film that may seem controversial for the time where it found itself. The film appeared in 1971, four years prior to the declaration of the National Emergency of 1975 and at a time when the Naxalite insurgency was at its peak. In Rakesh's narrative, Mallika and her ailing mother (who dies over the course of time and action) remain at the periphery throughout the play while Kalidas travels to the metropolitan centre of Ujjayini (never shown in the play). The centre carries a sense of doom for the margin and the marginal existence. It claims Kalidas for the wider readership and the public sphere while Mallika recedes into the steadily declining mise-en-scène. The centre sends the horse-riders, the learnt men, the princess and her associates, the information-gatherers with anthropological interests in the idyllic village, and they are unable to make inroads into the life at the margin. Kalidas succumbs to the demands of the Empire and the latter's preconceived role for the poet laureate. Even though the play never leaves for a change of scene beyond the interiority of Mallika's home, it is not the usual chamber-drama; instead, it creates a sense of profound disaffection and unease, unexplored till then in the world of Hindi theatre. Kaul follows the text really closely, as revealed through the narrative and the dialogues.

As the play (and the film) progresses, Kalidas's promotion to the position of the regional governor of Kashmir meets with a widespread revolt against the Empire. Even though the details of it remain ambiguous till the very end, rumours of Kalidas fleeing the scene after the loss in the battlefield circulate. Kashmir, the disputed territory, rises in revolt. Kaul, while adapting it, retains the pervasive sense of ambiguous exchanges and rumours. He went on to make a film on Kashmir in the following decade. *Before My Eyes* (Mani Kaul, 1989), the film on Kashmir, appeared a few years before the insurgency/militancy in that region that changed its history (and that of the Indian state) forever.

Sequences, interiority

Mani Kaul's camera remains static to such an extent that it makes his viewers uncomfortable. The deliberately claustrophobic interiority appears like an often darkened stage on which Kaul's *figures* exit and enter. Characters are often seen framed against the only window that opens up the interior space to the outside world of occasional 'freedom', the hilly landscape that characterizes the region and yet it remains undefinable. Big close-ups of fragmented body parts fill the screen, the lighting often changes within the interior space. The screen goes dark from time to time, the characters merely 'recite' their dialogues, they refuse to 'act' in front of the camera. Amrit Gangar, during a personal communication, referred to the way in which Kaul recorded the soundtrack first and added it to the film later.[18] The production conditions and strategies of Kaul, thus, contributed to the idiosyncratic mode of acting. Kaul dedramatizes theatre here, even though he follows the text closely. The politics of Rakesh and Kaul surfaces in several sequences, some of which will be located here.

Six minutes into the film, we encounter the centre/margin binary through the most profound sense of premonition possible. The screen is filled with the two women in Kaul's text, Mallika (Rekha Sabnis) and Ambika, her mother. Transitioning from her frontal close-up in the preceding shot, here, Mallika turns her face away from the audience, with her gaze following the world that is viewed outside the window frame on the left. Ambika, on her right, puts up her stern, expressionless face, with the mother-daughter duo expressing the perpetual yet subterranean discord that characterizes their relationship. From the off-screen space, sounds of horses' hooves invade the film. The sound produces unease, a sense of discord. It sounds more like what Ritwik Ghatak, the auteur who mentored Kaul during his days at the Film and Television Institute of India (FTII), termed as 'metaphoric sounds', the creative uses of which 'do not belong to the visible' (Ghatak 2000, 76–7).

As the conversation progresses, in the following shot, they are framed from outside the window, as if incarcerated within, and it becomes one of those rare instances where Kaul's camera moves out of the deliberately claustrophobic mise-en-scène. The mother narrates how the horsemen in the off-screen, sonic space connote the arrival of the 'royal servants' (in Dharwadker's translation, 'royal court officials'), the marauding troops that invariably carry a sense of impending doom, an ill-omen that may bring in a war or an epidemic

Figure 9.1 Mallika and Ambika converse on the invading sounds of the Empire.

(Figure 9.1). The 'men' of the Empire, from the metropolitan centre, bring annus horribilis to the periphery. The onslaught of the Empire soon reveals itself in the narrative and proves fatal for Mallika.

Much later in the film, with Kalidas's uneventful return to the village (in the narrative) and to the diegetic space of the interior (within the filmic text), a significant shift of space becomes visible. Kalidas, the representative of the Empire, has fled an insurgent Kashmir, as the narrative informs us through rumours. Towards the end, Kalidas recounts the epic and lyrical narratives of his own, offering parallels with his and Mallika's lives from the distant past, narrating how the past lives and Mallika as muse led to the formation of his literary 'characters'. Kalidas's confessions arrive in a disembodied voice as the camera arrests the hilly terrain, the picturesque, misty landscape framed outside the interior (Figure 9.2). The off-screen voice emerges from the past, expressing despair and Kalidas's inability to hide the latter. But the despair remains within the dialogue, not in the way they are being spoken. With the camera standing still, looking at the 'picturesque' exterior, landscape in the mist, Kalidas states how time is more powerful than desire, with time flowing through the extended shot à la Tarkovsky.[19]

Figure 9.2 Kalidas's voice traverses over the hilly landscape.

Within the interior, with occasional flashes of the outside, Kaul's figures refuse to be/remain actors. Their expressionless recitation, ambiguous, somewhat vacant looks (often away from the camera and the audience, even from the co-actor at times) may remind one of Kaul's perpetual fascination for and engagement with Robert Bresson and the latter's insistence on rejecting 'actors' in favour of *modèle*/'models'. Bresson reimagined the actor as an object or a mere 'visual element' (Crisp 1993, 312–13), with the latter's 'automatic, naturalistic movement and vocal tones and rhythms' having 'indeterminate' meanings (Burnett 2017, 151). Kaul recalled how his meeting with Bresson in Paris resulted in an indelible mark on him:

> 'Gesture comes before meaning'. Bresson said in English in answer to a question about his repetition of takes. The mechanism was a trap, which at the end must disappear. These words never left me afterwards.. . . Yet you come across not one who has entirely renounced the 'actor', or acting for that matter. (Kaul 2018, 34)

And, not surprisingly, Bresson's distinction between models and mere actors in his iconic *Notes on the Cinematograph* involves the question of interiority:

> HUMAN MODELS:
> Movement from the exterior to the interior. (Actors: movement from the interior to the exterior.)
> The thing that matters is not what they show me but what they hide from me. (Bresson 2016, 11)

Kaul's models/figures hide their faces, expressions, news of uprisings and move to the interior. In an apparently 'apolitical' play set in the distant past, they recite their words and frustrate the viewer who expects an immediate response to the contemporary or the movements within Mohan Rakesh's play-text. This is not unusual or unexpected from Kaul, as Bresson's idiosyncratic, militant rejection of cinema as photographed theatre must have resonated with him.[20] Unlike his explicitly political contemporaries, he is not considering theatre as an 'intuitive choice'. Kaul's choice of actors might also be noted here for its distinctiveness from theatre. Rekha Sabnis, Mallika in Kaul's film, played the same role on stage for Satyadev Dubey's 1964 production starring Dubey himself and Amrish Puri. Sabnis's performance in that production has been described as 'distressingly immature', something that 'flattened the play's serious resonances' (Dharwadker 2016, 42). In Kaul's film, the acting skills needed in the theatre seem redundant. Instead, he uses the play-text, depriving it of its theatricality, making it more ominous at times, allowing the tumultuous politics to storm its way around (and occasionally through) the interior.

Epilogue

Kaul's camerawork and mise-en-scène confine themselves to the interior, the intensity of Kaul's interiority becomes deliberately claustrophobic at times. His off-screen space is often ominous, it threatens the interior with sonic and figural invasion. It reminds me of how Jean Louis Schefer, the figural film-philosopher who inspired Deleuze, considered cinema itself as interior history, cinema existing within the spectator as an 'ultimate chamber where the hope and ghost of an *interior history* circulate' (2016, 17, emphases original). Here in Kaul, such an interior history and its spectral presence manifest in unusual ways, harbouring his anti-state politics four years prior to the cataclysm of 1975.

The sequences above seem *autonomous*, their political connotations not revealing themselves easily, neither through images nor through their contributions to the narrative, if any. Unlike overtly political cinematic practices in the long 1970s, *Ashadh Ka Ek Din* and its images exist independently as Kaul's politics remains apparently ambiguous, with its ambiguity posing challenges for film criticism. The 'reciprocal autonomy' of cinema and politics becomes evidence for the transformative here, it transforms our expectation for an immediacy of political experience into an aesthetic experience.

From 'dictatorship' to dictatorship

The dynamics of alien and 'legitimized' authoritarianism in 1980s popular Hindi films

Dibyakusum Ray

The popular cinematic output of the 1980s of India, marked by the historical precarity of posited between the 1970s and the 1990s, has been perceived as 'belabored, discontinuous, and poorly executed . . . [where] [p]owerful themes in contemporary politics are diffused' (Virdi 2003, 105). Arguing over a generalized concept of filmic aesthetics, Virdi's comments are germane. Films like *Shaan* (1980), *Inquilaab* (1984), *Karma* (1986), *Hukumat* (1987) or *Mr. India* (1987) – all major box-office success of their release years – wantonly display divisive, masculinist, jingoist or schlocky values; made starker in contrast to the politically charged, populist cinema depicting radical social transformation (Madhava Prasad 1997, 118) in the 1970s (like *Deewar* (1975) or *Sholay* (1975)). The prosaicness of the 1980s canon is further enhanced by the presence of the 'Bollywoodization' of the film industry itself during the neoliberal drive brought in by the 1990s, its scholastic fecundity embodied through the writings of Rajadhyaksha, Dwyer and so on. Through the filmic canon discussed in the following space, it is argued that through their pulpiness, melodrama and unabashed moral orthodoxy, the 1980s films are important 'aftertexts' of the 1970 to 1980s Indira Gandhi regime, and a potent antecedent of the millennial filmic ideology. I will further argue that the films mentioned above hold a unique view on 'dictatorship', thus becoming an important archive of the lingering effects of the National Emergency (1975–7) on public consciousness. How did the reactions to the Gandhi regime influence the 'villain' characterization of 1980s Hindi popular cinema? How was the 'hero' –

as a foil to the former – symbolizing the post-Emergency attempt at national integration? How does the hero/villain dynamics foretell the emergence of a 'nationalist' vigilante militia? This chapter attempts to answer these questions by considering the 1980s films a site of sociopolitical remaking of ideology.

Political precarity marked the very essence of the 1980s, effectively making it an ideological liminality posited between the social-mobilizing of the 1970s (Jha 2003, 48) and the globalized of the 1990s (Malhotra and Alagh 2004, 28). In other words, Indian politics of this decade oscillated between the decadent ideals of Nehruvian socialism and the looming neoliberal drive, already infiltrating a significant part of the Western economy, including the Reagan-era United States (Harvey 2007, 1). The backlash of the National Emergency (1975–7) and other political extremities of Indira Gandhi's first government was mighty, ultimately resulting in her humiliating defeat in the 1977 general elections by an immense margin of 200 seats. And yet, the coalition government that came to power after her was ousted within three years in favour of Gandhi's second term as the Prime Minister (1980–4) – an event Guha has described as 'the "end of ideology" in Indian politics': 'previous polls were fought and won on the planks of democracy, socialism, secularism and non-alignment. In 1980, however, Mrs Gandhi spoke not of the abolition of poverty but of her ability to rule' (Guha 2017, 428). Widely argued to be the waning decade of the Nehruvian 'democratic socialism' that adhered to the demands of a multilingual and multicultural society (Bayly 2015, 606), and the initiation of the political authoritarianism now rampant in India, the 1980s can thus be seen as the manifestation of a spectre of dictatorship. Faced with separatism within and outside the Indian Union (especially in Punjab, Assam, Bihar and then undivided Andhra Pradesh), the Gandhi government intensified military activities throughout the country, which finally resulted in the assassination of the Prime Minister in 1984, resulting in the Sikh pogrom (1984) that claimed thousands of lives. The reason I term the scenario a spectral dictatorship is this overall sense of abandonment, threat and oppression irrespective of the corporeal presence of the 'dictator', a situation (albeit in a different context) termed as the 'dismemberment' and 'detongue-ing' of the nation by Eduardo Galeano (1986, 17).[1] India, in all its socio-economic facets, faced stagnancy during the 1980s (which arguably intensified with the 1990s neoliberalism). Concurrent to the ethnic fault lines, the economic disparity was high – the GDP growth of 1980–90 experienced a spike unprecedented in national history (Panagariya 2004, 3), but a detailed analysis reveals that the growth was focused on specific sectors and areas, and by no means homogeneous. Retrospective studies show that economic inequality rose as dramatically as the growth from the mid-1980s and employment, healthcare and habitat growth started to show a declining trend.[2] The decadence, however, was undercut by several reformist and resistive endeavours, which probably affirms the presence of authoritarianism, as alternative social practices emerge on a large scale specially when dissent is subjugated to dictatorship's 'defining reality' (Corner 2016, 417). In the 1980s, there was a rising awareness and militancy among the caste and class minorities regarding their socio-economic rights. Change – judicial and social – was visible in gender relations as well, with several emancipatory laws, bills and punitive measures being adopted to safeguard women's rights and autonomy, now perceived as the rise of feminism in India (Ghadially 2007). Thus, the decade was fragmented into often-colliding values of 'liberalism' and 'authoritarianism', and this ethos drives the socio-politics of the 1980s, reflected through narrative bewilderment, crisis, paranoia and desperate resolutions through the contemporary filmic canon. The narratives are simultaneously marked by individual agency, national integration and so on adjusting with dictatorial centrism and authoritarian intervention.

Chronologically and thematically, the first film of my interest is a trailblazer of the 1980s cinematic trend. Aesthetically, *Shaan* (1980) is emblematic of the general outlandishness of contemporaneous Hindi popular films – transnational villains, fictional gadgetry, superhuman action sequences. More importantly, however, the film signals the transition from the 1970s 'angry young man' – a cinematic trope of overt vigilante themes with clear sympathy for the proletarian anti-hero fighting smugglers and corrupt elements bred by the state system. This departure is important regarding the aftertextuality of the Gandhi 'dictatorship' and the mass trend of dissociating itself from the former. 'With the disaggregation of the sociopolitical order . . . (came the) disidentification with the "socialist" program in the national project' (138) for the middle class, writes Madhava Prasad (1997), hinting at why it was necessary to jettison Nehruvian ideals from public memory altogether as a one-off, discordant, aberrant entity (thus alienating the very ideals of Nehruvian socialism by extension). One of the primary socio-moral distinctions of the 1980s was the rise of a militantly nationalist bourgeois populace, which has since turned into the dominant political apotheosis of

India, especially parallel to the strengthening of the right-wing Bharatiya
Janata Party. In place of the lone-wolf, amoral and rebellious vigilante (the
angry young man), in the 1980s, we have the middle-class family acting as the
guardians of the state border, social avenger and lawmaker, their main enemy
being some geopolitical alien terrorist-dictator who wanted to disrupt both.
The film depicts Amitabh Bachchan and Shashi Kapoor as aimless middle-
class youths, finding their bearing after the death of their eldest brother, an
honest lawman, murdered by a sadistic international crime lord, Shakaal.
Visually similar to Ernst Stavro Blofeld from the James Bond universe and
wearing a uniform vaguely reminiscent of a SS-Gruppenführer,[3] Shakaal is a
character without a back story, is racially indistinguishable and rules over a
lonely island 300 kilometres off the Indian mainland with an iron grip. He
also has a confounding effect on the subjects/henchmen, who follow him
with unquestioning, almost robotic doggedness. Beneath the green island in
the middle of the turquoise bay, Shakaal sits at the centre of his kingdom of
secret elevators reaching into the underwater facility, futuristic gadgets, CCTV
cameras and indecipherable backlit panels, echoing the modern dictators
of history 'relying on the infrastructure of the modern state and the most
advanced technology available' (Leese 2016, 218).[4] This 'dictatorial otherness'
of Shakaal is eventually invaded by the loyal national subjects (the protagonist
duo) who destroy every bit of it. The familial – consisting of the newly reformed
brothers avenging the breakage of their ideal family – wins over the alien as the
nation neutralizes its threat and establishes conservative-nationalist rendering
of modernity (Qayum and Ray 2011, 250–1). Moreover, at the climax of
Shaan, a strong argument in favour of extrajudicial, masculine vigilante
methods is presented. Having defeated Shakaal, the heroes momentarily argue
about killing him off as an avengement. A faint counterargument arrives in
the form of the widowed sister-in-law, who pleads with them to uphold the
sovereign law: 'I have learned to respect the law from my dead husband, and
taking the law in one's own hand is not respectful.' The vigilantes pause for a
second, emblematic of democracy's vacillation between liberal recourse and
instantaneous counterstrike. The dictator, however, expedites the conclusion
as he attempts to flee, prompting the heroes to shoot him down, giving the
protagonists a free hand in delivering nationalist justice whenever and however
they see fit.

Shaan hence initiates the trend of sharply otherizing the dictator, thus absolving the nation of its complicit role of bringing the Indira Gandhi 'autocracy' upon itself through electoral mandate. On the obverse, we now have a model of popular authoritarianism; the family-bound vigilante protagonists with a licence to deliver retribution for the sake of national security with assumed mass support (Corner 2016, 413). The 1980s popular cinema's spectatorship, in this sense, was a laboratory of dictatorship's reabsorption, where instead of the titular dictatorial figures (dismissed as aliens or aberrant elements of society), we have a legitimized 'voluntary mass participation in and support for dictatorial regimes' (Lim 2005, 325). This legitimization, in the case of *Shaan*, is granted by the orthodox bourgeois family structure. In the next film (another Amitabh Bachchan starrer), *Inquilaab* [Revolution] (1984), the legitimization is bestowed by something more direct: dictatorial politics, chosen over publicly mandated politicians. In other words, *Inquilaab* advocates a violent dispatch of democratically elected representatives and the supplanting with a berserker demagogue who will become the next chief minister, extra-electorally. 'Totalitarian movements are possible wherever there are masses who for one reason or another have acquired the appetite for political organization' (1951, 311) – Arendt's words are befitting the narrative arc of Amarnath (Bachchan), an educated but jobless youth who is also a fan of delivering vigilante justice over the long-winding judiciary process. He is politically adopted by the scheming leader of the opposition party, Shankar Narayan, who makes Amarnath a cop to target and wipe out his competitors while maintaining his facade of poverty alleviation and moral uprightness. The seeming critique of extrajudicial encounters (a staple during the Gandhi regime (Chaudhuri 1977, 1134–42)) and the capitalist-politics entente (once elected, Narayan chooses his principle funder, the billionaire Seetaram, as the state's Home Minister) is upended in the second half of the film, when Amarnath – as per Narayan's plan – becomes the titular head chief minister of the state. In the first cabinet meeting in an isolated room, the new CM double-crosses the ministry. He angrily chides the entire cabinet as corrupt and fallen, then opens fire on them from a hidden automatic weapon, killing all. Closely following the massacre, Amarnath is confronted by his wife, who promptly forgives him for his service to the nation. The same theme of redemption continues in the very final minutes of the film. The police, transporting an arrested Amarnath, are faced with an angry mob demanding their popular CM's release. Amarnath pacifies the crowd, declaring that although he has failed to do anything constructive in terms of the economy or infrastructure, he has 'purged' the nation of political leeches who were the sole reasons behind the nation's woes, ending his speech with an impassioned 'Long Live Revolution' cry. *Inquilaab* thus repeats the tropes of *Shaan*, treating electorality as expendable by aiding the figurative dictatorship. The shadow of the Gandhi ministry looms large over Shankar Narayan's gang (the public support, the socialist rhetoric, the corruption underneath), and this identifiability presupposes their downfall, especially to the 1980s audience. Oddly prescient of Indira Gandhi's assassination by her closest aides in the same year, the film's narrative then hails Amarnath's dictatorial and extra-legal purging of social malcontents, proving 1980s India's ideological incumbency for autocracies with a broad appeal that 'hijack the democratic process' (Matovski 2021, 3). Amarnath, posing as a liberator of people, thus subliminally comes closer to a dictator through his disdain for judiciality, social justice and democracy as such, and each of his actions is welcomed by the film's narrative and its audience. The film's commercial popularity grants its ideology further legitimacy: *Inquilaab* was one of the biggest hits among 1984-released Hindi films (Figures 10.1 and 10.2).

The 1980s Hindi popular canon, especially that of the action-adventure genre, thus repeatedly talks about a figurative autocracy in the guise of

Figure 10.1 Chief Minister Amarnath about to assassinate the entire ministerial cabinet, purging the nation of corruption.

Figure 10.2 Militia chief Vishwa Pratap Singh bullet-paints the map of India, around the cowering terrorist Dang.

revolutionary change, violent uprising and anti-electoral takeovers. The villains in these films are majorly caricatures of pop-cultural dictators that are menacing but expendable, with a distinctive asocial, unrealistic vibe. The protagonists, on the other hand, are rugged nativists from bourgeois to petit-bourgeois backgrounds and ever-ready to continue the unbroken and continuous iron grip on their respective milieus that, in Arendtian terms, 'represents the vantage point from which totalitarian developments are introduced' (Arato 2002, 482). This chapter argues that the purported political 'change' after Gandhi – as represented through films – is perhaps predictive of an even more pervasive authoritarianism in the near future (some may argue this prediction to have been fully realized in post-2014 India). Such predictions, discounting our main case studies, are rife in the 1980s films. For example, 1987's highest grosser *Hukumat* (*The Reign*) presents a villain called Deen Bandhu Deena Nath (roughly translated: Poor's Friend Poor's Saviour) – the nom de guerre of corrupt ex-cop Mangal Singh. From bent police to fake philanthropist-millionaire, Singh's life history (which is a departure from Shakaal's rootless otherizing) is as ironic as his alter ego's name. Rather than the alien villain, he is depicted as a low-level crook rising the crime syndicate's ladder, his cowardice ill-hidden by his forced swagger. *Hukumat*'s seemingly strong critique of the general lawlessness of the era[5] (Singh was a corrupt cop and a mastermind behind his constituency's crimewave) is undercut by the cartoonish nature of D. B. D. N. – his high-pitched voice, his private army in berets, his loudly Western attire and his parallel government of 'Shanti Nagar' (Peacetown) inside an otherwise sovereign nation. Against this absurd farceur stands upright cop Arjun, whose feud against the tyrant starts with the former's concern for his family but soon changes into a nationalist statement. Arjun shoots D. B. D. N. in public, then hails his dead son (killed by D. B. D. N's goons) as a martyr of the country before submitting himself to the law for manslaughter. The double legitimization – family revenge as nationalist cause and public homicide as patriotic duty – cements Arjun's position parallel to Amarnath as both are projected as the most suitable violent emancipators of the current system of governance. The same happens in the case of *Mr. India* (1987) as well, where, in addition to the theme of vigilante justice, we have a furtherance of technocracy as an anti-dictatorial device. The 1980s, which was the economic precursor of neoliberalism, saw the initiation of a large array of technological commodities in the liberalizing market, and technological skills were made an essential attribute in the expanding professional horizon (Pinches 1999) in the same decade. On the other hand, as we've seen in *Shaan*, gadgetry and machine-reliance was a trope of abject villainy (underwater lair, auto-sliding doors, inscrutable digital console, spinning chairs, torture devices etc.), presented in stark visual contrast with the quiet, nondescript middle-class homes. *Mr. India* initially seems to be adhering to this antithesis by pitching hapless middle-class youth, Arun Verma, against the exotic, megalomaniac, psychopathic terrorist Mogambo. Desperate to save his family and home, Arun – as noted by Ray and Radhakrishnan – 'has to become a champion of both India's forthcoming techno/liberalization projects and national defence: also suggested by his name change from Arun Verma to Mr. India' (Ray and Radhakrishnan 2024, 22). Arun shakes off the bourgeois gadget-phobia by embracing the power of the bracelet – an indigenously devised technology by Arun's father – that serves in vanquishing the outlandish villain by making its wearer invisible to the naked human eye. With the bracelet's aid, Arun is shown to have a godlike status in the country where nothing is beyond his purview, no crime goes unpunished in his reign. This status is further mythologized when, in a wacky fight sequence, the invisible Arun uses the Hanuman idol to deter the enemies, signalling an appropriation of technology for religious authoritarianism. Mogambo is defeated in the due process, but the omniscient Hindu icon Mr India's shadow looms large over the country, striking fear into the hearts of the dissenters. Indicative of the surveillance, intrusion and infiltration of state power into personal peripheries now prevalent in post-millennial India, *Mr. India* thus opens up a new possibility for the figurative dictatorship of the post-Indira Gandhi era.

So far, we have talked about the absorption of dictatorial values by the bourgeois family, anti-electoral leader and tech-savvy entrepreneur. These experimentations with democratic and dictatorial forms bring us closer to the third and final articulation of popular authoritarianism: the militaristic vigilantism in *Karma* (1986). Rana Vishwa Pratap Singh, an ageing jailor-turned-covert commando, lost his family as well as the band of prisoners in his charge in an attack carried out by international terrorist Dr Dang (a Shakaalian figure commanding a large army, Dang has every visual similarity to the ruler of a military junta). Repeatedly metaphorized as a microcosm of a united Indian populace, a trinity of the jail-inmates of Hindu–Muslim–Christian origin join the militia of Hindu patriarch Vishwa to carry out a retaliatory attack. The militia, however, faces a narrative conundrum: patriotism versus personal gratification. The reason I have posited *Karma* at the culmination of this paper is this apparent self-critique that actually furthers the film's advocacy for military authoritarianism. Two of the prisoners in Vishwa's band, as it turns out, have respective romantic interests which deter them from their violent cause. *Karma* brings this vacillation to the forefront during a verbal confrontation between Khairuddin (a member of Vishwa's band) and Vishwa himself – a key exchange of dialogue I have explicated elsewhere as well (Ray and Radhakrishnan 2024). Khairu pleads with Vishwa to let the other two prisoners 'live', stressing that they are not 'dogs' to the nationalist cause, and Vishwa is merely using them to avenge his slain family 'just like a cunning politician'. Vishwa angrily refuses, chiding Khairu as confused and cowardly, counter-stressing that the prisoners in his charge were every bit like a family to him, and he is fighting to avenge his uncountable 'children' who also represented the tortured nation to him. Khairu grudgingly concedes, and later in the film, the two wayward romantics dedicate themselves to the militia's cause completely, their choice made easier when their respective lovers join Vishwa as well. This *fated* subsumption of individualism into militarism sets *Karma* apart from the rest of the canon, as it represents the nation's desire to form a fully belligerent existence against the perceived 'dictators'. The militia's criminal regressions and terroristic backgrounds (its members were all violent criminals before they landed in jail) are all forgiven as they align themselves with the Hindu authoritarian patriarch who commands an army of his own. At the conclusion of the film, two armies clash, Vishwa kills Dr Dang, and the nation pays homage to the fallen comrades. The film, along with the preceding case studies, thus makes a clear preference for the weaponized, criminal-infested national militia over the racially undetermined, exotically named 'alien' dictator (Figure 10.2).

The 1980s popular Hindi film canon, thus, is an important experiment with post-Gandhi democracy as well as extant cinematic tropes. There is a clear attempt to break free from the 1970s tradition of class-radicalism and socialist themes, replaced by a new authoritarianism legitimized by various sociopolitical sections – bourgeoisie, electoral politics, tech-savvy entrepreneurs and the military. There is also a clear denial of the dictatorship as something identifiable and rooted in the democratic structure. It instead imagines the literal dictator as a farcical and absurdist figure, and conjures a figurative one who is hailed as an emancipator but evokes unquestioned authoritarianism with his purging technique. In other words, 1980s India was the initiation of a mass-legitimized superheroic iconism in central politics that will be strengthened with the advent of neoliberalism and right-wingerism during the 1990s. Hence, conclusively, the 1980s Hindi films are indeed 'bad' films, but it is because they reflect a 'bad' time. Collectively, these films provide a deft commentary on the 'issues of knowledge and power, and so raise broader social and political questions' (Perkins and Verevis 2014, 6).

The long 1970s

Anjan Dutt as archive, some interfaces

Kaushik Bhaumik

The massification of the Indian public in the 1970s forms the fragile, almost imperceptible armature of what I have to say about Bengali actor, musician, filmmaker Anjan Dutt as an archive of the 1970s, starting in the 1970s and then carrying forth the resonances of that decade into the post-revolution Thermidor following the Emergency and the Left capturing power in Bengal. Recent revisions of the idea of the post-French Revolution Thermidor see it as not necessarily conservative but as actually the birth of the modern idea of plural ideologies and ideas existing side by side (Baczko 1994; Mason 2015). Dutt's own remarkable twisting and turning around ethical choices throughout his life in times of remarkable ideological turbulence would uphold this revisionism against the extreme view of the Thermidor as conservative. Instead, we shall see, Dutt's career as a multimedia pop artist takes forward the radical noise of the 'shock of the global', to quote the title of a book about the 1970s co-edited by an eminent contemporary historian, as no other Indian artist of the 1970s did (Ferguson et al. 2011).

The 1970s

The signs were there for all to see. Above all, the epochal general elections of 1971 swept Indira Gandhi to power with an unprecedented majority against the legitimate wing of the Congress (O). If there is one event of the 1970s (and indeed that of post-Partition Indian history) that requires immediate research and study, it would be this election. What this election introduced was the idea of the mass in Indian everyday life and politics. By 1972, this mass was further consolidated towards the cult of the PM in the wake of the Indian army's victory in East Pakistan that led to the birth of Bangladesh. Cinema reacted to this political history very quickly and in the blink of an eye 1970s Bombay cinema, by then in full splendour of colour, was representing the masses on the streets, in slums, on construction sites, in the countryside and so on. Not Bachchan's cinema really, but before that, in 1974, in a Rajesh Khanna blockbuster such as Manmohan Desai's *Roti* or the Shashi Kapoor starrer *Chor Machaye Shor* or the Manoj Kumar blockbusters such as *Shor* and *Roti Kapda Aur Makaan*. *Masala* cinema excesses may very well be seen as a valorous attempt by cinema, restricted by conventional European scale frames, to contain the excesses of unwieldy masses – the excesses that we know would magically turn the tables on Indira Gandhi within four years of her spectacular victory, both electoral and over the colonial nationalist old guard within the Congress Party.

The idea of the mass was not just a spectacle of vast numbers. There was a massification of many registers of the Indian everyday, with massification being an intensity and speed of doing things outwards, away from the particular, in packs of cult public consumption of material things. There was mass scale higher education as well as mass scale film-watching in cinema halls with capacities of 1,000 and above. There was the beginning of mass middle-class residence in flats. Cars shrank in size – Ambassador giving way to Fiat – indicating the onset of a proper Western-style consumer society around nuclear families, paving the way for a further shrinkage to the size of the earliest Maruti cars. We see a sudden rapid massification of consumer desires around radios, telephones, cars, refrigerators, flats, cultural magazines, paperbacks, comfortable train travel for work and leisure and even travel by air and so on. All these things, of course, not in absolute terms, but in a relative scale of exponential growth in sectors of consumption. One might even argue that the desire for Hollywood films and art-house films too would be massified as compared to earlier decades. Television would merely cap this development as decades wore on and push this rational, frugal middle-class consumer society towards a demonic consumerist society within a span of two decades.

Subtler, more emotive things were up for massification. For one, the idea of "love marriage" was preceded by a more publicly sexualized logic of courting.

One has still not properly understood the revolutionary impact the pill and IUD would have on the sexual mores of both the young and adults in this period. Or, for that matter, the growing legitimacy of divorces among the middle classes. The number of 1970s Bombay films that broach the idea of divorce is considerable. One could say all lifestyle and consumer behaviour was tending towards massification. Even smoking pot was and maybe even trekking in the hills. Some less, some more, but it was only a matter of time before things would plateau in a *general* field of standardized mass consumerism – a mass becoming population.

Anjan Dutt

Dutt says that for the first time in his life he is ready to get down on the streets to protest against Hindu Right political forces threatening to take over Bengal. He says he will do so because he feels these forces pose an ultimate threat to his sense of being modern, his modernity forged by an angular countercultural radicalism against all stable positions, the countercultural radical being defined by the anti-architectural stance of having the right to question everything. He says that if he had not been sixteen in 1970, none of this would have happened.

For Dutt, the 1970s meant playing up rootlessness through a radical persona of being politically edgy while at the same time being a roadie rockstar, as a brazen transgressive subversion of Bengali *bhadralok* tradition, while performing urban chaos itself the place to be in through one's life. There is in Dutt's persona as music star, actor and filmmaker the hint of transgressive moral danger, a promise that things will always be shaky and unstable when he is around, expressing the occult libidinal desires of a mass society repressed by stifling tradition. This *image* of derring-do to question every morality against pleasure, a promise of social structures being shattered by a desirous body brooking no prohibition, promising the ruination of the desiring body in extreme *jouissance* bordering on cannibal desire, its ruination in borderline ambiguities of carnality wanting to go public and at the last moment withdrawing into conservatism, is the very 'dark' openness, that, has as its flipside, the ability to remain receptive to a plurality of material pleasures as trickster-as-connoisseur.

Thus, there is across Dutt's work a shapeshifting 'actor' – his songs are cinematic too, his son+image complex imbued with embodied 'liveness' and autobiographical immediacy – I have experienced this in my life, or I have experienced this as a milieu in which I have been immersed in very deeply. Now an alcoholic dirty man, next an Americanized hipster, then a middle-class door-to-door salesman returning home after a hard day's work, then a corrupt bourgeois patriarch, then again a corrupt policeman. Or sometimes a rockstar promising wild sexual encounters, sometimes a maudlin middle-class lover ruminating about lost love. And of course . . . a *bhadralok* – as the book's ontological social function – deterrence as pacifism, tarrying before acting. The multiplicity of white light refracted by the Dutt prism can even become a young boy or many religions – Christianity and Islam.

Thus, this is a multimedia extravaganza of differing accents, the authenticity of which is borne out by the only possible measure of such things – the mass public, cutting across class or caste, age, gender, religion, countries, cultures and, above all, personalities, publicly announcing that Dutt's songs and films or plays express their life experiences to a T. The artist's shapeshifting documents the 1970s' *ground* of political radicalism – a society cracking along different lines of desire in intense individuation. Sex, music and revolution are all media for this crumbling – equally. Or rather, as one may extrapolate from Althusser – cultural, not political, economy might articulate the determination by the economic in the last instance, something that Baudrillard demonstrates masterfully – as any anthropologist knows, culture is the medium of economic distribution of value, sense value (Althusser 1985; Baudrillard 1976; Ranciére 2013).

At the turn of 1968, Herbert Marcuse postulated the idea of a post-revolutionary 'Psychic Thermidor' countered by the pre-rational, by an *instinctual* life that rebirths the rebellious spirit in conservative times. When the Dialectic flattens towards universal instrumental reason, then the way out is something more ersatz, *instinct* (Habermas 1980). The world is alive in a million ways, now directly accessible in a 'permissive society', creating anxiety but also challenging intelligence to twist and turn intuitively to surf the unstable. Each moment of the persona is a play of light refracting into many *avatars|avatars* polarized back into Dutt – theatre, philosophy, insurgency, sex, alcohol, cigarettes, cinema, cosmopolitan hip, *noir* fiction, Bengal, America, Rabindra sangeet, rock, folk. Significantly, Marcuse's 'instinct' overlaps with key contemporary philosophical ideas – Deleuze's *larval* (Deleuze 1994) or earlier still Simondon's plane of the Super-individual where the Individual synthesizes the terror of Pre-Individual unformed sense perceptions (Grosz 2017). Or Lyotard's *figure*. Or even Scott Bukatman's 'terminal identity' as the self-as-pixel-containing-all-data (Bukatman 1993).

Thus, Westernization or Americanization was never at stake for Dutt, but rather being modern, owning up to everything he has been passionate about. Radical corporeal movements are symptoms of a struggle against a prohibitive cultural unconscious in favour of honestly belonging to *my* world. As Harald Szeemann, the legendary art curator who introduced Conceptual Minimal art to the world in the seismic 1969 *Live in Your Head: When Attitudes Become Form* show at the Kunsthalle Bern, would say:

> Hippiedom, rocker existence, the use of drugs had to come to affect the behaviour of a young generation of artists. (Szeemann 1969)

While extreme corporeality is generally a singular act, in Dutt's case this wildness is not just a literally rocking personality but above all an attempt to be the fracturing surface of a unified surface, a total epoch, into many faces. Therefore, the wild surface of Dutt's work, the many people Dutt is in mass noise, is more a matter of desire-for-difference on a single plane of history. This results in three *political* outcomes – first, it destroys the idea that the public face of the 'historically significant' be unified, *uniform* and above all sober or wild only in political excitation in ideologies; second, it plays the ontology of the political as just *image* of persona to its hilt, emptying it of any substance, showing up the full force of the political as charismatic image, not distracted by idealism – the only responsibility in pop is to get the *effect* right; and finally, he shows up the political as a ghostly spread of affect, a vague after-image of mass noise, impossible to 'represent' in discrete ideologies. Indeed, this *not taking sides* becomes a sign of *political probity* for the young from the 1970s onwards. The mass wants to see *all* as the ground for politics; the mass knows all *sides* lead to instrumental reason.

Nimbleness is of the essence here. Dutt forever chooses nimble bodies to act in his films (here, he continues his mentor Mrinal Sen's project of working with the youth body of the times). And he says an actor must know how to act, jump, run, dance, sing, play musical instruments. In short, an actor must be able to roll with the warping flux of mass noise, unpredictable all the way. A world of partial objects, fleeting but strong reflections, a field of continuously blooming different subject-object relationships – *subjectiles* and *objectiles*, affectively affirmed serially as aesthetic truths (Cache 1995). This is a world beyond ideology's rote-memory-learnt traditions of truth, a world where the individual considers living all differences as authenticity. Dutt has repeatedly emphasized the need of the moment as the creation of intelligent middling popular culture – modern, material, hip. He invokes Marx admiringly – everything must change. And Mao – the smaller contradiction can sometimes become the greater contradiction.

Therefore, the great gift American pop endowed the 1970s with – if everything must change and the small becomes the big, this can only mean that from now on all will be pop. And all politics will be a battle of the *image* since, in pop, there is no time for images to become flesh or discourse. Thus, this chapter is not about Dutt, the person, but Dutt as a series of images projected by him as the ground of Indic histories from the 1970s onwards. This chapter is about delicious paradoxes of the senses in pop, where if Che's face as an image has some political substance, then Dutt invoking a Naxal revolutionary somewhere politicizes the image of Dutt playing a man addicted to seducing young girls elsewhere. Thus, this chapter is about monstrous subliminal images in the mutual inflection of pop *avatar*s. Such is the 'Truth' of the politics of our times . . . beginning 1970s. Think of a 'terrorist chic' porn film like Bruce LaBruce's *Raspberry Reich* that fantasizes a raunchy Wilhelm Reich-inspired gay revolution in the Baader-Meinhof Complex (Selzer 1979). Or in another register, the disco carnal funk of Isaac Hayes speeded up becomes the syncopated excitement of an intense car chase. Deleuze and Guattari define pop as an ideal assemblage that allows you to make maximum connections across differences – high or low, animal or human, genders, cultures and so on (Deleuze and Guattari 1987).

Thus, the Dutt persona is an archive of a new public *individual* and cascading generations who would remain forever youthful from the 1970s onwards. The pop revolution of the middle class rebelling against the older reformist political order meant older regimes of rites of passage giving way to a generalized life in a pop 'culturalism' of sorts, *to define one's life not by timeless morality but by endless being-washed-away by pop media flows* that are by definition youthful. Szeemann, about his *Attitudes* show – he works towards a museum of obsessions. He would note in his curatorial note:

This new artwork incorporated from this social anti-form the tendency to contemplate, on the one hand, on the other hand, action based on the glorification of the physical and creative ego.

Szeemann observes about the art at the *Attitudes* show that it consists entirely of 'attitudes' to *everything* as culture – the city, industry, garbage, every commodity and, above all, 'nature'.

The 'action' Szeemann refers to above is obviously in the same register as the 'instincts', Marcuse's antidote to 'Psychic Thermidor'. A city might be mapped in a sort of Duchampian electric contemplation of things at certain 'banal' sites, exploding consciousness, liberating the unconscious – the city composed of 'readymade' sites and the physical performance of affects, the creative ego, responding to sites are simultaneous affairs (Roberts 2007). One recalls the 'live' youthful wildness of the famous tram sequence in Mrinal Sen's *Interview* – anti-form is the structure of the everyday. The city everyday has become pop 'attractive' to be caught live casually and presented as cinema to audiences (Gunning 1990). There is not much difference between Duchamp signing the urinal to make it an artwork and the live camera capturing the banal as 'attractive' cinema. The General Intellect is now clever enough to be stimulated by such a thing (Dyer-Witheford 1999).

Cinema as archive

It was at the start of the Thermidor of the 1980s, with the CPI (M) firmly in political power in Bengal, that Dutt began his career as a film actor. Previously, Dutt had descended to Calcutta at the turn of the 1970s, after a public school education at St Paul's School in Darjeeling, followed by a career on the Calcutta stage as an experimenter of radical theatre – Genet, Sartre, Weiss, above all, Brecht, as well as radical versions of Shakespeare, among others. Mrinal Sen, the doyen of Marxist filmmakers in India, would through the decade restlessly circle around the sites of social turbulence, post-Naxalbari, to see what was transpiring in such sites. Cast after Sen saw Dutt at the rehearsal of Peter Weiss's *Marat/Sade* at the Max Mueller Bhavan, Calcutta, the actor's turn in *Chalchitra* won for him the Best New Actor award at the Venice Film Festival of 1981, with Italo Calvino heading the jury. The film introduced a new restless urban young body tramping the streets of Calcutta, more loosely articulated than actors of earlier times portraying radical youth temperaments, such as Dhritiman Chatterjee. This body has now turned its radical eye to journalism in cue with a general shift of youth radicalism towards media as the site of a new politics. From then on, Dutt would become an intimate collaborator of Sen's, a friend and a frequently contrarian interlocutor right until Sen's death in 2018 (Bhaumik 2023).

In Dutt's films, the city of Calcutta, gifted to him by filmmaker Mrinal Sen, as Dutt would put it, and honed by his training in theatre under the radical experimenter Badal Sircar in the 1970s, who told him to soak in Calcutta, the lives of its people, in order to be a good actor (Katyal 2015), is always a principal character as 'cognitive map' of the city through deep personal experience in postmodern noise (Jameson 1990). This is almost *flânerie* as theatre technique and a training in shapeshifting across the mass, taking on all its personae as a new politics of a flatter and *intimate* democracy. Deleuze and Guattari speak of the positive, life-affirming primal desire of wanting to be multiplicity in the enchantment by difference, the marvellous. Acting would now need a leap of faith into multiplicity, to dispel the illusion that there is some void in the universe. Pop means there is no void.

Here, I take up about two documents that are literally Dutt's archive of the 1970s – his 2012 film *Dutta vs Dutta* and his script for the unmade film *Ghare Baire 71* written a little before that. *Dutta vs Dutta* chronicles autobiographically Dutt's coming of age in the 1970s amidst the genteel decline of family fortunes, the familial order being torn apart by his lawyer father's alcoholism and adultery, the youth of the family turning to Naxalism and a generalized 1970s Calcutta of marijuana-smoking countercultural radical intellectuals (sometimes gay), defined by anti-Vietnam protests, Sartre, Che and Communist Party of India (Marxist-Leninist) (CPI [M-L]) armed insurgency among many other things. The film ends with Dutt telling his father, now paralyzed in a wheelchair, that he has been offered a role in a film by Mrinal Sen. In a key scene, Dutt, playing his own father, an ardent supporter of Indira Gandhi, goes to jail for obstructing the police wanting to search his house for a hidden Naxalite (who, of course, is there, having been given shelter by Dutt the character).

Inasmuch as this absurdist episode is an affectionate *redux* of hard histories, it also hints at lines being blurred between dogmas, of reality being more complex and many-faceted than political histories of the time would admit.

Indeed, the film points out towards an *arché*-political that places feudal-bourgeois decline, Bengali insurgency, American counterculture, smoking pot, homosexuality, adultery 1970s style and so on as equal constituents of the political era defined by a *generalized* radical sensorium, as equal makers of Anjan Dutt as an archive of the 1970s (Gourgouris 2017). More explicitly, there is a hidden history of a general public turbulence that such movements draw upon, of public empathies of patronage, support and shelter driven by the simple dictum — this is wrong. Or, more enigmatically, the divides within the State itself. Pop, for Dutt, is perpetually bent. One might say pop is forever queer.

Ghare Baire 71 was planned as an adaptation of Tagore's novel that had earlier been adapted by Satyajit Ray, but now updated for 1970s Calcutta, more particularly to the ethos of the Naxal movement. Nikhilesh was supposed to be a liberal right-of-centre lawyer, while Sandip was slated to be a charismatic but cynical Naxalite. Bimala was to be a suburban girl who blooms through her affair with Nikhilesh into a short-haired, pot-smoking, pop music-listening countercultural feminist. Undoubtedly inspired by real people Dutt knew in the 1970s, the proposed film was going to be yet another opening up of the political to a plurality of social and cultural forces of the 1970s beyond the organized political, a complex palimpsest of monstrous alliances happening against the grain of ideology. Dutt was, to paraphrase Deleuze, intent on buggering the official 'party' line of analysis of the 1970s from behind.

Dutt is adamant about his opposition to violence as a political solution to things. He says he was moulded by the famous Sartre-Camus debate about revolutionary violence, with him siding with Camus against Sartre (Aronson 2005). He attended the famous Calcutta Maidan rally of 1969, where Charu Majumdar announced the formation of the CPI (M-L). Majumdar's speech left Dutt unimpressed (Samaddar 2018). But in all this, he is emphatic about learning a lot from the Naxal movement, which taught him what was wrong with the political order in India. And despite his opposition to political violence, Dutt says he admires the Baader-Meinhof for their almost juridical mode of armed revolution as well as for their pop heroism (remember Thomas Dellert's silkscreen painting made for Warhol around the photographs of RAF members?) (Dirke 2008) against the questionable loose dogmatic class analyses of Indian history @ Naxalbari.

Dutt would, in the 2000s and 2010s, become a leading filmmaker of a new generation of Bengali cinema with critically and commercially successful films such as *The Bong Connection, Chalo Let's Go, Madly Bangalee* and *Ranjana Ami Ar Ashbona* (referring to the title of what is probably Dutt's most iconic song). These films launched the careers of young filmmakers such as Srijit Mukherjee and Mainak Bhaumik, as well as the acting careers of many who would top Bengali cinema in the years to come. *Ranjana . . .* won a National Award for Best Bengali Feature, a Special Jury Award for Dutt himself and a National Award for Best Music for his son Neel Dutt. There is in Dutt's films an abiding sense of *duty* to show up the playful flamboyance of confused youth desire, as there is a duty towards playing up *jouissance* in the material excesses of the modern, its amoral beauty, a beauty that is mostly visible in the decadence of failed corporeal radicalism, of which the vampire is the greatest symbol. His films are almost as a rule filled up with many *individuating* presences caught 'live' in a canny telescoping of actor autobiography and film character, all going in different directions, materially and corporeally. This is an 'extreme' cinema marked by compassion, almost like the romantic excess of the corporeal and psychic decadence of a Cocteau film.

Poetry or Music as archive

The 1990s saw the full political fruition of the 1970s circulating in Dutt's biography. He became part of a new generation of Bengali pop music performers who galvanized mass audiences towards newer and more open expressions of material desires. Dutt says that he had not been impressed with the avant-garde extremism of Hungryalist poets of the 1960s (Bose 2023). Instead, he found the political song-making of a Dylan, a Seeger or a Cohen more conducive towards producing a radical mass populist music. However, he says Hungryalists like Sandipan Chattopadhyay and Dipak Majumdar had been his mentors in the 1970s by way of introducing him to world literature and music. Neither was Dutt impressed with the pop civic music of a band such as Moheener Ghoraguli, who had a cult following through the 1970s and 1980s. Moheener bridged the history of Bengali poetry and lyric writing across the *gana-sangit* of the Indian People's Theatre Association (IPTA), the *Kallol Jug* of Jibanananda Das and Naxalbari, while the Hungryalists revolted against Tagore and *Kallol* poets through a gritty deconstructive poetry of sounds and words of sensorially or sexually repressed bodies, bodies ground down by deprivations of the senses – hunger, labour, boredom, Puritanism (Bhattacharya 2017; Banerjee 2019). Dutt's music bumps along the spectrum – Dylan materialist irony or Hungryalist gruff carnal directness.

Dutt's own moment of cultural megastardom began ambiguously as he responded to the mass public popularity of Suman Chattopadhyay's pop music. Chattopadhyay remains a friend of Dutt's till date. On the one hand, Chattopadhyay held, as Dutt did, that Bengali music had not lived up to radical times, paving the way for his music inspired by Dylan's 'A Hard Rain's a-Gonna Fall', a Dylan that Dutt too swears by. On the other hand, Chattopadhyay was heavily inspired by the gruff scatological liberatory grind of Hungryalism. Dutt and Chattopadhyay are both legacies of *a* Calcutta of the 1960s, the Calcutta of Ginsberg and the Hungryalists, inflected by the radical poetics of the Beats, and of the beginning of Dylan's long-standing friendship with *baul* singers, first made explicit on the cover of *John Wesley Harding* (Bose 2016). Again Szeemann speaking about the artists in the Bern show:

> It is significant that some of the main representatives come from the American West Coast, which is particularly exposed to Eastern influences. (Szeemann 1969)

But there was much else of America circulating in 1970s Calcutta or Bengali culture – *noir*, Vietnam, Afro-Cool, Brando, Dean, Sinatra, Elvis, The Beatles, Scorsese, Coppola, Pacino, De Niro. But also a new Europe defined by new cultural stars such as Peter Weiss and Peter Brook and by a completely revamped radical reading of Brecht through a non-Marxist lens – the Brecht of radical bodily performances, the American Brecht of Kurt Weill's jazz. This is a vanguard moment for the Americanization of the radical Indic body, something that is now commonsensically ubiquitous in our times.

Of course, music would inextricably weave the fabric of Dutt's cinema. *Ranjana Ami Ar Ashbona* starred giants of Indian rock music such as Amyt Datta, Nondon Bagchi and Lew Hilt in lead roles. Bagchi and Hilt had been members of the legendary Calcutta rock band High that Dutt mentions admiringly when speaking of the music around him in the 1970s (Bhatia 2014). *Madly Bangalee, Ranjana* . . . and *Ami Ashbo Phirey* are set around rock bands. *Madly* . . . remains probably the best ever Indian film about the vicissitudes of the formation of a young rock band. In *The Bong Connection*, Dutt would court controversy and adulation in equal measures with a pop version of Tagore's *Pagla haowa*, leading to the acceptance of Tagore's music modulated to contemporary sounds as an acceptable mutation of the Bengali sonosphere.

More ontologically, all of Dutt's cinema is placed precisely in those 'story situations' in which the sentiments of his songs unroll, while his music is profoundly cinematic. *All is image.* We can here speak in Benjaminian terms of a *synaesthetic unconscious* (Gordon 2021), where the body on a *schizo walk* (Deleuze and Guattari 1977) absorbs the patterns in the noise of the city in all the registers of the senses. The Jamesonian cognitive mapping becomes a synaesthetic thing, something recalling Henri Lefebvre's *rhythmanalysis* project, where the body becomes a repository of the diverse rhythms that compose a city (Lefebvre 2004). As Scott Burton in his essay on the 'new' in Szeemann's 1969 show wrote:

> Art has been veritably *invaded* by life, if life means flux, change, chance, time, unpredictability. (Burton 1969)

Here, the real sense of Szeemann's epochal show's name would be literalized, both before and after the colon: *attitudes* will become form – a synaesthetic cognitive territory, captured in a particular attitude, would become a situational song or a film; the attitude arising from living in the *head*, from intense cerebro-sensory immersion in certain attractive situations (Szeemann 1969). This synaesthetic, defined by the *attitude*, is Anjan Dutt as a figure of history.

Dutt spoke at length about how he rebelled against orchestral arrangements of Bengali political and pop music, which on the whole favoured a generalized collective horizon for music or maudlin individual sentimentality. For him, the rock guitar and drums were better suited to the feverish excitement of life in cities, better suited to express the radical hopes, desires and frustrations of the massified individual living in a bewilderingly confusing and tough urban context. What Dutt's cinema and music catch is the 1970s urban as a peculiar distribution of bodies in the standardization of urban life – voices, gazes, things consumed, the same bus and tram travelled on every day, a job as a standard life horizon, the standardized horizon seen out of windows, as well as standardized expressions of suffering and disappointment, all measured as a set configuration of *distances* that remains more or less the same since the 1970s. In short, new urban myths. In short, Calcutta biopolitics acting and singing out – son(g)+image. The pop-ular of a mass becoming pop-ulation.

Only time will show how significant Dutt's interpellation of the masses by his wild pop, his making them dance excitedly in Dutt-as-their-own-*self-image*, was to the fall of the CPI (M) government in 2011. Dutt would make the divide between Partha Chatterjee's political society and Bengali *bhadralok* society less prominent. Even the neo-Bhadralok of the drawing room NRB cinema of the early 2000s, so eloquently analyzed by Moinak Biswas, would be part of this moment (Biswas 2011). Dutt's pop political importance for contemporary Bengali history would culminate in the sonic aesthetics of the 2014 *Hokkolorob* students' movement at Jadavpur University.

Dutt, the 1970s, concepts

First and foremost, Dutt's artistic career alerts us to the immediate need to jettison readings of the contemporary Indic as British postcolonial. It is above all American. Indeed, Dutt's own biography shows this transition from a British postcolonial at St Paul's, Darjeeling, to an Americanized Indian youth culture that took full flight in the 1970s. America brought two remarkable things into the Indic youth unconscious – pop and hipness defined by art historical things such as Happenings (which too were Duchampian in the sense of being defined by entropy, a deflation of the symbolic order) (Mercer 2007; Kaprow 2003). While the Happenings were an explicit part of Dutt's theatrical training, a new hip in becoming-everyday was very much an American contribution to Indian urban culture, an ambiguous interface of the insurgency of street pop|a discourse of defeat or defiance of bourgeois etiquette in pacifism (Bose 2020). A cool simplicity as intelligence, as the brain expressing itself in sharp pop ways, filling the senses-in-time sublimely – the essence of avant-garde as attitude. Think interface – Miles Davis's sartorial transformation from gentlemanly suit to aggressive street pop of World Music, *c.* 1970; James Dean jeans as White American working-class hip; and Che military fatigue.

Cultural history's entropic move into pop opened up the body across hierarchies of value to a 'general' noise that would, by definition, be, first, intermedial, since no single medium could express all the creative urges inspired by this noise in some totalizing *Gesamkunstwerk*, and second, a relentless production of artwork with everyday materiality *to fill the empty time of entropy*, a practice definitive of Conceptual artists' work. Dutt's manic serial production of pop would substantially answer to this description – the tribalism of the Global Village described by Marshall McLuhan, responding to mysterious signals from things in the noise through wild artmaking (McLuhan and Powers 1989). As my teacher of archaeology and anthropology, Shereen Ratnagar, had once remarked – in a village, they are always making things with their hands out of anything lying around. Indeed, Harald Szeemann would describe his curation as 'spiritual guest work' for the artists, and he himself would be described as a shaman of sorts by observers. Enigmatically, one of the sections of the *Attitudes* show would be called 'Mysticism and Shamanism' at first and would then be changed to 'Individual Mythologies' (Birnbaum 2005). By extension, one could say that the new pop artist of the 1970s was a shaman of sorts, playing the untotalizable noise of pop histories. The individual now becomes an entire system of mythologies that earlier would need a collective to enact.

The dark glasses by which Dutt is universally recognized. His totemic mask. The opacity of the look created by the dark glasses is the screen where the face relentlessly changes looks. The interface home|noise. One explodes out of repression in desire as a serial projection of *avatar* images, for the noise insists we totalize it in order to find a home there. Dutt inaugurates history as a flight of *figures* through scenarios, something described so marvellously by Jean-Francois Lyotard in his work on the postmodern condition (Lyotard 2011). Here, we don't get symbolic figures of ideology but merely gestures of radical energy in ecstasy of escaping the repressive apparatus. It is oculocentric even if synaesthetic, in line with Walter Benjamin's formulation of the *optical unconscious* as defining modernist urbanity (Krauss 1993) as well as with Bergson's dictum – matter is image (Bergson 1990; Herzog 2000). It is this oneiric simulacral *figure* fleeing across media noise that unifies Dutt into a single face remembered as a *readymade* in the mass unconscious – his dark glasses, which asks a single question, *always* – why do you want to look like the *avatar* I am? Why does your sexual wantonness of pop dance desire the mask of a Naxalite?

Here, we encounter a figure who occupies all positions in pop noise without belonging to any/one. Marcuse's *Psychic Thermidor* in the flattening of the

Enlightenment would imply a taking up of a Bartleby position as described by Deleuze of refusing to take sides with respect to all programmatic discourse – I would rather not. In *Chaalchitra Ekhon*, Dutt's paean to his cinematic mentor, Mrinal Sen, on his centennial year, a *redux* of his first film with Sen, there is an intense re-figuration of two aspects of their friendship – Dutt's resistance to Communism in his youth despite all irrational Death Drive attractions and Sen's gift of Calcutta to his young actor. Dutt turns Bartleby with respect to the ideologies of his time, and in that freedom, he is going to trawl the city for its 'attractions' intensely to push the system towards the White Light of exhaustion that alone can ensure the openness of a system to a future. But above all, to seduce and then 'betray' by not taking sides, a Bartleby in *jouissance* at variance with Deleuze's more stuck-up figure. Betrayal in the sense of defining seduction as exchange on the plane of the noise of ill-defined desire but *never* a politics to belong. Above all, the 'betrayals' that the new individual must sustain to live up to one's own potential in multiplicity. For one must enjoy many things and not get stuck in some idealized one. Jameson's definition of the postmodern by schizophrenia. Wisdom will follow if the betrayals are done well, ethically.

In short, to always betray the *image* of idealism, the audience's habitual belief that Eros must belong, to the point of *looking* cynical only to be redeemed by giving up. A betrayal that accuses idealism by forgiving the world for not giving us enough courage to exit the misery of belonging. This is a defeat accepted in a 'global' pacifism, where the *individual* totalized in pop knows he or she can destroy the world but does not, bowing to an ineffable 'historical' demand, a kindness way beyond the petty demands of conventional historical consciousness. It is when the sentiment 'Everybody I love you' sung out as the 1970s began, an 'everybody' which is literal and could only be felt as such in the world address of the American pop counterculture, is defeated that such a unilateral pacifism arises. With the failure of one's exhortations to the 'everybody' to:

Open up, open up
Baby let me in (Stills and Young 1970)

The only idealism here is defining peace in the world as every individual having *every thing* and the *everything* . . . on one's own terms, an impossible ideal, hence forever deferred. Instead, there are only passages here between various *avatar*s in pop noise, in-betweens that are only irony – Bartleby escaping capture saying, 'I am not that'. One is reminded of the great Nam June Paik's life interface of pop – split screen|Zen. What then holds this thing together is the thing with which Habermas finishes his piece on Marcuse – Marcuse on a hospital bed telling Habermas – look, I know wherein our most basic value judgements are rooted – in compassion, in our sense for the suffering for others (Habermas 1980). We are reminded of Lacan's enigmatic *nirvana* principle, where the foundational madness of our neural lives nevertheless somehow holds on in living on, resonant with the Buddha's philosophy of compassion as *nirvana*.

Rosalind Krauss very importantly characterizes early video art as narcissistic in that it endlessly fed back the artists' presence onto the video monitor. Then, she goes on to point out: narcissism is characterized, then, as the unchanging condition of perpetual frustration (Krauss 1976). This is because, at some point, the artist realizes the video image is a constructed one, not the artist as an authentic presence. Warhol is who would take Krauss's point to a radical conclusion – if the artist is impossible on the screen, then one might as well jettison the artist and replace him or her with fetish objects that too are the 'face' of the artist inasmuch as the artist identifies totally with the fetish. Instead of the self, a procession of endless pop images as *avatar*s of the artist. And by that token, the erotic attraction towards Che image, the revolutionary Bartleby opting out of 'Party' revolution, can be replaced by Che doing porn. Tagore being bestial, the Tagore whom Ritwik Ghatak celebrated as knowing more Bengali swear words than anyone else. Disguise, pastiche, betrayal. Mechanized Bakhtinian carnival of high becoming low automatized. The spectrum between the endless pop video apps of our time and Warhol's self-as-soup-can on the edge of exploding with a 'pop', going extinct.

The frustration of finding all versions of the self as 'constructed', the impossibility of the authentic/stability leads to the only solution possible – to become the world in manic pop desire/love for the world. The ego of *knowing* the world is jettisoned for an ego of *loving* the world . . . to the point of self-extinction – that old sacrificial logic of our finite body exhausted by multiplicity, or madness or Foucault experimenting with AIDS death and so on. Deleuze and Guattari say pop isn't easy – it's schizophrenia that begins with hypochondria. Indeed, only great compassion for the self-as-the-world can hold multiplicity together, the artist's self-compassion that mirrors the audience's need for self-compassion to survive the splitting in pop in an electronic openness. Through the concert/film the world becomes compassion/peace. Dutt's cinema and music has only one aim through the image of the artist falling apart in pop noise – to tell those feeling fear, guilt or despair in the excess of mass culture – don't kill yourself over these things, be compassionate towards yourself.

The spectres of the 1970s in Dutt/archive

The core of the logocentric archive of history – institutions defined by ideology – either as fetishized idealized political discourses or governance are in pop replaced by an irrational centre – *a shamanic flickering point giving off ever-transforming sensory pulsations*. Not power flowing centrifugally towards a name, but difference itself as kaleidoscopic centripetal signals. This is what abides in place of the 'archivable', names that stabilize history – cinema, music, literature, the State, politics, sexuality and so on – the nameless ghost in the machine. The name 'Anjan Dutt' does not correspond to the classical archive of names. Instead, like in *I'm Not Here*, the name is a spectral projection of masks, disguises, and forgeries that invite us to play along rather than stabilize the senses in older discourses of 'historical importance' – the old ethical hero of history *as image* who will teach us to be ideal people in a very old moral sense. The aim is to escape the name/passport photo, identity, as the wellspring of both nation and conventional politics of citizenship. One dreams of crashing the archive ontologically – relentless disguise cannot form a state/society since the identifiable citizen or individual is impossible. What we get instead is an archive of a population shapeshifting under the cruel pressure of relentlessly 'attractive' materiality, pop playing the intensity of nature, forcing the population to look flux – the Mission Impossible of pop histories. Here, we need to respond to Jason Lindsey postulating the Baudrillardian simulacrum, the pop, the *figure*, as the proper political expression of the 'silent majorities'. For the *figure* has force, indeed the memory of the force of all previous revolutionary desires, indeed their *essence*, always a synaesthetic image-in-multiplicity (Lindsey 2007).

Dutt-as-archive-of-the-long 1970s is a unique one that has lived up to the potential of the pop noise that the decade inaugurated in all its multifarious possibilities. As the most exhaustive definer of the truth of politics as continuously producing differing images defined by an *art of intensive intentions* of the time (Szeemann's term for what art of his time should have been all about (Biryukova 2017)), however imperfectly and sketchily. Across the many Thermidors of modern Indic histories – a global post–Second World War Thermidor, the post-Nationalist Thermidor, the Bengal Thermidor of the CPI (M) in power, and now the post-liberalization Thermidor defined by the rise of the Hindu Right Wing. Only this archive has singularly sublimated the pop *political potential* of the 1970s to *historical significance* on the *mass scale popular* as well as critical acclaim. Dutt's is a remarkable artistic career, very definitely a pop 'minor' art in all respects, say, to the 'Major' of Satyajit Ray's classical-modern multimedia genius (Deleuze and Guattari 1986). He takes the liveness of Sen's cinema to create an art of pop *kinesis* between radical bodies but jettisons Communism towards the individual, pop, taken to White Noise. He has done this in the radical frontal, in the urgency of the excess of pop and in its perpetual slipping away as well as in the urgency of the political moment intersecting with something as banal as the urgency of the blooming erotic young body. 'Perhaps the only quality that unifies the artists in this show is their urgency', writes Burton in the Catalogue for *Attitudes*. And this pop urgency, un-focusable, defines the 'new' of the time – Counterculture, May 68, Vietnam (Burton 1969).

It is a lifetime's crafting of life across many hard decisions – not to leave Calcutta for the West or Bombay (when most of his creative cohort had left Calcutta by the 1990s); to survive the rejections of his career as an actor and retain his creative drives. Szeemann says of the European component of his show – the lack of a centre always prompts more artists to stay in their hometowns and against all ideas of the respective society (Szeemann 1969). The 'hometown' has become multiplicitous in the interface: pop revolution of historical critique|the massification of cities in the failure of reformist developmentalism. But the flipside of multiplicity's multi-hued glory is an artisanal working away to live up to this glory – to make one's body become the everyday bodies of labour, defeat, desire and disappointment and their monstrous opposites. Above all, the artisanal sustains a 'place' in some irrational affect flow in a world falling apart. What 'acting' is all about. An ambiguous interface opens up – acting as shapeshifting into sweaty and dusty labour in the bored everyday|pop as actor shapeshifting across the Eros of sensory urban material excesses. This is a new politics of labour in the highest or most intense contradictions of Capital. The way it should always be – pop.

But let us also see the Dutt as the pop intermedial flexible heart of digital cyberspace, pop noise centralized is also Capital centralized to unprecedented scales. Let us think of totalizing culture to the frontiers of White Noise as the operational logic of cyberspace – form glitching into White Noise. Thus, the real *political* here lies in *sustaining* the excess of pop in the analogue human body at the intensities of cyberspace. In sustaining radical Individuation at all costs against all social pieties. Pop as long preparation for cyberspace. Cyberspace as the archive of merely the points of sustenance of pop noise – from Dutt to the hacker. An Individual is conceived in the womb of the 1970s' Liberation of history into pop, whose vague outlines we can now begin to see in contemporary cyberscape cultures – Web 2.0, the pop *avatar* of cyberspace, built on subsuming all extinctions of heroisms-as-pop until the Big Bang. The final One of human history.

A certain history of Bengal has long since gone ahead into advanced decline. The key enigmatic archival question to be asked is: How does the decline of an entire culture come to be encompassed by *One* figure of redemption of the repressed youth wildness living hypocritically in Hindu/Tagorean/British postcolonial Bengal when all had gone to America from the 1970s onwards? What was that historic moment of the 1990s when this repressed history of America in Bengali (and even Indic) senses came to be centred around Dutt's cultural superstardom in absolutely singular ways? But also, to wonder why it is that of all the postmodern stars India has produced since the 1970s, Dutt is the only artist from the 1970s generation who has archived the *proper form* of the 'Truth' of the global pop India became in the 1970s. Finally, what is this long historical transition beginning in the 1970s that Dutt symbolizes for the public over *such a long time*? A temptation to be destroyed by one's pop desires abides, so revolutionary was pop exploding in the 1970s, a 'Truth' that none can negate in honesty to one's times.

A 'final' ontology of universal freedom was reached in the 1970s, against the always opting for defining revolution as conventional politics instead of taking up the challenge of pop revolution – opting for the socialist bullet instead of being destroyed more radically by multiplicity, abbreviating the hubris of tragedy as a social thing instead of the original meaning of tragedy in being destroyed by the nature gods, the *arché*-tragedy – dying in overstimulus in nature within us – our senses. Culturally, pop achieves the return of the nature gods by flattening value hierarchies and letting in various degrees of the popular and avant-garde noise to define history, to push the formation of singular objects as high cultural value towards anti-form, chaos. There is an honesty in pop that restores tragedy to its original sense as cosmic noise, nature as madness – Led Zeppelin, against the grammar of tragedy as staged theatre where history is conveniently made anthropocentric in the social *against* nature. Pop's championing the *deeply personal neural individual* over symbolic sociocentrism thus abolishes the division between Reason and nature and restores the human to the One.

The One becomes an enigmatic mathematical calculus of the flux of the colonial/global histories of Bengal/India – the Enlightenment project begins in colonial Calcutta/India, it keeps on ending in the persona of a single star who alone encompassed the radical pop potentials of that project, by instinctively staying on in Calcutta against the tide of the times. The talismanic figure of this 'late style' of Bengali modernity in extinction is the poetics of a figure that communist Mrinal Sen and pop Anjan Dutt share substantially – the *ulongo* man – the shamelessly naked man, cannibal, the bestial, who wants to throw off all structural/architectural constraints and perform instinctual impulses randomly (Said 2007). Sen famously recounted on multiple occasions, as autobiography and film-scenes-as-quotation, his story of going completely naked in front of a mirror when frustrated with his job as a salesman, and Dutt uses this word many times in his songs to critique social Puritanism – one has to get naked to have sex, and one dies naked, so why censor. To go pop in wanton nakedness – electric connections with *all* the fetishes of one's desire at once – *ulongo* as shaman. To play pop extinction as the individual true to history.

One is reminded of an *ulongo* interface – *Chalchitra*-as-interface: the bestial nakedness of *Marat/Sade* instigating the Left to forcibly shut down Dutt's performance of the play, leading Dutt to do the film|Sen making Dutt sustain his story enacted right at the beginning of the film, wickedly testing his neophyte actor. With a difference of course – Sen says 'I am angry', I want to tear off my clothes, Dutt says 'I am too desirous', I want to tear off my clothes. Somewhere the two intersect. To become animal in the sudden desire to believe that humans have a natural ecology free from Capital, to realize this is make-believe and make a film/become an actor instead. An archival conundrum – *ulongo* exterior (the classical archive yielding nothing)/shamanic interior (the pop archive yielding only fakes).

The year is 1980 – the long 1970s commences its interminable archival journey towards extinction.

Notes

Foreword

1 See, in particular, the discussion of the work of Jason Stanley in Hediger and Simon (2024).

2 On the neo-colonial undertow of the neo-conservative project for the export of democracy, see Muppidi (2012).

3 For a study of Indian-Swiss film/tourism relations, see Schneider (2024, 27–40).

Introduction

1 Snehalata Reddy (1932–77), better known for her role in *Samskara* (1970), the celebrated Kannada New Wave film made by her husband Pattabhirama Reddy, was subjected to imprisonment without trial during the Emergency. Her chronic asthma deteriorated, and the lack of medical attention led to her death a few days after her release.

2 Ashish Rajadhyaksha deployed this expression in the context of Andhra Pradesh's Chunduru massacre of 1991, where an act of defiance of caste within the exhibition space led to violence against Dalits. He also referred to the nomadic, bohemian life and death of John Abraham, whose existence contributed to the making of his iconic last film *Amma Ariyan* (1986) (Rajadhyaksha 2000: 295).

Chapter 1

1 Open letter by K.A. Abbas to M.K. Gandhi in *Filmindia* (October 1939), reprinted in Bandyopadhyay (1993).

2 Supreme Court of India, *Ramesh S/O Chotalal Dalal vs Union Of India & Ors* on 16 February 1988.

3 Report of Khosla Committee on film Censorship, Section 8.40, p. 122.

4   Supreme Court of India, *K.A. Abbas vs The Union Of India & Anr* on 24
     September 1970, para 7.

5   *K.A. Abbas vs The Union Of India & Anr*; emphasis mine.

6   Sanjiv Shah, who joined FTII in late 1977 (admissions had been delayed due to
     the 1977 strike, which was followed by yet another strike a month after he joined)
     and left in 1982, recalls that the 'apolitical nature of the student body as a whole'
     was especially notable, coming as he did from Ahmedabad, which had during
     the 1973 Navnirman movement seen both Centre for Environment Planning
     and Technology (CEPT) and National Institute of Design (NID) 'forbidding the
     students from engaging with the protesters'. Shah sees the difference between
     these and institutes that had started to 'impart education for professions that were
     not mainstream' and so 'were seen as esoteric, and which somewhere attracted
     the more privileged, and the larger organized political groups saw little gain in
     engaging with these institutes. And these institutes promoted, even revelled in,
     exclusion of the outside'. Email to the author dated 20 November 2021.

7   Both this and the following quotation are from Shah (2014, 198, 227).

8   See Anil Mehta on the need for 'co-authorship' acknowledgment with
     cinematographers at https://www.youtube.com/watch?v=wrqOO1R2LXo.

9   See, in particular, battles by screenwriters and music composers that led in
     2012 to significant amendments to the Copyright Act, 1957. Anjum Rajabali
     and the Progressive Writers Group (PWG) within the Film Writers Association
     fought for writers retaining their right over screenplays and lyrics, leading to
     an amendment to Section 18 of the Act, asserting that 'the author of the literary
     or musical work included in a cinematograph film shall not assign or waive
     the right to receive royalties to be shared on an equal basis with the assignee
     of copyright for the utilization of such work in any form other than for the
     communication to the public of the work along with the cinematograph film
     in a cinema hall'. Likewise, the movement of the Indian Performing Rights
     Society (IPRS) to amend the copyright law to address song remixes led to the
     amendment of Section 31-c (Statutory License for Cover versions).

10 All quotations are from Satyajit Ray's controversial essay, 'An Indian New Wave?',
     in *Our Films, Their Films*, 81–99.

11 See Steyerl (2016).

12 Report of Committee on Public Undertakings (1975–76), 3–4.

13 Report of Committee on Public Undertakings (1975–76), 16.

14 Supreme Court of India, *Ramesh S/O Chotalal Dalal vs Union Of India & Ors* on
     16 February 1988.

Chapter 2

1 New Delhi: Ministry of Information and Broadcasting, Govt. of India, August 1977.

2 *All India Reporter*, Supreme Court section (1971), 495.

3 *Report of the Enquiry Committee on Film Censorship* (1969), para 8.11.

4 The censorship rules were framed by the bureaucrats through powers vested in them by the Cinematograph Act 1952. The Cinematograph Act was an umbrella document, and the Censorship Rules were the means to operationalizing it. Moreover, the CBFC also formulated 'Guidelines' outlining subjects that were unacceptable. The Rules and Guidelines are part and parcel of the same mechanism. These are revised periodically.

5 *White Paper* (1977), 84. Note that films certified 'U' can be shown to any audience while films certified 'A' can be shown only to persons above eighteen years of age.

6 N. S. Thapa, who was the Regional Officer of the Bombay Regional Office between 1972 and 1976, reminisces that *Sholay* was granted an 'A' certificate by the Examining Committee on account of excessive violence. 'Even before I reached the office, G P Sippy's man was there asking for a withdrawal of the application. Next day, a top politician called to tell us to pass the film without referring it to the revising committee. . . . I was shocked by the political interference in the work of the Board and returned to my original post at FD' [Quoted by Shoma A. Chatterjee in her article 'Scissorhands' in *The Statesman*, 8th Day (Sunday Magazine), Calcutta, dated 11 July 2004].

7 The director reminisces: 'During the Emergency in 1975, the film *Aandhi* was banned. I was at the Moscow Film Festival where the film was to be shown. I received orders that the film had been banned and must not be shown at the festival. We were also told that all posters and publicity material must be removed' (Gulzar, Nihalani, and Chatterjee. 2003, 425).

8 *White Paper* (1977), 85.

9 *White Paper* (1977), 85–7.

10 *White Paper* (1977), 85.

11 As told by Shabnam Sukhdev, daughter of S. Sukhdev, to Dr Camille Deprez in 2015. https://digital.lib.hkbu.edu.hk/documentary-film/sukhdev.php (accessed 21 December 2023).

12 *White Paper* (1977), 97–8.

13 *White Paper* (1977), 89–100.

14 Report of the Regional Board of Film Censors, Hyderabad, September 1975 and *Deccan Herald*, 15 August 1977.

15 *The Hindu*, 6 February 2020.

16 *Indian Express*. 16 September 2010.

17 As Anand revealed in a symposium organized by the Indian Institute of Mass Communication and Directorate of Film Festivals on 10 January 1979, during the 7th International Film Festival at New Delhi (*Symposium* 1979, 130).

18 'I do not know the reason, but one of the members unofficially informed me that it might injure the prestige of India in the international world', as Utpalendu revealed at the aforementioned symposium on 9 January 1979, during the 7th International Film Festival at New Delhi (*Symposium* 1979, 107).

19 *Frontier* (Weekly edited by Samar Sen), Calcutta, 29 July 1978.

20 *Times of India*, 2 February 1982.

21 *Times of India*, 8 August 1984.

22 *Hindustan Times*, 12 September 1985.

23 *Indian Express*, 11 April 1989.

24 A quasi-judicial body, which, if appealed to, could examine and overturn CBFC rulings. FCAT verdicts were binding on CBFC. Only the judiciary could retain or overturn FCAT verdicts. FCAT is now defunct.

25 Bhaskar Ghosh's article "Cuts, Snips and Bans" in Gulzar, Nihalani, and Chatterjee (2003).

26 *Times of India*, 27 September 1998.

27 *Times of India*, 20 July 1994.

28 *Times of India*, 20 July 1994.

29 Press Release of *People's Media Initiative*, 4 March 2003.

30 www.AFP/sify.com, 7 August 2004.

31 Details available on www.patwardhan.com.

32 Report of the Committee of Experts chaired by Shyam Benegal. https://mib.gov.in/sites/default/files/Shyam_Benegal_committee_Report_compressed_0.pdf. Retrieved on 19 April 2019.

33 https://www.scconline.com/blog/post/2021/03/27/judicial-censorship/. Retrieved on 19 April 2019.

Chapter 3

1 In common parlance, 'adda' is a place for a free-for-all discussion among like-minded members of a group. In 2011, filmmakers Surjo Deb and Ranjan Palit made a documentary titled *Adda: Calcutta, Kolkata*, which was screened at several film festivals around the world. *Kolkatar Adda* is a Bengali book edited

by Samarendra Das (2002) and *Adda!: The College Street Coffee House* is a Kindle book in English authored by Mala Mukerjee and Jael Silliman (2020). India Coffee House is one of the cultural landmarks of India. Bidi is a type of cheap cigarette of unprocessed tobacco wrapped in leaves.

2 The case of Amrit Nahata's film *Kissa Kursi Ka* is well known for how its prints were destroyed by the government during the Emergency.

Chapter 4

1 For a general history of the Emergency and Jayaprakash Narayan (JP) movement, read Chandra, Mukherjee, and Mukherjee (2008, 311–30). For specifics, read Sinha (1977), Tarlo (2003), Chandra (2003), Prakash (2018), Nandy (1980, 112–30), Kaviraj (1986, 1697–708), Rajagopal (2011, 1003–49.)

2 Also see, Ramakrishna (1976, 1 and 10). In a meeting, Shukla urged the filmmakers 'to eschew narrow and selfish money-making ways and demonstrate their social and national responsibilities'. He also told the industry 'not to lean too much on Government but to solve their own problems', and 'to show initiative and enterprise' (10). For details on the negative impact of censorship policy, see 'Production Work Plummets Down, Flow of finance halts in Bombay', 1976. The flow of funds, both from financiers and distributors, had virtually halted, resulting in over 200 pictures in Hindi in various stages of production being stranded and the launching of new films coming down drastically. The worst hit were casual workers like junior artistes, technicians and musicians. This was happening as financiers were not sure of the fate of the film they would help produce.

3 Some of the popular Hindi films during this period include *Sholay, Deewar, Aandhi, Julie, Jai Santoshi Maa* (all from 1975), *Kabhi Kabhie, Kalicharan, Mehbooba, Laila Majnu, Chhoti Si Baat* (all 1976), *Amar Akbar Anthony, Dharam Veer, Shirdi Ke Sai Baba*, and *Dulhan Wahi Jo Piya Man Bhaaye* (all 1977). Veena Das wrote an essay on the unprecedented popularity and commercial success *Jai Santoshi Maa* received, after *Sholay* and *Deewar*. See Das (1981, 43–56).

4 The censorship on films was also extended to film journals, which were advised 'to evolve a code of self-regulation' with the assistance of the chairman of the Censor Board and the Chief Press Censor (152). As per guidelines drawn up by the Press Information Bureau, 'journals would not comment on or even mention, films that were refused certificates by the Censor Board, or make any reference

to difficulties faced by individual producers or actors as a result of government orders' (154). Such control was extended to publicity material as well.

5   While *Kissa Kursi Ka* and *Aandhi* have been widely covered, *Andolan* does not find much mention. On a preliminary search done on Google, one gets few clips from the movie, mostly its songs, and the first seven minutes of the feature film on YouTube. Directed by Lekh Tandon, the film starred Rakesh Pandey (*Sara Aakash*-fame) and Neetu Singh. The film is dedicated to the 'Immortal Sons of Mother India who, with their unique sacrifices, gave us the right to live in an atmosphere of freedom'. The movie narrates the story of a revolutionary during the Quit India movement (1942). It goes into flashback and is narrated by an old man to a bunch of youngsters sitting in a public park. As credits scroll down, images of revolutionaries like Chandra Shekhar Azad, Madan Lal Dhingra, Ram Prasad Bismil, Sukhdev, Rajguru, Bhagat Singh and many others show up, with Bismil's poem *Dar-o-Diwar Pe Hasrat Se Nazar Karte Hain*, played in the background. Another song, written by Verma Malik and sung by Manna Dey, *Majlum Kisi Qaum Ke Jab Khwab Jaagte Hain*, depicts British excesses against revolutionaries and celebrates the desire for freedom and sacrifice for the nation. It does not take much time to understand why the film came under the censor's scanner during Emergency.

6   The original *KKK* was completed and ready to be released as early as 1974. Amrit Nahata, the producer, was a Congress Member of Parliament (MP) at that time. The release of the film was delayed due to its heavily political overtones. Nahata was reported to have said that, 'he felt somebody must speak out from within the party against all that they thought was wrong. But others in the group said no, not yet. He agreed, saying, "I'll keep quiet inside the party but not within my own medium. So I made the film."' See Vasudev (1978, 170).

7   Popular Hindi films were screened on television to distract people from attending JP's meeting. See *White Paper on Misuse of Mass Media* (1977, 75), for details.

8   Also see '"Kissa" New Version will be Exactly as it was Made Originally', *Screen*, 5 August 1977, 1 and 4. Amrit Nahata told in a press conference that, 'while he felt a sense of futility at the destruction of his film after it had been confiscated by the Government of India in 1975, after a lot of introspection, he had come to the conclusion that, if he did not make the film again, he would be doing "precisely what its destroyers wanted me to do – to submit to tyranny"'. He directed the remake himself and used more stage artistes in the new version of the film. Interestingly, while responding to a question, Nahata said that he had approached the FFC in 1967 or 1968 for a loan to make the earlier version of the

film, 'but the then FFC Chairman, Mr. Himmatsinghji, had told him that the FFC did not consider it a suitable subject'. (4).

9   Also see 'Tax Relief for "Andolan" in Five States' (1977, 14); *Andolan* Release Poster (1977, 23); and '"Andolan" has Fine Music, Thrilling Action' (1977, 4). *Andolan* was exempted of entertainment tax in Assam, Kerala, Maharashtra, Chandigarh and Rajasthan. *Andolan* makers also had approached the FFC for financial aid but were refused assistance.

10 See Tiwari (2018–19, 848–58).

11 Desai (1977a, 1 and 10). Also see 'Welcome' (1977, 8).

12 Also see 'Guild Hails Morarji Desai's Leadership; Wants Autonomous Status for HPF, FFC', 4.

13 Arun Kaul and Mrinal Sen used the word 'New Cinema' in their 'Manifesto on New Cinema' (1968) to describe the alternative cinema movement in India. This 'New' cinema had certain common, universal characteristics – no stars, no songs (music, yes), story and filmmaker (auteur) as the defining elements of the feature film, on-location shooting, low budget, high production value, disciplined and on-time completion of the film (but no money, no private producers ready to finance such films that did not have a 'commercial' prospect). With a pre-history going back to the 1940s, New Cinema is supposed to have finally arrived in 1969 with Mrinal Sen's Hindi feature film *Bhuvan Shome*.

14 FFC was an autonomous body working under the MIB, government of India, since 1960. It was formed under the Articles of Association and was primarily promotional in its role, financing young and independent filmmakers. FFC got merged with NFDC when the latter started functioning in 1980. NFDC continues to support 'independent' cinema through its Film Bazar venture. Both FFC and NFDC, played a key role in providing all kinds of institutional support that young filmmakers needed since the 1960s, in terms of finances, equipment and production support.

15 See Rajagopal (2011, 1003–49).

16 The chapter where he discusses this particular incident is titled "Deadly Discipline, When Trains Ran On Perfect Time"

17 Also see Biradar, '"Prison Diaries"'. Historian Uma Chakravarthi made a documentary film titled *Prison Diaries* on Snehalatha's life, using a diary that Snehalatha maintained while in jail. The documentary can be viewed on YouTube, 'Prison Diaries', https://www.youtube.com/watch?v=Qm-DJ7XhP0w &ab_channel=PSBTIndia (accessed 29 November 2023). The film is produced by the Public Service Broadcasting Trust (PSBT).

18   Also see 'Karanjia's Resignation Regretted' (1976, 3).

19   I. K. Gujral was replaced by Vidya Charan (V. C.) Shukla as Minister for Information and Broadcasting on 28 June 1975. See 'Shukla Wants New Sense of Discipline in Film Industry', 15. In his 'articulate and frank speech', Shukla said that the government was very anxious to treat the film industry as 'a vital industry in the economy of the country' and invited them to enter a new era of co-operation and mutual trust. He demanded a sense of discipline in the industry. He also warned film journals and journalists against indulging in character assassination and scandal mongering. Shukla also said that TV would be used 'to build up the nation on proper lines'. It was going to 'tell our farmers how to produce more and housewives how they can rear their children better' ('Shukla Wants New Sense of Discipline in Film Industry' 1975, 15).

20   For more details on how the FFC's position as a patron of purposeful cinema got affected under Shukla, see 'FFC's Untold Story' (1977, 45).

21   Loans for films like *Aakrosh* and *Tarang* were sanctioned in the backdrop of these recommendations.

22   In 1975, before the Emergency, when questions were asked in Parliament about producers failing to repay loans, increasing amounts of outstanding and doubtful loans, and the writing off of bad debts, I. K. Gujral pleaded that FFC should not be judged from its outstanding loans alone, but from whether they had been able to influence the Indian cinema scene as a whole or not. He said that it should be remembered that FFC encouraged films which helped in the development of aesthetic taste and possessed a great deal of cultural value. See 'FFC's Finances: Mr. Gujaral's Clarification' (1975, 15).

23   The incidence of mass resignation had happened by then.

24   B. K. Karanjia had resigned on 12 April 1976. Jagdish Parikh was appointed as acting chairman after Karanjia's resignation, and as chairman in September 1976. He was reported to be a management expert with a special interest in film, travel, tourism and orienting industries. He was a governor on the board of the Asian Institute of Management in the Philippines. 'FFC Chief' (1976, 4). Hrishikesh Mukherjee, Dr. D. R. Rangnekar, Dr. Narayana Menon and Ali Sardar Jafri, members of the Board of Directors, resigned on 28 April 1976. *Annual Report & Accounts 1974–75* (1976, 1).

25   One lakh in the international numeral system is one hundred thousand.

26   Also see p. 22, 27, and 44–6 for more details.

27   Also see 'Govt. to Set Up NFC by October, New Film Policy Being Evolved, Says Gujral' (1973, 1 and 8).

28 One crore in the international numeral system is ten million.

29 See *Report 1980–81* (1981, 38).

30 See 'Govt. to Merge 3 Film Corporations' (1979, 5).

Chapter 5

1 When India got independent, it reintroduced a colonial law of the compulsory showing of 'approved' films to build an audience for its documentary films. Theatre owners got into one-sided 'block-booking and blind-booking contracts' with FD to screen its films in lieu of the mandate of screening documentary films before commercial films.

2 The period after the Emergency also saw the publication of the 'White Paper on the Misuse of Mass Media During the Internal Emergency', in August, as FD faced several accusations about its operations during the period. One of the major concerns raised in the White Paper was about the commissioning and purchase of films during the Emergency, which bypassed the usual routes and exceeded average costs, along with the notorious 'Film 20' series.

3 The term 'negotiation basis' refers to when FD contacted selected producers, some of whom do not belong to FD's designated panel of outside film producers, and then negotiated the terms of the production of films.

4 Some other films were about the New Apprenticeship Scheme, Human Dignity (Shivendra Sinha), Youth Power (Sohrab Boga), Higher Production (N. K. Issar) and Wastage in Government Expenditure.

5 Each OP was supposed to be assigned one film at a time, a regulation that was ignored concerning Sukhdev. He was assigned one film after another, as mentioned in the 'White Paper' (1977), including a film on Meghalaya, *After the Silence*, *Thunder of Freedom*, *Four Great Filmmakers* and *For What Are You Voting*. (Out of these, only *Thunder of Freedom* and *After the Silence* appear to have been completed and exist in the FD catalogue.)

6 It turns out that his film was assigned to the lowest bracket of Rs. 50,000. At his plea for more money or more film assignments in a handwritten letter to Mushir Ahmed, he was finally given Rs. 55,000 for his film, on par with B. D. Garga and Sohrab Boga.

Chapter 6

1 The power of the archive is discussed, most famously, by Jacques Derrida ([1995] 1996) and Michel Foucault ([1969] 2002).

2 Orality, here, is expressed in two forms: the testimony and the anecdote. While testimony bears the weight of evidence, the anecdote resists it with vehemence.

3 The particular reasons for which the testimonies are found to be unreliable are not mentioned by the authors.

4 Apart from these, other official sources may include police archives, judicial papers and records from other discrete wings of the bureaucracy with their own record management systems.

5 Clarity here refers to a comprehensive image of all parts of society, including public life.

6 This is written from the perspective of archivists, not research scholars. The authors suggest that this might enable archivists to 'capture more material even in unpromising situations' (231).

7 For a critique and discussion, see Lionel Gossman's (2003).

8 For instance, the United States Holocaust Memorial Museum houses a large collection of oral and written testimonies.

Chapter 7

1 For more on the FD's so-called golden age, see, for instance, chapters six and seven of Sutoris (2016), Kaushik (2017, 103–23), and Kishore (2018, 222–35).

2 In addition to the compulsory exhibition policy, FD films were also screened using mobile exhibition vans managed by the Directorate of Film Publicity. The FD claimed to have as many as 12,900 permanent and touring cinemas in its distribution circuit, reaching a weekly audience of 10 million. Mohan (1990, 25).

3 Jaffrelot and Anil (2020, 96). The literature on the Emergency of 1975–7 is vast but somewhat scattered. Besides *India's First Dictatorship,* the major academic monographs include Chandra (2003), Tarlo (2003), Hewitt (2007), Prakash (2019), and Plys (2020).

4 Devi (1998, vi). See also Devi (1997).

5 Mohan (1976). Reproduced in Mohan (1984, 83–4).

6 Figures from Jaffrelot and Anil (2020, 76).

7 I am reminded of Lee Schlesinger's remarkable ethnographic observations about a Maharashtrian village's scepticism about Emergency rhetoric that led him to

a dispassionate conclusion, straight out of a Hindi village novel: 'Most Indian rituals are orally constituted, and hence any public or political speaking may be easily construed as one more formulaic exercise. The mantras must be chanted, but the results will depend on invisible forces, will not be immediate, and perhaps will not be at all.' Schlesinger (1977, 628–9).

8   For instance, the *Report of the Study Group on the Welfare of Weaker Sections of the Village Community* (1961); the *Report of the Committee on Distribution of Income and Levels of Living* (1969a); and the *Report of the Committee on Untouchability, Economic and Educational Development of the Scheduled Castes* (1969b).

9   The history and significance of the 1970s as a populist moment in postcolonial India is explored in Chatterjee (2020). For the popular Hindi cinema's response to the 1970s as a moment of crisis, see Prasad (1998, 117–60). The post-Nehru populist turn in the Hindi public sphere is clearly visible in the anthology of Hindi-language speeches, political pamphlets, poetry and essays from the Emergency-era compiled by the Bihar State Archives: Karna (2016).

10   Prasad (1998, 117–216). See also, Rajadhyaksha (2009, 231–54).

11   Kaushik (2017, 112). See also Kishore (2018).

12   Both documents are reproduced in Mohan (1984, 53–5 and 96–103).

13   On Sukhdev's contrapuntal insertions in *Thoughts in a Museum* (1968), see Vasudevan (2022, 360–85).

14   S. Sukhdev, interviewed by Mohan Bawa. Reproduced in Mohan (1984, 43).

15   *Documentation of Emergency Period in India (June 1975 till March 77).* Microfilm, Center for Research Libraries, Chicago. 'Jhoote Prachar Ki Asliyat', *Documentation of Emergency Period in India*. MF-11985 SAMP r.1. The same sense of a sharp, immutable divide between propaganda aligned with the state and the literature of resistance can be observed in early anthologies of Emergency-era writing: for instance, Dissenting Voices (1977) and Perry (1983).

16   Indeed, one of the most significant long-term impacts of the Bihar movement was to clear the space for new kinds of coalitions that included Hindu nationalist factions, ending their 'political untouchability' (to use L. K. Advani's term). See, for instance, Anderson and Clibbens (2018, 1729–73); Rajagopal (2003, 2797–8); and Jaffrelot (2015).

17   Myrdal (1968, Vol. 1, 34). Myrdal's personal observations about the loss of optimism in Indian planners are scattered between pp. 257–304; Tyler (1977), Mitra (2004, 117). The experiences of female prisoners during the Indian 1970s have been the subject of an extraordinary wave of recent scholarship: Roy (2011, 2012). Kamra (2013), Sen (2018, 917–41), and Scott (2018, 270–86); Narayan (1977). For his paranoia about the Emergency as a Soviet plot, see pages 3–4, 6, and 72.

Chapter 8

1 In early 2001, I made a documentary on the link between urban memory and catastrophic events. The film titled *Delhi Diary 2001* dealt with two moments from the city's recent past. These were the Emergency and the massacre following Indira Gandhi's assassination in 1984. I was interested in the relationship between memory and the everyday and how ordinary lives located in various parts of the city encountered and retained the traces of spectacular events. In revisiting that moment, I realized how I was trying to excavate something at a time when online activity and social media had still not taken the shape it has today. Today the context is different – the Emergency has a ubiquitous online presence, where concentration and convergence of information seem to be the norm.

2 Indira Gandhi won the 1971 Lok Sabha election from Rae Bareli, defeating socialist leader Raj Narain, who later challenged the decision. On 12 June 1975, the Allahabad High Court convicted Gandhi of electoral malpractices; she was debarred from Parliament, and a six-year ban on her holding any elected post was imposed.

3 Tarlo offers a vivid account of the record room in the Municipal archives of a resettlement locality, consisting of almost 3733 personal files of land allotted to residents. Her term 'paper truths' is evocative of a gap between written records and the constant need for verification, interpretation, additional documents and oral testimonies.

4 For a discussion of the relevance of the 1974 railway strike, see Mudiar (2021).

5 For more on platformization, see Nieborg and Poell, T (2018).

6 Jayaprakash Narayan, known popularly as JP, led a movement against the Congress government's corruption that began in 1975. He called for total revolution and acquired substantial following among the youth. The force of the movement became one of the grounds used by Indira Gandhi to impose Emergency.

7 There are innumerable accounts of the way forced sterilization destabilized the family planning initiatives during the Emergency.

8 See Ahmed (2013) for an analysis of the violence in Muzaffarnagar.

9 For more details, see Mander, Chaudhury, Eqbal, and Bose (2020).

10 Some of Paul's other films are *Nayi Kheti* (New Harvest, 2013), *Shabd Kosh* (A Dictionary, 2014), *Long Hair Short Ideas* (2014), and *The Dreams of Cynthia* (2017).

11 The essay film is typically traced back to several twentieth-century film practices, like the work of Chris Marker and Harun Farocki, and occasionally even includes films like Dziga Vertov's *Man with a Movie Camera*. The term, however, has had

much greater currency since the digital turn, linked primarily to a new form of audiovisual expression made possible with easier access to camera and editing facilities.

12 Interview with Pallavi Paul, Berlin September 2023.

13 The thirty-second Freedom Lecture by Pallavi Paul, International Film Festival of Rotterdam https://www.youtube.com/watch?v=6656LzVHdvw

14 Paul had read Emma Tarlo's book during the making of the film and it is not surprising that her form addresses what was different about the archival imagination in the book

Chapter 9

1 In the context of South Indian popular cinema, its stardom, fan phenomenon and its ever-present association with electoral politics, M. Madhava Prasad coined the term 'cine-politics' (see Prasad 2014). I am refraining from explaining it as it is not relevant for the present context.

2 Figural thinking/criticism in cinema is a predominantly French and philosophically rooted (in Auerbach, Agamben and so many others) school of thought where figures (including shapes, forms, cliches, outlines, icons, emblems from art or cultural history, tropes, image clusters) constitute the most foundational unit of film criticism. For a comprehensive introduction to its theoretical framework, see Martin (2012). For the most significant and sustained use of this mode of criticism, see Brenez (2023).

3 For a detailed bibliography, see Panagia (2020, 107). For one of the most recent political theoretical take on cinematic and democratic, aesthetic and political representation, see Dienstag (2020).

4 Fernando Solanas and Octavio Getino's 'Hacia un Tercer Cine'/'Towards a Third Cinema' is perhaps the most seminal text of the time. But there were many other significant manifestos, cine-political calls for action across the Global South. Arun Kaul and Mrinal Sen arrived in the scene with their 'Manifesto of the New Cinema Movement' in 1968 India. For an anthology of many manifestos, see MacKenzie (2014).

5 Mariano Mestman researched extensively on these Third Cinema conferences and retrieved the recordings of the 1974 Third Cinema conference in Montreal. These recordings, apart from the Cinémathèque québécoise archive, can be found at the Instituto de Investigaciones Gino Germani, Faculty of Social Sciences, Universidad de Buenos Aires, Argentina. See Mestman (2014).

6   Jean-Pierre Brossard regretted the near-complete absence of representatives of Asian cinema in the Third Cinema conferences (Mestman 2007, 2).

7   In the autobiographical writings of Mrinal Sen, memories of his engagement and interactions with such Latin American filmmakers as Solanas, Glauber Rocha, Raymundo Gleyzer, Carlos Álvarez, Jorge Sanjinés, Patricio Guzmán et al. can be found. Visual references to/citations from Solanas and Getino's *La hora de los hornos* (*The Hour of the Furnaces*, 1968) can be located in Sen's films such as *Padatik* (*The Guerrilla Fighter*, 1973).

8   Ashish Rajadhyaksha draws our attention to formal transformations in political art and theatre as evident in the works of Badal Sircar, Vivan Sundaram, Somnath Hore and K. G. Subramanyan, among others (cited in Biswas 2020, 146–7).

9   For the histories of Film Finance Corporation (FFC) and/or the National Film Development Corporation (NFDC), see Tiwari (2024). Also, see Sudha Tiwari's contribution to this volume.

10 With a management guru like Jagdish Parikh at the helm of the affairs at the FFC, debates on profitability, return of the money invested in film projects and on loan/subsidy issues became significant. *Filmfare* and other magazines featured that.

11 Kumar Shahani's writings have been published with an introduction by Ashish Rajadhyaksha, Laleen Jayamanne has published her monograph on Shahani, curated his films in Australia and the Queensland Art Gallery (QAGOMA) has preserved Shahani's films. Book-length interviews with Kaul and Shahani have appeared in Hindi, and the one with Kaul has been translated in English as well.

12 New Literature/*Nai Kahani* movement in Hindi is associated with such names as Kamleshwar, Rajendra Yadav and Mannu Bhandari, apart from Mohan Rakesh.

13 I am referring to Mani Kaul's *Naukar ki Kameez* (*The Servant's Shirt*, 1999), which is based on Vinod Kumar Shukla's novel of the same name.

14 Kaul's 1980 film *Satah Se Uthata Aadmi* is based on Muktibodh's writings in an experimental, non-linear fashion.

15 For the hostile response to Kaul's apparent 'whitewashing' of Muktibodh's legacy, see Dadawala (2021, 11–12).

16 Peter Handke, the controversial Literature Nobel Laureate of 2019, wrote *Kaspar* in 1967, and it is often regarded as the most significant absurdist play from Europe after Samuel Beckett's *Waiting for Godot*.

17 As Dharwadker notes, the narrative of Kalidas abandoning Mallika, his muse, to her uncertain fate for the sake of achieving greatness in the Gupta court

seems to be uncannily represented in the performance history of the play. The two protagonists (Kalidas and Mallika) were played by Om Shivpuri and Sudha Sharma (Shivpuri), respectively, in the iconic 1962 National School of Drama production of Ebrahim Alkazi. Om and Sudha, the thespian couple, got married, and the woman sacrificed the better part of her acting career for the sake of her domesticity, paving the way for her partner's greater success on stage and screen (Dharwadker 2016, 42–5). With this gendered history of its production, Dharwadker refers to it as the 'interpenetration of art and life' (2016, 45). In Kaul's adaptation, Om Shivpuri plays Vilom, the antagonist, which he also did in the 1973 stage production of the play for their group Dishantar (Dharwadker 2016, 40).

18 Personal communication with Amrit Gangar in Mumbai, 13 July 2024.

19 'Time flowing through the frame with dignity' as the most significant element in cinema is something that Andrey Tarkovsky believed in and expressed firmly, as opposed to the montage school, in his *Sculpting in Time* (Tarkovsky 1989, 120).

20 For more on Bresson's definitive assertions against filmed theatre, see Burnett (2017, 149). It might be noted how Bresson had an objection to the use of ornate theatrical décor and costumes even in an iconic film such as *Citizen Kane* (Orson Welles, 1941).

Chapter 10

1 Galeano talks about the civic-military dictatorship of Uruguay (1973–85).

2 '[A]n increase in the level of income inequality, in step with the robust economic growth over the observational period' (Ray 2022, 106) was observed by Stewart and Morales, complemented by Chancel and Piketty: 'top 10 percent and top 1 percent grew substantially faster than the average since 1980' (2019, S35).

3 This similarity has been previously noted by researchers before, like Lipka-Chudzik (2011) and Nath and Dowerah (2023). It is further argued that Shakaal parallels Blofeld in his alienism and machinations as well, especially since Blofeld is of mixed ancestry, lives in a bubble of futuristic technology and precipitates international war-like situations.

4 At the same time, this gizmoid array had an alienating effect on the average Indian viewer, especially since 1980–1 was only the initial years of adapting, absorbing and disseminating modern technologies in the industrial sectors, as mandated by the Congress government (Panagariya 2008, 92).

5   Tapan Kumar Ghosh writes a detailed description of the socio-political crisis of
    the 1980s and its effect on popular Hindi films rogue's gallery. '[O]fficers behaved
    as though they are not accountable at all to any public authority. The decisions
    to arrest and release certain persons were based on . . . political considerations'
    (Ghosh 2013, 94).

References

Preface

Badiou, Alain (2005), *Cinema as a Democratic Emblem*, trans. Alex Ling and Aurélien Mondon, Melbourne: Parrhesia.

Bhutto, Fatima (2019), *New Kings of the World. Dispatches from Bollywood, Dizi and K-Pop*, New York: Columbia University Press.

Chatterjee, Partha (2021), *The Truth and Lies of Nationalism,* New Delhi: Permanent Black.

Hediger, Vinzenz and Felix Simon (2024), 'Unauthorized Fictions: Political Conflict as Spectacle and the Question of Trust in the Age of Trump (w. Felix Simon)', in Rebecca Boguska, Guilherme Machado, Rebecca Puchta and Marin Reljic (eds), *Tacit Cinematic Knowledge: Approaches and Practices*, 241–64, Lüneburg: Meson Press.

Kracauer, Siegfried (1947), *From Caligari to Hitler. A Psychological History of German Cinema*, Princeton: Princeton University Press.

Mody, Ashok (2023), *India is Broken. A People Betrayed, from Independence to Today*, Stanford: Stanford University Press.

Mukherjee, Arun P. (2009), 'B. R. Ambedkar, John Dewey, and the Meaning of Democracy', *New Literary History*, 40 (2): 345–70.

Muppidi, Himadeep (2012), *The Colonial Signs of International Relations*, London: Hurst Publishers.

Przeworski, Adam (2019), *Crises of Democracy*, Cambridge: Cambridge University Press.

Rajadhyaksha, Ashish (1998), 'Who is Looking? Viewership and Democracy in the Cinema', *Cultural Dynamics*, 10 (2): 171–95.

Schneider, Alexandra (2024), '"I Am in Love, I Am in Love, I Am in Looove!": The Visual Economy of the Indo-Swiss-Film–Tourism Complex Around 2000', *Studies in South Asian Film & Media*, 16, Issue India–Europe Film Connections: 27–40.

Sen, Amartya (2012), *The Argumentative Indian. Writings on Politics, History and Culture*, New Delhi: Penguin.

Srinivas, S.R. (2006), 'Stars and Mobilization in South India: What Have Films Got to Do with It?', *Postscript*, 25 (3): 30–47.

Williams, Appleman (1982), *Empire As A Away of Life: An Essay on the Causes and Character of America's Predicament Along with a Few Thoughts about an Alternative,* Oxford: Oxford University Press.

Introduction

Banerjee, S. (1980), *In the Wake of Naxalbari: A History of Naxalite Movement in India,* Kolkata: Subarnarekha.

Bhowmik, S. (2009), *Cinema and Censorship: The Politics of Control in India,* Hyderabad: Orient Blackswan.

Chakrabarty, D. (2002), *Habitations of Modernity: Essays in the Wake of Subaltern Studies,* Chicago: University of Chicago Press.

Dhar, P. N. (2000), *Indira Gandhi, the 'Emergency', and Indian Democracy,* New Delhi: Oxford University Press.

Guha, R. (2008), *India after Gandhi: The History of World's Largest Democracy,* London: Picador.

Prakash G. (2019), *Emergency Chronicles: Indira Gandhi and Democracy's Turning Point,* Princeton: Princeton University Press.

Hewitt, V. (2008), *Political Mobilisation and Democracy in India: States of Emergency,* London and New York: Routledge.

Jaffrelot, C. and P. Anil (2020), *India's First Dictatorship: The Emergency, 1975–77,* New Delhi: Harper Collins.

Joshi, P. and R. Dudrah, eds (2014), *The 1970s and its Legacies in Indian's Cinemas,* Oxon and New York: Routledge.

Kapoor, C. (2016), *The Emergency: A Personal History,* Gurgaon: Penguin Books.

Kaviraj, S. (1986), 'Indira Gandhi and Indian Politics', *Economic and Political Weekly,* XXI (38–9): 1697–708.

Lockwood, D. (2020), *The Communist Party of India and the Indian Emergency,* New Delhi: Sage.

Mazzarella, W. (2013), *Censorium: Cinema and the Open Edge of Mass Publicity,* Durham: Duke University Press.

Nandy, A. (1980), 'Indira Gandhi and the Culture of Indian Politics', in *At the Edge of Psychology: Essays in Politics and Culture,* 112–30, Delhi: Oxford University Press.

Nayar, K. (2013), *Emergency Retold,* New Delhi: Konark.

Patra, P. and M. Kho Lim (2021), *Sine ni Lav Diaz: A Long Take on the Filipino Auteur,* Bristol: Intellect.

Prasad, M. M. (1998), *Ideology of the Hindi Film: A Historical Construction,* New Delhi: Oxford University Press.

Rajadhyaksha, A. (2000), 'Viewership and Democracy in the Cinema', in Ravi S. Vasudevan (ed.), *Making Meaning in Indian Cinema*, 267–96, Delhi: Oxford University Press.

Rajadhyaksha, A. (2009), *Indian Cinema in the Time of Celluloid: From Bollywood to the Emergency*, New Delhi and Bloomington: Indiana University Press.

Reynaud, B. (2019), *A City of Sadness*, London: BFI.

Tarlo, E. (2003), *Unsettling Memories: Narratives of the Emergency in Delhi*, Berkeley: University of California Press.

Tyler, M. (1977), *My Years in an Indian Prison*, London: Victor Gollancz.

Chapter 1

'A Conversation With Anil Mehta-On Cinematography and Influences, Part I' (2017), [Video] *Cinema Beyond Entertainment*, 11 May. https://www.youtube.com/watch ?v=wrqOO1R2LXo (accessed 15 February 2024).

Abbas, K. A. (1970), 'The Short and Long of It', *Close-Up*, 3 (5–6): 110–11.

Abbas, K. A. (1977), *I am Not an Island: An Experiment in Autobiography*, Delhi: Vikas.

Bandyopadhyay, S., ed. ([1939] 1993), 'Open Letter by K.A. Abbas to M.K. Gandhi', in *Indian Cinema: Contemporary Perceptions from the Thirties*, 141–45, Jamshedpur: Celluloid Chapter.

Basu, S. and S. Dasgupta, eds (1992), *Film Polemics*, 38, Kolkata: Cine Club of Calcutta.

'Bombay University Occupied!!, Story of a Student' (2015), *Asura*, 16 January. https://asuramagazine.wordpress.com/2015/01/16/bombay-university-occupied/ (accessed 15 February 2024).

Calcutta 71 (1972), [Film] Dir. Mrinal Sen, India: D. S. Pictures.

'Committee on Public Undertakings (1975–76): 79th Report: Film Finance Corporation', New Delhi: Lok Sabha Secretariat.

Gandhi, M. K. (1929), 'Young India', in *Collected Works of Mahatma Gandhi*, 45: 216–17, New Delhi: Publications Division Govt of India, 1999.

Gandhi, M. K. (1939), 'Harijan', in *Collected Works of Mahatma Gandhi*, 76: 378, New Delhi: Publications Division Govt of India, 1999.

Gandhi, M. K. (1947a), 'Speech at a Prayer Meeting', in *Collected Works of Mahatma Gandhi*, 98: 121, New Delhi: Publications Division Govt of India, 1999.

Gandhi, M. K. (1947b), 'Talk with Socialists', in *Collected Works of Mahatma Gandhi*, 95: 150, New Delhi: Publications Division Govt of India, 1999.

'K.A. Abbas vs The Union of India & Anr' (1970), Supreme Court of India, 24 September.

Kothari, R. (1988a), 'Integration and Exclusion in Indian Politics', *Economic and Political Weekly*, 23 (43): 2227.

Kothari, R. (1988b), *State Against Democracy: In Search of Humane Governance*, Delhi: Ajanta Publications.

Masud, I. (1980), 'Fierce Little Bushwar in the Indian Film World', *Is There a New Cinema Movement? Cinema Vision India*, 1 (3): 83–8.

Namjoshi, A. (1974), 'Should Students Run Universities?', *The Illustrated Weekly of India*, 16 June.

Pandian, M. S. S. (2014), 'Tamil Cultural Elites and Cinema: Outline of an Argument', *Economic and Political Weekly*, 49 (46): 952.

Prasad, M. M. (1998), *Ideology of the Hindi Film: A Historical Construction*, Delhi: Oxford University Press.

Prasad, M. M. (2014), *Cine Politics: Film Stars and Political Existence in South India*, Hyderabad: Orient Blackswan.

'Ramesh S/O Chotalal Dalal vs Union of India & Ors' (1988), Supreme Court of India, 16 February.

Ray, S. ([1976] 1994), 'An Indian New Wave?', in *Our Films, Their Films*, 81–99, New York: Hyperion.

Report of Committee on Public Undertakings (1975–76): 3–4.

Sen, M. (2003), *Over the Years: An Interview with Samik Bandyopadhyay*, 67, Kolkata: Seagull Books.

Shah, N. (2014), *And Then One Day: A Memoir*, 198, 227, New Delhi: Penguin Books.

Shah, S. (2021), [Email] Received by A. Rajadhyaksha, 20 November.

'Shukla's Twenty Month Reign of Terror: Industry Speaks Out At Last' (1977), *Screen*, 18 March.

Steyerl, H. (2016), 'A Sea of Data: Apophenia and Pattern (Mis-) Recognition', *e-flux*, April: 72.

Teevra Madhyam (1974), [Film] Dir. Arun Khopkar, India: Film and Television Institute of India.

Chapter 2

All India Reporter, Supreme Court section, (1971), Nagpur: All India Reporter Pvt. Ltd.

Gulzar, S.S., Govind Nihalani, and Saibal Chatterjee, eds. (2003), *The Encyclopaedia of Hindi Cinema*, Mumbai: Encyclopaedia Britannica (India) Pvt. Ltd. and Popular Prakashan Pvt. Ltd.

Mohan, Jag (1990), *Documentary Films and Indian Awakening*, New Delhi: Publications Division, MIB.

Ramnath, Nandini (2015), 'The Story Behind the Controversial Film *Kissa Kursi Ka* which was Banned during the Emergency', *Scroll*, 27 January. https://scroll.in/reel/702429/the-story-behind-the-controversial-film-kissa-kursi-ka-which-was-banned-during-the-emergency (accessed 22 June 2021).

Report of the Enquiry Committee on Film Censorship, (1969), New Delhi: Ministry of Information & Broadcasting.

Symposium on Cinema in the Developing Countries (1979), Delhi: Publications Division, Ministry of Information & Broadcasting.

Chapter 3

Cowan, Michael (2023), *Film Societies in Germany and Austria 1910–1933*, Amsterdam: Amsterdam University Press. https://www.aup.nl/en/book/9789463725477/film-societies-in-germany-and-austria-1910-1933.

Das, Samarendra, ed. (2002), *Kolkatar Adda*, Kolkata: Gangchil. http://archive.org/details/in.ernet.dli.2015.266932.

Gangar, Amrit (1989), 'Rumination', in *Celebrating Poesy of Cinematography: Alexander Dovzhenko*, 1–11, Bombay Screen Unit.

Magistrelli Plys, Kristin Victoria (2020a), *Brewing Resistance: Indian Coffee House and the Emergency in Postcolonial India*, Cambridge: Cambridge University Press.

Magistrelli Plys, Kristin Victoria (2020b), 'Spaces of Resistance: From Indian Coffee House to Tihar Jail', *Jamhoor*, 21 October. https://www.jamhoor.org/read/2020/10/21/spaces-of-resistance-from-indian-coffee-house-to-tihar-jail (accessed 27 June 2024). https://doi.org/10.1017/9781108490528.

Mukerjee, Mala and Jael Silliman (2020), *ADDA! : The College Street Coffee House*, Chennai: Notion Press.

Passek, Jean-Loup (2001), *Dictionnaire du Cinéma,* Paris: Larousse.

Rajadhyaksha, Ashish (2009), *Indian Cinema in the Time of Celluloid: From Bollywood to the Emergency*, 13320th edn, Bloomington: Chesham: Indiana University Press.

Rajadhyaksha, Ashish (2017), *Kumar Shahani – The Shock of Desire and Other Essays*, New Delhi: Tulika Books.

Chapter 4

'A Kind of Cinema Culture' (1976), *Filmfare*, 16–29 April.

'"Andolan" has Fine Music, Thrilling Action' (1977) *Screen*, 9 September, 4.

Andolan Release Poster (1977), *Screen*, 5 August, 23.

Annual Report 1975–76 (1976), Bombay: FFC Ltd., 36.

Annual Report 1976–77 (1977), Bombay: FFC Ltd., 5.

Annual Report 1977–78 (1978), Bombay: FFC Ltd., 5.

Annual Report & Accounts 1974–75 (1976), Bombay: FFC Ltd., 2, 7.

Barnouw, Erik and S. Krishnaswamy (1980), *Indian Film*, New York: Oxford University Press.

Biradar, Basav (2019), '"Prison Diaries": An Intimate Documentary on Anti-Emergency Activist Snehalatha Reddy', *The News Minute*. https://www.thenewsminute.com/article/prison-diaries-intimate-documentary-anti-emergency-activist-snehalatha-reddy-115075 (accessed 20 March 2020).

Barnouw, Erik and S. Krishnaswamy (1980), *Indian Film*, 2nd ed., 274, New York: Oxford University Press.

'Cabinet okays plan for film corpn. [*sic*]' (1974), *The Times of India*, 27 July, 3.

'Censors Ban 19 Films' (1976), *Screen*, 14 May, 1.

Chandra, Bipan (2003), *In the Name of Democracy: JP Movement and the Emergency*, New Delhi, New York: Penguin Books.

Chandra, Bipan, Mridula Mukherjee, and Aditya Mukherjee (2008), *India Since Independence*, New Delhi: Penguin Books.

Committee on Public Undertakings (1975–76) (Fifth Lok Sabha) Seventy-Ninth Report, Film Finance Corporation Limited (Ministry of Information and Broadcasting) (1976), Lok Sabha Secretariat, New Delhi, March.

'Continue the Revolution' (1976), *Filmfare*, 11–24 June, 35.

Dalmia, Yashodhara (1976), 'New Cinema: Another Hesitant Beginning?', *The Times of India*, 12 December, 13.

Das, Veena (1981), 'The Mythological Film and its Framework of Meaning: An Analysis of *Jai Santoshi Ma*', *India International Centre Quarterly*, 8 (1): 43–56. https://www.jstor.org/stable/23001935 (accessed 24 January 2019).

Desai, M. S. M. (1976), 'FFC Expands Its Activities, Distribution and Exhibition Wings Being Started', *Screen*, 26 November, 1.

Desai, M. S. M. (1977a), 'New Minister Will Promote Industry, Aim is No Control, Says Advani', *Screen*, 1 April, 1, 10.

Desai, M. S. M. (1977b), 'Shukla's 20-Month "Reign of Terror", Industry Speaks Out at Last', *Screen*, 18 March, 1.

'FFC and IMPEC merged with National Film Development Corporation' (1979), *Bulletin on Films*, June, XXIV, No. 6, 1.

'FFC Chief' (1976), *Screen*, 1 October, 4.

'FFC's Finances: Mr. Gujaral's Clarification' (1975), *Screen*, 21 March, 15.

'FFC Infra-structure strengthened, Says its Chairman, Expansion Plans' (1977), *Screen*, 16 September, 1 and 14.

'FFC's Role' (1976), *The Times of India*, 25 March, 8.

'FFC's Untold Story' (1977), *Filmfare*, 13–26 May, 45.

'For the film industry A New Dawn' (1977), *Filmfare*, 15–28 April, 10.

'Govt. to Set Up NFC By October, New Film Policy Being Evolved, Says Gujral' (1973), *Screen*, 29 June, 1 and 8.

'Govt. to Merge 3 Film Corporations' (1979), *The Times of India*, 3 June, 5.

'Guild hails Morarji Desai's Leadership; Wants Autonomous Status for HPF, FFC' (1977), *Screen*, 1 April, 4.

'Indira Jaap in Mazdoor Zindabaad (1976)' (2009), *At the Edge*, 29 October, http://8ate.blogspot.com/2009/10/indira-jaap-in-mazdoor-zindabaad-1976.html (accessed 15 February 2019).

'Karanjia's Resignation Regretted' (1976), *The Times of India*, 21 May, 3.

Kaviraj, S. (1986), 'Indira Gandhi and Indian Politics', *Economic and Political Weekly*, 21 (38–9): 1697–708, http://www.jstor.org/stable/4376158 (accessed 24 February 2016).

Mazzarella, William and Raminder Kaur (2009), 'Between Sedition and Seduction: Thinking Censorship in South Asia', in Raminder Kaur and William Mazzarella (eds.), *Censorship in South Asia: Cultural Regulation from Sedition to Seduction*, 18, London, New York, New Delhi: Routledge.

Mohamed, Khalid (1976), 'FFC Plans to Change the Pattern of Aid', *The Times of India*, 25 November, 7.

Nandy, Ashis (1980), 'Indira Gandhi and The Culture of Indian Politics', in Ashish Nandy (ed.), *At The Edge of Psychology: Essays in Politics and Culture*, 112–30, Delhi: Oxford University Press.

'No Let Up in Censorship, Says Dayal' (1976), *Screen*, 21 May, 1 and 4.

Personal Interview with Kumar Shahani (2016), New Delhi, 3 May.

Personal Interview with Saeed Akhtar Mirza (2018), Mumbai, 27 June.

Prakash, Gyan (2018), *Emergency Chronicles: Indira Gandhi and Democracy's Turning Point*, New Delhi: Penguin Viking.

Prasad, M. M. (1988), 'The State in/of Cinema', in Partha Chatterjee (ed.), *Wages of Freedom: Fifty Years of the Indian Nation-State*, Delhi: Oxford University Press.

'Production Work Plummets Down, Flow of finance halts in Bombay' (1976), *Screen*, 18 June, 1.

Rajagopal, Arvind (2011), 'The Emergency as Prehistory of the New Indian Middle Class', *Modern Asian Studies*, 45 (5): 1003–49. https://www.jstor.org/stable /25835711 (accessed 9 August 2018).

Ramakrishna, R. (1976), 'New Film Policy Being Formulated – Shukla', *Screen*, 14 May, 1 and 10.

Report 1977–78 (1978), Ministry of Information and Broadcasting, Government of India, New Delhi, 32.

Report 1980–81 (1981), Ministry of Information and Broadcasting, Government of India, New Delhi, 38.

Saari, Anil (1973), 'FFC May Lose New Functions, Another Body for Stock, for Export, Import in Offing', *Screen*, 21 December, 1.

Saari, Anil (1974), 'Politician May Head NFC', *Screen*, 24 May, 1.

Saari, Anil (1976), 'FFC Told to Encourage Historicals', *Screen*, 28 May, 1.

Saari, Anil (1977), 'Pat for Industry from "J.P.," and Morarji', *Screen*, 1 April, 1.

Sen, Mrinal (2006), *Always Being Born*, New Delhi: Stellar Publishers.

Shahani, Kumar (2015), 'The Necessity of a Code (1975)', in Ashish Rajadhyaksha (ed.), *Kumar Shahani: The Shock of Desire and Other Essays*, 115, New Delhi: Tulika Books.

'Shukla wants new sense of discipline in film industry' (1975), *Screen*, 22 August, 15.

Sinha, Sachchidanand (1977), *Emergency in Perspective: Reprieve And Challenge*, New Delhi: Heritage Publishers.

Tarlo, Emma (2003), *Unsettling Memories: Narratives of India's Emergency*, Delhi, London, Hurst: Permanent Black.

'Tax Relief for "Andolan" in Five States' (1977) *Screen*, 5 August, 14.

'The Proposed Film Corporation' (1972), *Filmfare*, 17 November.

'Thematic Classification of Feature Films Made during the Last Five Years,' *Bulletin on Film*, A Monthly Digest for Official Use, January-March 1978, Vol. XXII, Nos. 1–3, National Documentation Centre on Mass Communication, New Delhi.

Tiwari, Sudha (2018-2019), 'The Political, Public, and Popular: Hindi Film Songs of Emergency', in *Proceedings of the Indian History Congress*, 79th Session, 848–58, Delhi: Indian History Congress.

Vasudev, Aruna (1978), *Liberty & License in the Indian Cinema*, New Delhi: Vikas Publishing House Pvt. Ltd..

'Welcome' (1977), *Screen*, 1 April, 8.

'What F.F.C. Should Do' (1976), *Screen*, 16 April, 6.

Chapter 5

Barnouw, Erik and Subrahmanyam Krishnaswamy (1963), *Indian Film*, New York: Columbia University Press.

Battaglia, Giulia (2018), *Documentary Film in India: An Anthropological History*, London: Routledge.

Garga, Bhagwan Das (2007), *From Raj to Swaraj: The Non-Fiction Film in India*, New Delhi; New York: Viking.

Government of India (1966), *Report of the Committee of Broadcasting and Information Media on Documentary Films and Newsreels*: 'Chanda Committee Report', New Delhi: Ministry of Information and Broadcasting.

Government of India (1976a), Films Division Internal Production file, [N.A] *FDP*, 'Production of Film on 'Naya Daur/We Have Promises to Keep', Mumbai: Ministry of Information and Broadcasting.

Government of India (1976b), Films Division Internal Production File, *3/11/76 FDP*, 'Production of Film on Subjects of National Importance-Bonded Labor', Mumbai: Films Division of India, Ministry of Information and Broadcasting.

Government of India (1977a), Films Division Internal Production file, *10/7/77 FDP*, 'Query Regarding Production of Films from Independent Producers and Production of Morale-Boosting Films', Mumbai: Films Division of India, Ministry of Information and Broadcasting.

Government of India (1977b), 'Mass Media in India', in *White Paper on Misuse of Mass Media*, New Delhi: Publications Division.

Gupta, Akhil (2012), *Red Tape: Bureaucracy, Structural Violence, and Poverty in India*, Durham: Duke University Press.

Hull, Matthew (2012), 'Documents and Bureaucracy', *Annual Review of Anthropology*, 41: 251–67.

Indian Institute of Mass Communication (1976), *Film 20-A Study of Audience Reaction in New Delhi Cinema Houses*, New Delhi: IIMC.

Jayasankar K. P. and Anjali Monteiro (2015), *Fly in the Curry: Independent Documentary Film in India*, New Delhi: Sage Publications.

Kaushik, Ritika (2017), 'Sun in the Belly': Film Practice at Films Division of India 1965–1975', *BioScope: South Asian Screen Studies*, 8 (1): 103–23.

Mathur, Nayanika (2016), *Paper Tiger: Law, Bureaucracy and the Developmental State in Himalayan India*, New Delhi: Cambridge University Press.

Mohan, Jag (1976), 'Bonded Labour: To The Editor, 11 December', *The Times of India (1861–2010)*, 21 December, ProQuest Historical Newspapers.

Our Film Critic (1962), 'Films and the Emergency', *The Statesman,* 16 December.

Tarlo, Emma (2003), *Unsettling Memories: Narratives of India's Emergency*, Berkeley and Los Angeles: University of California Press.

Times of India (1976), '180 Feature Films Made on 20-Point Plan', *The Times of India (1861–2010)*, 20 May, ProQuest Historical Newspapers.

Chapter 6

Agamben, G. (1999), *Remnants of Auschwitz: The Witness and the Archive*, New York: Zone Books.

Andhi (1975), [Film] Dir. Gulzar, India: Mehboob Studio.

Anjaria, U. (2014), 'Relationships Which Have No Name: Family and Sexuality in the 1970s', in P. Joshi and R. Dudrah (eds), *The 1970s and its Legacies in India's Cinemas*, 23–35, New York: Routledge.

Aziz, Z. u. N. (2016), 'Passages from India: Indian Anti-colonial Activism in Exile, 1905–20', *Historical Research*, 90 (248): 404–21. https://doi.org/10.1111/1468-2281.12175.

Benjamin, W. (1968), 'Theses on the Philosophy of History', in H. Arendt (ed.), *Illuminations*, 253–64, New York: Schocken Books.

Chakravorty, S. (2019), 'Silenced Archives and Archived Voices: Archival Resources for a History of Post-independence India', in M. Moss and D. Thomas (eds), *Do Archives Have Value?* 89–104, London: Facet Publishing.

Derrida, Jacques ([1995] 1996), *Archive Fever: A Freudian Impression*, Chicago: University of Chicago Press.

Dhar, P. N. (2000), *Indira Gandhi, the 'Emergency', and Indian Democracy*, Oxford: Oxford University Press.

Douglas, J. (2015), 'A History of Postmortem Images and the Role of Recordkeeping in Grieving', Paper Presented at *Seventh International Conference on the History of Records and Archives (I-CHORA7)*, The University of Amsterdam, 29–31 July.

Doval, N. (2015), 'Narrating Emergency: Bollywood's Silence', *LiveMint*, 22 June. https://www.livemint.com/Politics/nekps5jmvsxxLbVwaYyrXP/Narrating-Emergency-Bollywoods-silence.html (accessed 17 February 2023).

Duarte, M. E. and Belarde-Lewis, M. (2015), 'Imagining: Creating Spaces for Indigenous Ontologies', *Cataloging & Classification Quarterly* [online], 53 (5–6): 677–702. https://doi.org/10.1080/01639374.2015.1018396.

Fineman, J. (1989), 'The History of the Anecdote', in H. A. Veeser (ed.), *The New Historicism,* 49–76, New York and London: Routledge.

Foucault, Michel ([1969] 2002), *The Archaeology of Knowledge*, London and New York: Routledge.

Ghaddar, J. J. and Caswell, M. (2019), 'To Go Beyond': Towards a Decolonial Archival Praxis', *Archival Science*, 19 (2): 71–85. https://doi.org/10.1007/s10502-019-09311-1.

Gilliland, A. J. and M. Caswell (2016), 'Records and their Imaginaries: Imagining the Impossible, Making Possible the Imagined', *Archival Science*, 16 (1). 1 March. https://escholarship.org/uc/item/4fd6t5mb (accessed 4 September 2023).

Gossman, Lionel (2003), 'Anecdote and History', *History and Theory*, 42 (2): 143–68.

Harris, V. and S. Hatang (2000), 'Archives, Identity and Place: A Dialogue on What It (Might) Mean(s) to be an African Archivist', *Canadian Journal of Information and Library Science*, 25 (2–3): 41–60.

Hedstrom, M. (2010), 'Archives and Collective Memory: More than a Metaphor, Less than an Analogy', in T. Eastwood and H. McNeil (eds), *Currents of Archival Thinking*, 163–80, Santa Barbara: Libraries Unlimited.

Jaffrelot, C. and P. Anil (2020), *India's First Dictatorship: The Emergency, 1975–1977*, New York: Oxford University Press.

Joshi, P. (2015), *Bollywood's India- A Public Fantasy*, New York: Columbia University Press.

Kapoor, C. (2016), *The Emergency: A Personal History*, New Delhi: Penguin Books Limited.

Khanna, A. (2019), *Words, Sounds, Images: A History of Media and Entertainment in India,* New Delhi: Harper Collins Publishers.

Nasbandi (1978), [Film] Dir. I. S. Johar, India: Yash Raj Films

Nora, P. (1989), 'Between Memory and History: Les Lieux de Mémoire', *Representations*, 26: 7–24.

Poduval, S. (2014), 'The Affable Young Man: Civility, Desire, and the Making of a Middle Class Cinema in the 1970s', in P. Joshi and R. Dudrah (eds), *The 1970s and its Legacies in India's Cinemas*, 66–87, New York: Routledge.

Ranjani Mazumdar (2007), *Bombay Cinema : An Archive of the City*, Minneapolis: University Of Minnesota Press.

Roti, Kapda, aur Makaan (1974), [Film] Dir. Manoj Kumar, India: Vishal International Productions Pvt. Ltd.

Schwartz, J. M. and T. Cook (2002), 'Archives, Records, and Power: The Making of Modern Memory', *Archival Science*, 2: 1–19. Dordrecht: Kluwer Academic Publishers.

Shakti (1982), [Film] Dir. Ramesh Sippy, India: M.R. Productions

Sholay (1975), [Film] Dir. Ramesh Sippy, India: Sippy Films

The Indian Memory Project. https://www.indianmemoryproject.com/ (accessed 1 December 2023).

The Long Emergency. https://www.longemergency.demx.in/ (accessed 12 November 2023).

The Partition Archive. https://in.1947partitionarchive.org/ (accessed 1 September 2023).

Thomas, D. and Fowler S. eds, *The Silence of the Archive*, London: Facet Publishing.

Trouillot, M. R. (1995), *Silencing the Past: Power and the Production of History*, Boston: Beacon Press.

White Paper on Misuse of Mass Media During the Internal Emergency (1977), New Delhi: Controller of Publications.

Yale, Elizabeth (2015), 'The History of Archives: The State of the Discipline', *Book History*, 18: 332–59.

Chapter 7

Advani, L. K. (2002), *A Prisoner's Scrap Book,* New Delhi: Ocean Books.

Anderson, Edward and Patrick Clibbens (2018), '"Smugglers of Truth": The Indian Diaspora, Hindu Nationalism, and the Emergency', *Modern Asian Studies*, 52 (5): 1729–73.

Brady, Thomas F. (1965), 'India: The Year of Hunger and Ideological Changes', *New York Times.*

Chandra, Bipin (2003), *In the Name of Democracy: JP Movement and the Emergency*, New Delhi and New York: Penguin.

Chatterjee, Partha (2020), *I am the People: Reflections on Popular Sovereignty Today*, New York: Columbia University Press.

Dadawala, Vikrant (2022), 'The Films Division of India and the Nehruvian Dream', *South Asia*, 45 (2): 220–35.

Desai, A. R., ed. (1986), *Agrarian Struggles in India After Independence,* New Delhi: Oxford University Press.

Desai, Morarji (1979), *The Story of My Life,* Vol. 3, New Delhi: Macmillan.

Devi, Mahasweta (1997), *Dust on the Road: The Activist Writings of Mahasweta Devi,* trans. Maitreya Ghatak, Kolkata: Seagull Books.

Devi, Mahasweta (1998), *Bitter Soil,* trans. Ipshita Chanda, Kolkata: Seagull Books.

Dissenting Voices (1977), New Delhi: People's Union for Democratic Rights.

Documentation of Emergency Period in India (June 1975 till March 77). Microfilm, Center for Research Libraries, Chicago.

Eleyaperumal, l. (1969), *Report of the Committee on Untouchability, Economic and Educational Development of the Scheduled Castes,* New Delhi: Department of Social Welfare.

Frankel, Francine (1971), *India's Green Revolution: Economic Gains and Political Costs*, Princeton: Princeton University Press.

Hewitt, Vernon Marston (2007), *Political Mobilization and Democracy in India: States of Emergency*, London and New York: Routledge.

Indian Institute of Public Opinion (1966), *Monthly Public Opinion Surveys* 12 (3): 29–34.

Jaffrelot, Christophe (2015), 'Who Mainstreamed BJP?', *Indian Express*, 21 July.

Jaffrelot, Christophe and Pratinav Anil (2020), *India's First Dictatorship: The Emergency, 1975–77*, New Delhi: Harper Collins.

'Jhoote Prachar Ki Asliyat', *Documentation of Emergency Period in India.* MF-11985 SAMP r.1.

Kamra, Lipika (2013), 'Self-Making Through Self Writing: Non-Sovereign Agency in Women's Memoirs From the Naxalite Movement', *South Asia Multidisciplinary Academic Journal*, 7. https://doi.org/10.4000/samaj.3608.

Karna, Mahendra Narayan, ed. (2016), *Bihar Andolana,* Vol. 1–8 [The Bihar Movement], Patna: Bihar Rajya Abhilekhagara Nidesalaya.

Kaushik, Ritika (2017), '"Sun in the Belly": Film Practice at Films Division of India 1965–1975', *BioScope: South Asian Screen Studies*, 8 (1): 103–23.

Kishore, Avijit Mukul (2018), '"You've Told Me that Three Times Now": Propaganda/anti-propaganda in the Films Division India Documentary, 1965–75', *The Moving Image Review & Art Journal (MIRAJ)*, 7 (2): 222–35.

Kudaisya, Medha (2015), 'Developmental Planning in "Retreat": Ideas, Instruments, and Contestations of Planning in India, 1967–1971', *Modern Asian Studies*, 49 (3): 711–52.

Mahalanobis, P. C. (1969), *Report of the Committee on Distribution of Income and Levels of Living*, New Delhi: Planning Commission.

Mitra, Asok (1984), 'The Indian Documentary Film in 1967', in Jag Mohan (ed.), *S. Sukhdev: A Documentary Montage*, 49, New Delhi: National Film Archive of India.

Mitra, Joya (2004), *Killing Days,* trans. Shampa Banerjee, New Delhi: Kali For Women.

Mohan, Jag (1976), 'Review of "After the Silence"', *Socialist India,* 27 November.

Mohan, Jag, ed. (1984), 'Personal Postscript', in *S. Sukhdev: A Documentary Montage*, 172. New Delhi: National Film Archive of India.

Mohan, Jag (1990), *Documentary Films and National Awakening*, New Delhi: Ministry of Information and Broadcasting, Government of India.

Myrdal, Gunner (1968), *Asian Drama: An Inquiry into the Poverty of Nations,* Vols. 1–3, New York: Pantheon.

Narayan, Jayaprakash (1961), *Report of the Study Group on the Welfare of Weaker Sections of the Village Community,* New Delhi: Ministry of Community Development and Corporation.

Narayan, Jayaprakash (1977), *Prison Diary 1975*, Bombay: Popular Prakashan.

Patwardhan, Anand (1989), 'Waves of Revolution', *Deep Focus*, 1 (4): 68.

Perry, John Oliver (1977), *Dissenting Voices,* New Delhi: People's Union for Democratic Rights.

Perry, John Oliver, ed. (1983), *Voices of Emergency: An All-India Anthology of Protest Poetry of the 1975–77 Emergency*, Bombay: Popular Prakashan.

Plys, Kristin (2020), *Brewing Resistance: Indian Coffee House and the Emergency in Postcolonial India*, Cambridge and New York: Cambridge University Press.

Prakash, Gyan (2019), *Emergency Chronicles: Indira Gandhi and Democracy's Turning Point*, Princeton and Oxford: Princeton University Press.

Prasad, M. M. (1998), *Ideology of the Hindi Film: A Historical Reconstruction*, New Delhi: Oxford University Press.

Rajadhyaksha, Ashish (2009), *Indian Cinema in the Time of Celluloid: From Bollywood to the Emergency,* Bloomington and Indianapolis: Indiana University Press.

Rajagopal, Arvind (2003), 'Sangh's Role in the Emergency', *Economic and Political Weekly,* 38 (27): 2797–8.

Report of the Committee on Distribution of Income and Levels of Living, headed by P. C. Mahalanobis (1969a), New Delhi: Planning Commission.

Report of the Committee on Untouchability, Economic and Educational Development of the Scheduled Castes, headed by L. Eleyaperumal (1969b), New Delhi: Department of Social Welfare.

Report of the Study Group on the Welfare of Weaker Sections of the Village Community, headed by Jayaprakash Narayan (1961), New Delhi: Ministry of Community Development and Corporation.

Roy, Mallarika Sinha (2011), *Gender and Radical Politics in India: Magic Moments of Naxalbari,* New York: Routledge.

Roy, Srila (2012), *Remembering Revolution: Gender, Violence and Subjectivity in India's Naxalbari Movement,* New Delhi: Oxford University Press.

Roy, Srirup (2007), *Beyond Belief: India and the Politics of Postcolonial Nationalism,* Durham and London: Duke University Press.

Sarang, Vilas (2006), 'Return', in *The Women in Cages,* 177–89. New Delhi: Penguin.

Saxena, Sarveshwar Dayal (1976), 'Lal Cycle', in *Jangal Ka Dard* [The Jungle's Pain], 49. New Delhi: Rajakamala.

Schlesinger, Lee I. (1977), 'The Emergency in an Indian Village', *Asian Survey,* 17 (7): 628–9.

Scott, Gemma (2018), '"Women Will Have to Fight This Battle": Political Prisoners Under India's Emergency, 1975–77', *Contemporary South Asia,* 26 (3): 270–86.

Sen, Atreyee (2018), 'Torture and Laughter: Naxal Insurgency, Custodial Violence, and Inmate Resistance in a Women's Correctional Facility in 1970s Calcutta', *Modern Asian Studies,* 52 (3): 917–41.

Shah Commission of Inquiry (1978), *Interim Report 1, Interim Report 2,* and *Final Report,* New Delhi: Government of India, Controller of Publications.

Sinha Roy, Mallarika (2011), *Gender and Radical Politics in India: Magic Moments of Naxalbari,* New York: Routledge.

Sutoris, Peter (2016), *Visions of Development: Films Division of India and the Imagination of Progress,* New Delhi: Oxford University Press.

Tarlo, Emma (2003), *Unsettling Memories: Narratives of the Emergency in Delhi,* Berkeley: University of California Press.

Ministry of Home Affairs (1969), *The Causes and Nature of Current Agrarian Tensions* (1969), New Delhi: Ministry of Home Affairs.

Tyler, Mary (1977), *My Years in an Indian Prison*, London: Victor Gollancz.

Vasudevan, Ravi (2022), 'Infrastructures of Political Address: The Film and Media Archive', in Neepa Majumdar and Ranjani Mazumdar (eds), *A Companion to Indian Cinema*, 360–85. Hoboken: Wiley.

Verma, Nirmal (1989), *Raat Ka Reporter* [The Nocturnal Reporter], New Delhi: Rajkamal.

White Paper on the Misuse of Mass Media During the Internal Emergency (1977), New Delhi: Controller of Publications.

Williams, Raymond (1977), *Marxism and Literature*, Oxford: Oxford University Press.

Chapter 8

Ahmed, H. (2013), 'Meanings of Violence', *Economic and Political Weekly*, 48 (40): 10–13.

Alter, N. (2019), *The Essay Film after Fact and Fiction*, New York: Columbia University Press.

Baron, J. (2014), *The Archive Effect: Found Footage and the Audiovisual Experience of History*, London: Routledge.

Bulletin on Film, Vol. XXIV, Nos. 1, January 1979.

Chatterjee, A. P., Thomas Blom Hansen, and Christophe Jaffrelot, eds (2019), *Majoritarian State: How Hindu Nationalism is Changing India*, New Delhi: Harper Collins.

Chun, W. H. K. (2011), 'Crisis, Crisis, Crisis, or Sovereignty and Networks', *Theory, Culture & Society*, 28 (6): 91–112.

Corrigan, T. (2011), *The Essay Film: From Montaigne After Marker*, Oxford: Oxford University Press.

Doane, M. A. (2001), 'Information, Crisis, Catastrophe', in M. Landy (ed.), *The Historical Film: History and Memory in the Media*, 269–85, New Brunswick, New Jersey: Rutgers University Press.

Fuller, M. and E. Weizman (2021), *Investigative Aesthetics: Conflicts and Commons in the Politics of Truth London*, New York: Verso.

Gitelman, L. (2014), *Paper Knowledge: Toward a Media History of Documents*, Durham: Duke University Press.

Goodman, S. and L. Parisi (2010), 'Machines of Memory', in S. Radstone and B. Schwarz (eds), *Memory: Histories, Theories, Debates,* 343–59, New York: Fordham University Press.

Hilderbrand, L. (2007), 'Youtube: Where Cultural Memory and Copyright Converge', *Film Quarterly*, 61 (1): 48–57.

Mander, H., A. A. Chaudhury, Z. Eqbal, and R. Bose (2020), *Living Apart: Communal Violence and Forced Displacement in Muzaffarnagar and Shamli*, New Delhi: Yoda Press.

Mudiar, J. (2021), 'Why the 1974 All-India Railway Strike Is Relevant Even Today', *The Wire*, 8 May. https://thewire.in/rights/why-the-1974-all-india-railway-strike-is -relevant-even-today (accessed 24 June 2024).

Nandy, A. (1995), 'Emergency Remembered', *The Times of India*, 22 June.

Nieborg, D. B. and T. Poell (2018), 'The Platformization of Cultural Production: Theorizing the Contingent Cultural Commodity', *New Media & Society*, 20 (11): 4275–92.

Prakash, G. (2018), *Emergency Chronicles: Indira Gandhi and Democracies Turning Point*, New Delhi: Penguin Viking.

Rascaroli, L. (2017), *How The Essay Film Thinks*, Oxford: Oxford University Press.

Reddy, C. G. K. (2014), *The Baroda Dynamite Conspiracy: The Right to Rebel*, New Delhi: Orient Blackswan.

Russel, C. (2018), *Archiveology: Walter Benjamin and Archival Film Practices*, Durham: Duke University Press.

Scott, L. (2019), 'In Search of Lost Time on YouTube', *The New Atlantis*, 59 (Summer): 13–20.

Tarlo, E. (2003), *Unsettling Memories: Narratives of India's Emergency*, New Delhi: Permanent Black.

Chapter 9

Biswas, M. (2020), 'Film, Revolution, Politics: Criticism in the Seventies', in P. Chatterjee (ed.), *After the Revolution: Essays in Memory of Anjan Ghosh*, 138–63, Hyderabad: Orient Blackswan.

Biswas, M. (2021), 'Thinking with Cinema: Mani Kaul Reading Deleuze', in B. Bose (ed.), *Humanities, Provocateur: Towards a Contemporary Political Aesthetics*, 84–94, New Delhi: Bloomsbury.

Brenez, N. (2023), *On the Figure in General and the Body in Particular: Figurative Invention in Cinema*, trans. T. Fendt, London: Anthem Press.

Bresson, R. (2016), *Notes on the Cinematograph*, trans. J. Griffin, New York: New York Review of Books.

Burnett, C. (2017), *The Invention of Robert Bresson: The Auteur and His Market*, Bloomington: Indiana University Press.

Comolli, J. L. (2015), *Cinema against Spectacle: Technique and Ideology Revisited*, trans and ed. D. Fairfax, Amsterdam: Amsterdam University Press.

Crisp, C. (1993), *The Classic French Cinema, 1930–1960*, Bloomington: Indiana University Press.

Dadawala, V. (2021), 'Gajanan Madhav Muktibodh and the Passing of Soviet India', *South Asia: Journal of South Asian Studies*, 44 (6): 1090–113.

Dalmia, V. (2008), *Poetics, Plays, and Performances: The Politics of Modern Indian Theatre*, New Delhi: Oxford University Press.

Daney, S. (2022), *The Cinema House & the World 1: The Cahiers du Cinéma Years 1962–1981*, trans. C. Pichini, California: Semiotext(e).

Dave-Mukherji, P. (2016), *Ebrahim Alkazi: Directing Art*, Ahmedabad and Delhi: Mapin Publishing and Art Heritage Gallery.

Dharwadker, A. B. (2016), 'Introduction', in M. Rakesh, *One Day in the Season of Rain*, New Delhi: Kindle edn, Penguin.

Dienstag, J. F. (2020), *Cinema Pessimism: A Political Theory of Representation and Reciprocity*, New York: Oxford University Press.

du Baecque, A. (1991), *Les Cahiers du cinéma: Histoire D'une Revue Tome II: Cinéma, tours détours 1959–1981*, Paris: Cahiers du Cinéma.

Fairfax, D. (2021), *The Red Years of Cahiers du Cinéma (1968–1973)*, Amsterdam: Amsterdam University Press.

Ghatak, R. (2000), 'Sound in Cinema', in *Rows and Rows of Fences*, 74–9, Kolkata: Seagull Books.

Kaul, M. (2018), 'On Robert Bresson', in S. Debuysere and A. Sen (eds), *The Rambling Figures of Mani Kaul*, 34, Brussels: Courtisane.

Law, H. L. (2021), *Ambiguity and Film Criticism: Reasonable Doubt*, Basingstoke: Palgrave Macmillan.

MacKenzie, S. (2014), *Film Manifestos and Global Cinema Cultures: A Critical Anthology*, Berkeley: University of California Press.

Majumdar, R. (2021), *Art Cinema and India's Forgotten Futures: Film and History in the Postcolony*, New York: Columbia University Press.

Martin, A. (2012), *Last Day Every Day: Figural Thinking from Auerbach and Kracauer to Agamben and Brenez*, New York: Punctum Books.

Mestman, M. (2007), 'Entre Argel y Buenos Aires. El Comité de Cine del Tercer Mundo (1973/1974)', *laFuga*, 5: 1–8.

Mestman, M. (2014), *Estados Generales del Tercer Cine. Los documentos de Montreal, 1974*, Buenos Aires: Red de Historia de los Medios-Prometeo.

Oudart, J. P. (1996), 'Cinema and Suture', in N. Browne (ed.), *Cahiers du Cinéma Vol 3: 1969–1972 The Politics of Representation*, 45–57, London: Routledge.

Panagia, D. (2020), 'Attending to Film: *The World Viewed* and Cinematic Political Thinking', *Discourse*, 42 (1–2): 81–111.

Patra, P. (2021), 'The Non-Populist Popular and the Cinematic Apocrypha', in P. Chakravarty (ed.), *Populism and Its Limits: After Articulation*, 231–48, New Delhi: Bloomsbury.

Prasad, M. M. (2014), *Cine-Politics: Film Stars and Political Existence in South India*, Hyderabad: Orient Blackswan.

Rajadhyaksha, A. (2012), 'Teaching Film Theory 2', *Journal of the Moving Image*, 11: 40–8.

Resmini, M. (2022), *Italian Political Cinema: Figures of the Long '68*, Minneapolis: Minnesota University Press.

Schefer, J. L. (2016), *The Ordinary Man of Cinema*, trans. M. Cavitch, P. Grant and N. Wedell, California: Semiotext(e).

Tarkovsky, A. (1989), *Sculpting in Time*, trans. K. Hunter-Blair, Austin: University of Texas Press.

Tiwari, S. (2024), *The State and New Cinema in Contemporary India 1960–1997*, Oxon and New York: Routledge.

Willemen, P. (1994), *Looks and Frictions: Essays in Cultural Studies and Film Theory*, Bloomington: Indiana University Press.

Chapter 10

Arato, Andrew (2002), 'Dictatorship Before and After Totalitarianism', *Social Research*, 69 (2): 473–503. http://www.jstor.org/stable/40971559 (accessed 24 June 2024).

Bayly, C. A. (2015), 'The Ends of Liberalism and the Political Thought of Nehru's India', *Modern Intellectual History*, 12 (3): 605–26. https://doi.org/10.1017/s1479244314000754.

Chancel Lucas and Thomas Piketty (2019), 'Indian Income Inequality, 1922–2015: From British Raj to Billionaire Raj?', *Review of Income and Wealth*, 65 (S1). https://doi.org/10.1111/roiw.12439.

Chaudhuri, Kalyan (1977), '"Law and Order" Killings', *Economic and Political Weekly*, 12 (29): 1134–42. JSTOR, http://www.jstor.org/stable/4365771 (accessed 24 June 2024).

Corner, Paul (2016), 'Non-Compliance, Indifference and Resistance in Regimes of Mass Dictatorship', in Paul Corner and Jie-Hyun Lim (eds), *The Palgrave Handbook of Mass Dictatorship*, 413–26, Siena, Seoul: Palgrave Macmillan.

Galeano, Eduardo (1986), 'The Dictatorship and Its Aftermath: The Secret Wounds', *Contemporary Marxism*, 14: 16–20. http://www.jstor.org/stable/29765866 (accessed 24 June 2024).

Ghadially, Rehana (2007), *Urban Women in Contemporary India: A Reader*, New Delhi: SAGE.

Ghosh, Tapan Kumar (2013), *Bollywood Baddies: Villains, Vamps and Henchmen in Hindi Cinema*, New Delhi: SAGE.

Guha, Ramchandra (2017), *India after Gandhi: The History of the World's Largest Democracy*, Kindle edn, New Delhi: Pan Macmillan India.

Harvey, David (2007), *A Brief History of Neoliberalism*, Oxford: Oxford University Press.

Jha, Priya (2003), 'Lyrical Nationalism: Gender, Friendship, and Excess in 1970s Hindi Cinema', *The Velvet Light Trap*, 51: 43–53. https://doi.org/10.1353/vlt.2003 .0007.

Leese, Daniel (2016), 'Rituals, Emotions and Mobilization: The Leader Cult and Party Politics', in Paul Corner and Jie-Hyun Lim (eds), *The Palgrave Handbook of Mass Dictatorship*, 2017–28, Siena, Seoul: Palgrave Macmillan.

Lim, J. (2005), 'Historiographical Perspectives on "Mass Dictatorship"', *Totalitarian Movements and Political Religions*, 6 (3): 325–31. https://doi.org/10.1080 /14690760500317669.

Lipka-Chudzik, Krzysztof (2011), 'Bodies, Bollywood and Bond: The Evolving Image of Secret Agents in Hindi Spy Thrillers Inspired by the 007 Franchise', *Acta Orientalia Vilnensia*, 12 (2): 31—46. https://www.journals.vu.lt/acta-orientalia -vilnensia/article/view/3934/2725 (accessed 24 June 2024).

Malhotra, Sheena and Tavishi Alagh (2004), 'Dreaming the Nation: Domestic Dramas in Hindi Films post-1990', *South Asian Popular Culture*, 2 (1): 19–37. https://doi .org/10.1080/1474668042000210492.

Matovski, Aleksander (2021), *Popular Dictatorships: Crises, Mass Opinion and the Rise of Electoral Authoritarianism*, Cambridge: Cambridge University Press.

Nath, Debarshi Prasad and Swikriti Dowerah (2023), 'The Icons of Unadulterated Evil: Bollywood Villains of the 1980s', *Quarterly Review of Film and Video*, 1–25. https://doi.org/10.1080/10509208.2023.2173474.

Panagariya, Aravind (2004), 'India's Trade Reform: Progress, Impact and Future Strategy', *International Trade*, 0403004. https://ideas.repec.org/p/wpa/wuwpit /0403004.html (accessed 24 June 2024).

Panagariya, Aravind (2008), *India: An Emerging Giant*, New York: Oxford University Press.

Perkins, Claire and Constantine Verevis (2014), *B is for Bad Cinema: Aesthetics, Politics, and Cultural Value*, New York: SUNY Press.

Pinches, Michael (1999), 'Cultural Relations, Class and the New Rich of Asia', in Michael Pinches (ed.), *Culture and Privilege in Capitalist Asia*, 1–56, London: Routledge.

Prasad, M. M. (1997), *The Ideology of the Hindi Film: A Historical Construction*, New Delhi: Oxford University Press.

Qayum, Seemin and Raka Ray (2011), 'The Middle Classes at Home', in Amita Baviskar and Raka Ray (eds), *Elite and Everyman: The Cultural Politics of the Indian Middle Classes*, 246–70, London: Routledge.

Rajadhyaksha, Asish (2003), 'The "Bollywoodization" of the Indian Cinema: Cultural Nationalism in a Global Arena', *Inter-Asia Cultural Studies*, 4 (1). https://doi.org/10.1080/1464937032000060195

Ray, Dibyakusum (2022), *Postcolonial Indian City-Literature: Policy, Politics and Evolution*, New York: Routledge Research.

Ray, Dibyakusum and Pooja Radhakrishnan (2024), 'From Domestic Guardian to the National Militia: The Familial, the National and the Middle Class in 1980s Popular Hindi Films', *National Identities*, 26. https://doi.org/10.1080/14608944.2023.2292689.

Virdi, Jyotika (2003), *The Cinematic ImagiNation: Indian Popular Films as Social History*, New Brunswick: Rutgers University Press.

Chapter 11

Althusser, Louis (1985), 'Contradiction and Overdetermination', in *For Marx*, 15–34, London: Verso.

Aronson, Ronald (2005), *Camus and Sartre: The Story of a Friendship and the Quarrel that Ended It*, Chicago: University of Chicago Press. https://press.uchicago.edu/ucp/books/book/chicago/C/bo3630360.html (accessed 16 July 2024).

Baczko, Bronislaw (1994), *Ending the Terror: The French Revolution after Robespierre*, trans. Michael Petheram, Cambridge: Cambridge University Press.

Banerjee, Tanmayee (2019), 'Kabir Suman: The Child and Father of Movements', in John Clammer, Meera Chakravorty, Marcus Bussey, and Tanmayee Banerjee (eds), *Dynamics of Dissent: Theorizing Movements for Inclusive Futures*, 53–65, New Delhi: Routledge.

Baudrillard, Jean (1976), *Symbolic Exchange and Death*, London: SAGE Publications. https://doi.org/10.4135/9781526401496.

Bergson, Henri (1990), *Matter and Memory*, New York: Zone Books. https://www.biblio.com/book/matter-memory-bergson-henri/d/1445345524 (accessed 16 July 2024).

Bhatia, Sidharth (2014), *India Psychedelic: The Story of Rocking Generation: The Story of a Rocking Generation*, Noida: HarperCollins.

Bhattacharya, Bhaswati (2017), *Much Ado Over Coffee: Indian Coffee House Then and Now*, 1st edn, New Delhi: Routledge.

Bhaumik, Kaushik (2023), 'Cinema Redux: Mrinal Sen's Anjan Dutt Films', Unpublished paper presented at 'Mrinal Sen and the Vicissitudes of Political Cinema, Annual Seminar of the Department of Film Studies, Jadavpur University.

Birnbaum, Daniel (2005), 'When Attitude Becomes Form', *Artforum International*, 43: 10.

Biryukova, Marina (2017), 'Reconsidering the Exhibition When Attitudes Become Form Curated by Harald Szeemann: Form versus "Anti-Form" in Contemporary Art', *Journal of Aesthetics & Culture* 9 (1): 1362309. https://doi.org/10.1080 /20004214.2017.1362309.

Biswas, Moinak (2011), 'Neo-Bhadralok Darpan', in Moinak Biswas (ed.), *Baromas*, 255–60, Kolkata: Baromas.

Bose, Brinda (2016), 'The Ginsberg-Dylan Express: Tangled Up in Vomit and Blues', *Cafe Dissensus*. https://cafedissensus.com/2016/06/16/the-ginsberg-dylan-express -tangled-up-in-vomit-and-blues/ (accessed 16 July 2024).

Bose, Brinda (2020), 'Slouching Toward an Aesthetics of Failure', *Aroop Journal*, 4: 15–20.

Bose, Brinda (2023), 'Poetry of the Indian Avant-Garde: An Intransigent Aesthetics', in Alfred J. Lopez and Ricardo Quintana-Vallejo (eds), *The Routledge Companion to Literature and the Global South*, 190–203, London: Routledge.

Bukatman, Scott (1993), *Terminal Identity: The Virtual Subject in Postmodern Science Fiction*, Durham: Duke University Press.

Burton, Scott (1969), 'Notes on the New', in Harald Szeeman (ed.), *Live in Your Head: When Attitudes Become Form: Works-Concepts-Processes-Situations-Information*, Bern: Kunsthalle Bern.

Cache, Bernard and Michael Speaks (1995), *Earth Moves: The Furnishing of Territories*. Writing Architecture, Cambridge, MA: MIT Press. http://www.gbv.de/ dms/bowker/toc/9780262531306.pdf (accessed 16 July 2024).

Deleuze, Gilles (1994), *Difference and Repetition*, trans. Paul Patton, New York: Columbia University Press.

Deleuze, Gilles and Guattari, Felix (1977), *Anti-Oedipus: Schizophrenia and Capitalism*, Minneapolis: University of Minnesota Press.

Deleuze, Gilles and Félix Guattari (1986), *Kafka: Toward a Minor Literature*, 9th edn, Minneapolis: University of Minnesota Press.

Deleuze, Gilles, Félix Guattari, and Brian Massumi (1987), *A Thousand Plateaus: Capitalism and Schizophrenia*, 2nd edn, Minneapolis: University of Minnesota Press.

Dirke, Sabine von (2008), 'The RAF as Trauma and Pop Icon in Literature since the 1980s', in Berendse Gerrit-Jan and Ingo Cornils (eds), *Baader-Meinhof Returns*, 103–23, Amsterdam: Brill. https://doi.org/10.1163/9789042032156_008.

Dyer-Witheford, Nick (1999), *Cyber-Marx: Cycles and Circuits of Struggle in High Technology Capitalism*, Urbana: University of Illinois Press.

Ferguson, Niall, Charles S. Maier, Erez Manela, and Daniel J. Sargent, eds (2011), *The Shock of the Global: The 1970s in Perspective*, Cambridge, MA: Belknap Press: An Imprint of Harvard University Press.

Gordon, Paul (2021), *Synaesthetics: Art as Synaesthesia*, New York: Bloomsbury Academic USA.

Gourgouris, Stathis (2017), 'Archē', in J. M. Bernstein, Adi Ophir and Ann Laura Stoler (eds), *Political Concepts: A Critical Lexicon*, 5–24, New York: Fordham University Press. https://doi.org/10.5422/fordham/9780823276684.003.0002.

Grosz, Elizabeth (2017), *The Incorporeal: Ontology, Ethics, and the Limits of Materialism*, New York: Columbia University Press.

Gunning, Tom (1990), 'The Cinema of Attractions: Early Film, Its Spectator and the Avant-Garde', in Thomas Elsaesser (ed.), *Early Cinema: Space, Frame, Narrative*, 56–62, London: BFI Publishing.

Habermas, Jurgen (1980), 'Psychic Thermidor and the Rebirth of Rebellious Subjectivity', *Berkeley Journal of Sociology*, 24/25: 1–12.

Herzog, Amy (2000), 'Images of Thought and Acts of Creation: Deleuze, Bergson, and the Question of Cinema', *In Visible Culture: An Electronic Journal for Visual Culture*, 3. https://ivc.lib.rochester.edu/images-of-thought-and-acts-of-creation-deleuze-bergson-and-the-question-of-cinema/ (accessed 16 July 2024).

Jameson, Fredric (1990), *Postmodernism, or, The Cultural Logic of Late Capitalism*, Post-Contemporary Interventions, Durham: Duke University Press.

Kaprow, Allan (2003), *Essays on the Blurring of Art and Life: Expanded Edition*, ed. Jeff Kelley, Berkeley: University of California Press.

Katyal, Anjum (2015), *Badal Sircar: Towards a Theatre of Conscience*, A Series of Contemporary Indian Playwrights, New Delhi: SAGE Publications.

Krauss, Rosalind E. (1976), 'Video: The Aesthetics of Narcissism', *October*, 1: 51–64. https://doi.org/10.2307/778507.

Krauss, Rosalind E. (1993), *The Optical Unconscious*, Cambridge, MA: MIT Press.

Lefebvre, Henri (2004), *Rhythmanalysis: Space, Time, and Everyday Life*, Athlone Contemporary European Thinkers, London: Continuum.

Lindsey, J. R. (2007), 'Rethinking the Political: Taking Baudrillard's "Silent Majorities" Seriously', *International Journal of Baudrillard Studies*, 4 (2), Online.

Lyotard, Jean-François (2011), *Discourse, Figure*, Minneapolis: University of Minnesota Press.

Mason, Laura (2015), 'Forum: Thermidor and the French Revolution (Part 1)', *French Historical Studies*, 38 (1): 1–7. https://doi.org/10.1215/00161071-2822832.

McLuhan, Marshall and Bruce R. Powers (1989), *The Global Village: Transformations in World Life and Media in the 21st Century*, New York: Oxford University Press.

Mercer, Kobena (2007), *Pop Art and Vernacular Cultures,* London: MIT Press.

Ranciére, Jacques (2013), *The Politics of Aesthetics: The Distribution of the Sensible*, London: Bloomsbury Academic.

Roberts, John (2007), *The Intangibilities of Form: Skill and Deskilling in Art after the Readymade*, London: Verso Books.

Said, Edward W. (2007), *On Late Style*, London: Vintage.

Samaddar, Ranabir, ed. (2018), *From Popular Movements to Rebellion: The Naxalite Decade*, London: Routledge. https://doi.org/10.4324/9780429026706.

Selzer, Michael (1979), *Terrorist Chic: An Exploration of Violence in the Seventies*, New York: Hawthorn Books.

'Shukla wants new sense of discipline in film industry', *Screen*, 15, 22 August 1975.

Stills, Stephen and Neil Young (1970), *Everybody I Love You,* New York: Atlantic Records. https://www.youtube.com/watch?v=lmc6w2k28y8 (accessed 16 July 2024).

Szeemann, Harald (1969), 'Curatorial Note – "Zur Ausstellung"', in *Live in Your Head: When Attitudes Become Form: Works-Concepts-Processes-Situations-Information*, Bern: Kunsthalle Bern.

'Thematic Classification of Feature Films Made during the Last Five Years', *Bulletin on Film*, A Monthly Digest for Official Use, January–March 1978, Vol. XXII, Nos. 1–3, National Documentation Centre on Mass Communication: New Delhi.

Index